Virgil's Homeric Lens

Routledge Monographs in Classical Studies

The Roman Garden
Katharine T. von Stackelberg

The Eunuch in Byzantine History and Society
Shaun Tougher

Actors and Audience in the Roman Courtroom
Leanne Bablitz

Life and Letters in the Ancient Greek World
John Muir

Utopia Antiqua
Rhiannon Evans

Greek Magic
John Petropoulos

Between Rome and Persia
Peter Edwell

Passions and Moral Progress in Greco-Roman Thought
John T. Fitzgerald

Dacia
Ioana A. Oltean

Rome in the Pyrenees
Simon Esmonde-Cleary

Virgil's Homeric Lens
Edan Dekel

Virgil's Homeric Lens

Edan Dekel

Routledge
Taylor & Francis Group
NEW YORK   LONDON

First published 2012
by Routledge
711 Third Avenue, New York, NY 10017

Simultaneously published in the UK
by Routledge
2 Park Square, Milton Park, Abingdon, Oxfordshire OX14 4RN

First issued in paperback 2014

*Routledge is an imprint of the Taylor & Francis Group,
an informa business*

© 2012 Taylor & Francis

The right of Edan Dekel to be identified as author of this work has been asserted by him in accordance with sections 77 and 78 of the Copyright, Designs and Patents Act 1988.

Typeset in Sabon by IBT Global.

All rights reserved. No part of this book may be reprinted or reproduced or utilised in any form or by any electronic, mechanical, or other means, now known or hereafter invented, including photocopying and recording, or in any information storage or retrieval system, without permission in writing from the publishers.

Trademark Notice: Product or corporate names may be trademarks or registered trademarks, and are used only for identification and explanation without intent to infringe.

Library of Congress Cataloging-in-Publication Data
Dekel, Edan, 1975–
  Virgil's Homeric lens / by Edan Dekel.
    p. cm. — (Routledge monographs in classical studies)
  Includes bibliographical references and index.
  1. Virgil. Aeneis. 2. Virgil—Knowledge—Greek literature. 3. Epic poetry, Latin—History and criticism. 4. Epic poetry, Greek—History and criticism. 5. Latin poetry—Greek influences. 6. Homer—Influence. 7. Homer. Iliad. 8. Homer. Odyssey. 9. Intertextuality. I. Title.
  PA6825.D455 2011
  873'.01—dc22
                                    2011005701

ISBN 978-0-415-89040-3 (hbk)
ISBN 978-1-138-80229-2 (pbk)
ISBN 978-0-203-80622-7 (ebk)

For my mother and father

Contents

	Acknowledgments	ix
1	Primary Colors	1
2	Iliadic Refraction	29
3	Odyssean Diffraction	63
4	Virgilian Reflection	90
	Notes	117
	Bibliography	139
	Index of Passages	153
	Subject Index	161

Acknowledgments

I would like to thank the many teachers, colleagues, students, and friends who have contributed to this book in various ways. In addition to providing valuable comments on early drafts, Ralph Hexter was instrumental in helping me hone my ambitious epic designs into a project of more reasonable scope and greater relevance. Mark Griffith, Ellen Oliensis, and Robert Alter also read earlier incarnations of this work and provided insightful criticism throughout. I am grateful to Michael Putnam and Joseph Pucci for planting the original seeds for this work many years ago during my time as an undergraduate at Brown University. I also owe special thanks to Joseph Pucci for reading and commenting on the manuscript at a crucial stage in the project. The manuscript was substantially revised during a happy year spent as a fellow at the Oakley Center for the Humanities and Social Sciences at Williams College, where Michael Brown and Rosemary Lane provided much assistance. I would also like to thank my colleagues in the Classics department at Williams, Meredith Hoppin, Kerry Christensen, Amanda Wilcox, Ben Rubin, and David Porter, for their enormous generosity and support throughout the project. My colleagues in Jewish Studies and Religion also offered valuable perspectives and encouragement, particularly Steve Gerrard, Sarah Hammerschlag, Ali Garbarini, and Denise Buell. Likewise, the students in my annual course on Virgil helped bring many important questions into specific relief. My debts to my longtime research partner and collaborator on so many projects, Gantt Gurley, are too numerous to list here. I also owe a special debt of gratitude to all the family and friends who supported me over the years, particularly my parents and brother, who sustained me in so many ways, and my daughter, Mai, who came into the world to inspire me during the very last stages of the project. Finally, this work would not exist without the boundless patience and optimism of my wife, Alexis Dekel. She is my ideal reader.

PERMISSIONS

Latin citations of Virgil are from the edition of R. A. B. Mynors, *P. Vergili Maronis Opera* (Oxford, 1969). Used by permission of Oxford University Press.

1 Primary Colors

One of the fundamental problems in the long history of criticism regarding Virgil's use of the two Homeric poems in the *Aeneid* is the failure to recognize that because there are three texts involved in the process, there are three distinct relationships. Traditionally, the two Homeric poems are mined for sources of allusions and echoes in the *Aeneid* independently of each other, but little attention is paid to the ways in which Virgil reads the interaction between the *Iliad* and *Odyssey* themselves. Virgil does not simply appropriate various Iliadic and Odyssean scenes, themes, similes, and individual lines; he is constantly engaged in the creative act of reading the two texts against each other. This reading is neither haphazard nor mechanical in its manifestation. Virgil is writing an epic in the Homeric tradition, so he locates a certain hierarchy already embedded in that tradition and proceeds to read the relationship between the two poems accordingly.

For Virgil, the two Homeric poems are not completely coordinate. As a poem about the hero's return from the Trojan War, the *Odyssey* necessarily positions itself as taking place after the *Iliad*, and as a consequence of the war described in that *Iliad*. But at the same time, the *Odyssey* is also an interpretation, or perhaps even a rendition, of the *Iliad*. Characters, themes, and conflicts from the war are evaluated and reconfigured as an authorative account of central Iliadic concerns. This book examines some specific ways in which Virgil uses the notion of the *Odyssey* as a reading of the *Iliad* and its aftermath to inform his own epic project, while constantly challenging the *Odyssey*'s claim to being the best reading of the *Iliad*. I aim to show that the *Aeneid* undertakes the *Odyssey*'s program of exploring multiple outcomes of the Trojan war while using the *Odyssey* itself to provide context for this exploration. Virgil positions the *Aeneid* in relation to the *Iliad* through the *Odyssey*'s own manipulations of the post-Iliadic experience.

In this first chapter, I will explore the history and methodology of Virgilian intertextual criticism starting with the commentators of late antiquity in order to reorient the underlying premise of bipartite, unidirectional influence of the Homeric poems on the *Aeneid*. By examining the links between discrete, local allusions and the comprehensive adoption of epic technique, and also treating the explicit demands of reading three distinct texts together as opposed to taking the Homeric poems as a univocal corpus,

2 Virgil's Homeric Lens

I will describe a system in which Virgil bases his own active interpretation and adaptation of Homer on the interaction between the *Odyssey* and the *Iliad* themselves. This design allows the *Aeneid* to process the content of both poems individually and taken together as a dynamic intertextual pair. Virgil uses the *Odyssey* both as a conceptual model for writing an intertextual epic and as a powerful refracting lens for the specific interpretation of the *Iliad* and its consequences.

intentio Vergilii

The relationship between the *Aeneid* and the two Homeric poems has been recognized for so long and so well as to be practically axiomatic. Indeed, many of the current generation of intertextual studies of Virgil have taken as their starting point the implicit view that this relationship is an established framework in which all sorts of other more surprising and revealing dialogues with Apollonius, Callimachus, Catullus, Lucretius, and Ennius take place. This has generally diminished the complexity and often startling vibrancy of the connection between the two canonical epic poets. The underlying principle of the axiom has not been substantially challenged since Servius first articulated it in the preface to his commentary on the *Aeneid* (Serv. *praef.*): "intentio Vergilii haec est: Homerum imitari et Augustum laudare a parentibus" ("Virgil's intention is this: to imitate Homer and to praise Augustus through his ancestors"). In a moment we will turn to the question of *imitatio*, but it is quite instructive to consider the ways in which this notion of "intention" frames the very history of the scholarship on and around the problem of Virgilian intertextuality.

For Servius, *intentio* certainly means "aim, purpose, intention," but this is a transferred meaning from the physical sense of "a stretching, straining" perhaps through the notion of "mental effort, concentration."[1] The act of recovering authorial intent is itself a kind of stretching of the text that bears the author's name. In the great debates about allusion and intertextuality in the study of ancient Roman texts, there has been an emphasis on the need to distinguish "real" allusions from accidental ones, that is to say, the intentional from the coincidental.[2] Setting aside epistemological issues about the irrecoverability of the author's intent, there is a more pressing issue at hand, namely, the difference between using allusion or intertextual reference as part of a poetic composition and having that composition's *raison d'être* actually be intertextuality. Servius' dictum is not so much a revelation about the inner workings of Virgil's mind as it is a bold definition of the very essence of the poem. He is setting up a model for reading Virgil that places the poet's own reading at the center of the analysis. We often take for granted that *imitatio* presupposes some act of *lectio*, but while the *imitatio* itself can be accidental, *lectio* requires both deliberate intent as well as *intentio* in the sense of "mental effort, concentration."[3]

Thus any identification of Homeric models, references, allusions, or interactions in the text of the *Aeneid* must presuppose a purposeful reading of the Homeric corpus, even if no individual intertextual reference can ever be labeled as intentional.

The notion of Virgil's *intentio* as a productive act of reading suggests a dynamic interaction with the Homeric poems, one that far exceeds individual allusions and borrowings. Servius himself already refers to one possible application of that productive reading in the second half of his statement, *Augustum laudare*. The *imitatio* need not be merely coordinate with the *laus*; it can also be a means of accomplishing it.[4] This too may prove to be an act of etymological "stretching" or "straining," as in the *intentio vocis* of Quintilian (*Inst.* 1.10.25), but nevertheless, the juxtaposition of Virgil's two masters, Homer the spiritual and poetic and Augustus the temporal, also seems to be a kind of dialogue between readings, one of literal text, the other of history and perhaps personality.

It is precisely this consummate readership that has so often fueled the *intentio* of Virgil in the legalistic sense of "accusation, charge": that the *Aeneid* is scarcely more than an imitation of Homer, and a pale one at that. The eighteenth- and nineteenth-century love affair with the "primitive" Homer as opposed to the "artificial" Virgil has at its very core the assumption of Homeric originality and Virgilian imitation.[5] The poet of the *Aeneid* was often viewed as a "harmonious plagiary," in the words of Byron,[6] but no serious attempt was made to investigate the precise nature of the alleged plagiarism.[7] Even once the oral hypothesis became prevalent in the twentieth century and helped shape the way in which we understand the composition of different sorts of epics, our terminology still reflected the old view when we referred to Homer as "primary" and Virgil as "secondary" epic.[8] But rather than disputing the terminology, we should embrace it for the essential truth that it embodies. For Virgil, the Homeric poems are primary not just because they are of the highest rank and earliest in time, but also because they are fundamental and radical in a way that encourages subsequent derivations from them. They are primary in the sense of primary colors, which, in the words of Isaac Newton, "cannot by any Art be changed, and whose Rays are alike refrangible."[9] Let me press briefly on this optical metaphor, to which I will return later in this chapter. The almost too fine distinction between the colors themselves and their eminently refractable rays suggests that the integrity of the source is just barely held together when the appropriate lens is applied. That is to say that, despite Newton's careful hairsplitting, the right art can and will alter not just the perception of a source, but the source itself.

This raises a difficult question for intertextual studies. Even if modern scholarship is more apt to locate the idea of an allusion or reference in the reader, or at least in the act of reading, than in the author's intention, there is still a common expectation of an historical, unidirectional system in which models cannot postdate their referents, that is, a system in which

4 Virgil's Homeric Lens

Virgil can refer to Homer, but not the other way around. Readings of a text that seek to reflect the "influence" of subsequent texts usually rely on the notion of the later texts revealing something that already existed in the earlier one, which skates dangerously close to reducing all interpretations to a reconstruction of authorial intention.[10] But at the same time, this practice again implicitly positions the author of the subsequent text as a critical reader of the prior one. If something in Virgil's text "uncovers" something in Homer's, then Virgil is practicing interpretation in his creative act. Even if we are unwilling to claim any direct knowledge of his particular intent while reading, a theory of reference that privileges the reader must acknowledge that all readings of Virgilian intertextuality presume readings of Homer. Once again, we are in realm of *intentio* as *lectio*, but we can push the argument even further. Since Virgil is not writing a critical analysis of Homer, but rather using his reading of the poems to activate his own epic project, it is not only the Homeric "borrowings" in the *Aeneid* that are relevant, but also the ways in which Virgil's other interests reflect back onto the Homeric models. If Servius' statement is to be understood as a definition of the poet's readings, then we must accept not only the idea of the *Homerum imitari* informing the *Augustum laudare,* but the converse as well. But this is already a reversal of the intertextual relationship: the reading of Augustus, and everything that is bound up with it, can serve as a model for the historically prior reading of Homer.

The point, of course, is that the two readings are in constant dialogue with each other throughout the *Aeneid*, and this idea of dialogue between readings furnishes a model for the relationship between the poem as whole and its two Homeric predecessors. "Secondary" Virgil is not simply receiving influence; he is actually changing the "primary" colors of Homer. Once the relationship is activated by Virgil, there can be no privileging of direction for the dialogue. No less a figure than Dante understands this point quite clearly when he models his own poem on Virgil's but, at the same time, figures his influence on Virgil by literally putting words into "Virgil's" mouth. Virgil does not introduce the figure of Homer into his poem, but he can put words into the mouths of Homer's characters, starting with Aeneas and including Hector, Priam, Andromache, Diomedes, and even the gods themselves. It seems impossible to read Poseidon's prophecy in the *Iliad* (*Il.* 20.307–8):[11]

νῦν δὲ δὴ Αἰνείαο βίη Τρώεσσιν ἀνάξει
καὶ παίδων παῖδες, τοί κεν μετόπισθε γένωνται.

and now the strength of Aeneas will rule over the Trojans,
and his sons' sons, who are born afterward.

without thinking of the *Aeneid* as a whole and especially the words of Apollo at Delos (*Aen.* 3.97–98):[12]

> hic domus Aeneae cunctis dominabitur oris
> et nati natorum et qui nascentur ab illis
>
> here Aeneas' house will rule all shores,
> and his sons' sons, and those who are born from them

Nowhere is a proleptic allusion more apt than in prophecy.[13] The Virgilian text not only expands the Iliadic one to encompass the whole world, but it also reconfigures the Homeric moment as a literary prophecy. What originally serves as a marker of the end of the House of Priam now becomes a statement about the continuity of the very texts in which Aeneas appears. The strength (*biê*) of Aeneas is domesticated into the house (*domus*) of his descendants. Moreover, Strabo reports a variant reading that makes the text of Homer quite literally allude to his successor Virgil (Strabo 13.1.53):[14]

> τινὲς δὲ γράφουσιν «Αἰνείαο γένος πάντεσσιν ἀνάξει,
> καὶ παῖδες παίδων,» τοὺς Ῥωμαίους λέγοντες.
>
> And some write, "the family of Aeneas will rule over all,
> and his sons' sons," meaning the Romans.

Here the *biê* has been supplanted by *genos*, which better approximates the *domus* of Virgil's text, and likewise *pantessin* instead of *Troessin* is a perfect match for the globalizing *cunctis*. The fact that no manuscript text of the *Iliad* records this variant may suggest that the emendation was recognized as a proleptic allusion and duly excised from the main tradition,[15] but nevertheless, this is a clear example of the kind of synchronic dialogue between texts that the *Aeneid* seeks to establish. Not only does Virgil put words into Homeric Aeneas' mouth, he also seems to have put words into Homer's text, if only for a while or in some strains of the tradition.

This ability to inscribe Virgil's own poem into the *Iliad* also highlights the inherent instability of Homer's text. We can only partially reconstruct the transmission of that text, but at the core of the issue is its primacy both in the oral-formulaic sense and in the sense that I have been attributing to Virgil's interaction with it. As oral compositions, the *Iliad* and *Odyssey* continued to evolve well after they were first committed to writing. The existence of the so-called "wild papyri," which often record greatly divergent readings, as well as the massive athetization program undertaken by Aristarchus and his followers, demonstrate that there is no reason to presume automatically a canonical text of Homer in the Roman period.[16] This would only make the "primary" texts more refractable in the hands of a skilled poet. Of course, I do not mean to suggest that Virgil had a modern critical understanding of the oral tradition (or textual tradition for that matter), but the idea of multiple variants existing simultaneously and with great frequency would surely encourage a freer kind of intertextual play than we might imagine when comparing relatively stable printed editions. We cannot recover the text of Homer in Virgil's time (or in any time) any more than we can reconstruct Virgil's own specific reading habits,[17] but we can recognize that a fluid tradition is very likely to inspire creative interaction, particularly when that tradition already contains rigorous intertextuality.[18] The interaction between the *Aeneid* and the Homeric poems is systematic and persistent to a degree that is matched only by the relationship between the *Iliad* and the *Odyssey* themselves.

While we seem to be beyond the age of viewing this systematic interaction as the prime evidence for the charge of mere *imitatio*, it is that very rigor that has driven the search for schematic models of the intertextual relationship. In this regard, one tendency has been to take a somewhat mechanical approach to the question of Homeric primacy and see the "secondary" *Aeneid* as a combination of one part *Iliad* and one part *Odyssey*. We will treat this dichotomy more thoroughly in the next section, but the deceptive simplicity of this model has inspired many to view it as a mere foundational layer and to search for the other active influences on the Virgilian project instead.[19] We cannot ignore these other relationships, but in order to appreciate their function in the overall composition, we have to reexamine the properties of the first layer. By moving away from a binary model, we can better understand the elaborate refractions taking place within the *Aeneid*.

Homerum imitari

If the *intentio Vergilii* is bound up with the notion of *lectio*, and more specifically with the idea of dialogical readings of Homer, then the bipartite model of the poem tends to suppress the effects of the alleged *imitatio* on the two primary sources, as well as the actual intricacies of Virgil's interpretative reading, in favor of structural symmetry. Once again we can turn to Servius for a succinct account of the traditional model of Virgilian *imitatio* (Serv. ad *Aen.* 7.1):

> in duas partes hoc opus divisum est: nam primi sex ad imaginem Odyssiae . . . hi autem sex qui sequuntur ad imaginem Iliados dicti sunt.
>
> This work is divided into two parts: for the first six [books] are said to be in the image of the *Odyssey* . . . moreover the six that follow are said to be in the image of the *Iliad*.

Servius, and nearly the entire subsequent scholarly tradition, have neatly divided the *Aeneid* into two halves along the lines suggested by the overall subject matter of those two poems, and further reinforced by what appears to be a literal restarting of the Latin poem at 7.37. This, however, raises two immediate difficulties for the traditional view.[20] First, this second proem makes the explicit claim that what follows is a greater task (*maius opus*) than what has come before (*Aen.* 7.45), which may still support a bipartite view of the poem's overall structure, but hardly supports the idea of an equal division in terms of stature. While generations of Latin students have been raised on the reading of *Aeneid* 1–6, presumably because these books are superficially more rich and varied, here Virgil proposes that Books 7–12 are the greater work. The famous lines by Propertius also seem to recognize the Iliadic component of the poem as the dominant one (2.34.65–66):

> cedite Romani scriptores, cedite Grai!
>   nescio quid maius nascitur Iliade.

> Yield Roman writers, yield Greek ones!
>   Something greater than the *Iliad* is being born.

At the time he wrote these lines, Propertius may have known little more than that Virgil was working on an epic poem (cf. Donatus *Vit. Verg.* 100–103), but they do demonstrate that Propertius is thinking of the *Aeneid* in Homeric, and specifically Iliadic, terms.[21]

Second, by beginning the proem at 7.37 rather than at 7.1, Virgil seems quite firmly to be denying a symmetrical model for the poem.[22] In the past, this was variously explained as a mistake by his editors,[23] or as a result of his unwillingness to disturb the ending of Book 6 with the final details of the journey.[24] More convincing is the notion that this mirrors the structural division of the *Odyssey*, where the first half of the poem (i.e., the journey) closes not at the end of Book 12 but at 13.92 with Odysseus asleep as the Phaeacians carry him home.[25] Since the book divisions of the Homeric poems are generally attributed to the Alexandrian editors, the charge of mistaken division is even more common, which would make an identical error by Virgil's editors an especially uncanny coincidence.[26] But setting aside the prehistory of the Homeric divisions, for Virgil the first half of the *Odyssey* would have ended as it does for us, with the final stage of the journey occupying the opening lines of Book 13, and consequently his own overlap must be seen as a crucial point of contact between the epics. We will examine the specific implications of this contact later,[27] but in terms of the traditional bipartite model, we can already see that the very architecture of the poem is set against any overly symmetrical reading.

We have, then, already two compelling reasons to question the conventional bipartite structure. On the one hand, the claim that the second part is a *maius opus* suggests a greater emphasis on the Iliadic model, while the asymmetrical overlap marks the *Odyssey* as the overall structural paradigm. But these are difficulties only if we are determined to see the *Aeneid* as a perfect binary product, a view that, though attractive on many levels, has long been complicated by the identification of various other structural patterns in the poem. In addition to the twofold division of six books, there is the tripartite division of the Dido story (1–4), Roman center (5–8), and tragedy of Turnus (9–12);[28] the six consecutive pairs model;[29] and the parallel panel model where Books 1 and 7, 2 and 8, and so on, correspond, and there is an accompanying alternation between the "light" odd-numbered books and the "dark" even-numbered ones.[30] Whether or not we believe these schematic theories to be accurate or useful for our understanding of the poem, it is at least clear that there is no need to see any one of these divisions as exclusive of the others.

Of course, Servius does not claim that the bipartite division is the exclusive architectural principle of the poem, but rather uses it to define the structure of the Homeric *imitatio*. In this regard, the asymmetrical effects created by the second proem are serious challenges to his model. But even formulations that do not impose any requirement of symmetrical dichotomy are problematic. Consider this analysis of the *imitatio* by Macrobius (*Sat.* 5.2.6):

> Iam vero Aeneis ipsa nonne ab Homero sibi mutuata est errorem primum ex Odyssea, deinde ex Iliade pugnas?
>
> Now truly did the *Aeneid* not borrow for itself from Homer first the wandering from the *Odyssey*, and then the battles from the *Iliad*?

Although there is no mention of specific book numbers or relative value of the parts, the model is still binary and sequential: the *Aeneid* borrows first from the *Odyssey* and then from the *Iliad*. Regardless of how much of the poem these borrowings occupy, the implication is that they are two distinct transactions. This further supports the view of the *Aeneid* as a construction or compound of the two Homeric poems. But a physical compound model is forced to account for the "reduction" of the forty-eight scrolls of Homer into the twelve books of the *Aeneid*–a process that at best might be called distillation, at worst, constriction. Either way, the overarching idea is a combination of two separate and unidirectional *imitationes* of the *Iliad* and *Odyssey*.

One major result of this early "analytic" view on the history of Virgilian scholarship is the long commentary tradition of identifying individual Homeric "parallels" in the text of the *Aeneid* without any interpretation of their significance in either their original or new context or of their implications for the overall project of Homeric *imitatio*.[31] This is, of course, a feature of many commentary traditions, not just the Virgilian one, but when the interaction between the texts is so intricate and persistent, it is particularly counterproductive to opt for a "juxtatextual" rather than an intertextual mode of analysis. Even when the connections are called allusions, there is still a tendency to read them as discrete moments of contact between texts rather than as part of a dialogic system. The binary model generates this particularization of the intertextual relationship because it encourages the view of the Homeric poems as static repositories of source material that can be extracted and then molded into the *Aeneid*. By thus privileging the local contact between the poems, the model further discourages any serious reevaluation of its own validity.[32]

While the separation of the two Homeric texts into the two halves of the *Aeneid* is only an implicit consequence of Macrobius' formulation, the sequencing of the poems seems quite explicit. He tells us that the poem first borrows the *error* from the *Odyssey* and subsequently the *pugnae* from the *Iliad*. His choice of words, however, is ambiguous, allowing for a much richer interpretation. While *error* surely refers to the physical wandering of Odysseus, both he and Aeneas are also "straying" from both the Trojan war and the *Iliad*. Furthermore, the transferred meanings of *error* ("mistake," "deception," "derangement or madness")[33] all figure prominently in both the *Iliad* and the *Aeneid*. We need only recall Laocoon's warning about the Greek horse (*Aen.* 2.48: *aut aliquis latet error*, "or some error lies hidden within") to see how the various *errores* set in motion by the *Iliad* both motivate the *Aeneid* and repeat themselves within it. The multiplicity of meaning generates the ironic effect of the passage, for the *error* lies not only in the deception of the Greeks within the horse, but also in the mistake of the Trojans who admit it within their walls.[34] Like the horse, the *Iliad* contains within itself the implicit destruction of Troy through the mistakes of its defenders, and above all through the deranging power of war exemplified by Achilles.

The *pugnae*, of course, are the literal battles of both the *Aeneid* and the *Iliad*, and the first ones Aeneas encounters are depicted on the walls of the temple of Juno (*Aen.* 1.456): *videt Iliacas ex ordine pugnas* ("he sees the battles at Troy in order"). The adjective *Iliacas* directs our attention to the city of Ilium and the Homeric poem that bears its name, and thus the ecphrastic moment establishes an Iliadic lineage for all the *pugnae* to come.[35] By physically deciphering the story of the Trojan war from the panels on the wall, Aeneas is actually reading the *Iliad* into the record of the poem. The equation is completed in the second proem, which uses the same word to describe the forthcoming battle in Italy (*Aen.* 7.40): *et primae revocabo exordia pugnae* ("and I will recall the beginnings of the first battle"). The sonic similarity of *ex ordine pugnas* and *exordia pugnae* in the same metrical position reinforces the connection, while *revocabo* and *primae* both look back to the earlier war and the "primary" Homeric account of it.

Likewise, the action of the *Odyssey* is directly motivated by the battles of the *Iliad*, but it offers its own conflicts as well. Macrobius' choice of *pugnae* rather than *bellum* once again points the way. The distinction between *pugna* and *bellum* is one of size and extent (a *pugna* can be part of a *bellum* but not the other way around), or alternatively, of a concrete event versus an abstraction (*bellum* as the state of war; the opposite of *pax*). But the primary meaning of *pugna* is single combat in battle (as at *Aen.* 12.54) or in a boxing match (as at *Aen.* 5.463) as its etymological derivation from *pux* (fist) would suggest. The broader meaning of a battle is then a natural expansion of the term. Although there are many *pugnae* in the *Iliad* in the sense of single combat, and even a famous boxing match (*Il.* 23.651–99), the word is equally suited to the *Odyssey*, which includes at least one fistfight (*Od.* 18.32–116) and, more importantly, features as its climax the *pugna* between Odysseus and the suitors. The emphasis on the individual combat thus provides a connecting thread between the central duels in all three poems.

In addition to these subversions of the rigid binary sequencing initially suggested by his statement, Macrobius may also offer us a way out of the problem of strict unidirectional intertextuality when he tells us that the *Aeneid* "ab Homero sibi mutuata est." The verb *mutuari* is often used in the sense of "to derive," as in a word or idea,[36] but its usual meaning is "to borrow." We often speak of languages "borrowing" a word or construction from others. In concrete terms, the implication of borrowing something is that one will return that very thing or some equivalent. This is the underlying concept of the English derivative "mutual." We can see then, that if the *Aeneid* borrows the *errores* and *pugnae* of the *Iliad* and *Odyssey*, then it must somehow return the favor. Once again, we are encouraged to read the relationship between the texts dialogically.

In this regard, we might consider a third ancient formulation of the interaction between the *Aeneid* and the Homeric poems, this time by Donatus in his life of Virgil (*Vit. Verg.* 75–76): "argumentum varium ac multiplex et quasi amborum Homeri carminum instar" ("a varied and complex subject and almost the image of both Homeric poems"). We might first question whether this is even a statement about that relationship, for if we understand *instar* as meaning something like "the equivalent in worth" or "counterpart,"[37] then this may be no more than a way of staking Virgil's claim to the highest rank of epic poetry. On the other hand, the juxtaposition of this claim with the description of the *argumentum* as *varium ac multiplex* suggests that this is actually a judgment about the overall structure and content of the poem. The use of *quasi* to apologize for the strength of the simile further supports the notion that *instar* means something more like "equal in magnitude" or "image," which echoes the *ad imaginem* of Servius' formulation.[38] But unlike with Servius or Macrobius, there is no strong sense of bifurcation. The use of *ambo* instead of *uterque* points to a more unified view of the relationship as does *multiplex* instead of the *divisum* in Servius.[39] Unfortunately, Donatus offers no further explication of that view, and its potential revision of the strict bipartite model seems not to have been activated in the subsequent commentary tradition.

Even if there is a more radical view lurking in Donatus' characterization of the poem, the framework is still the same one that Servius and

Macrobius are using: there is some equivalence between the *Aeneid* and the Homeric poems, and the bipartite composite model is designed to answer the problem of how to equate *ambo Homeri carmina* with one Virgilian poem. But this is precisely where the traditional model goes wrong: it does not actually attempt to see the whole *Aeneid* in relation to both the *Iliad* and *Odyssey*, but rather sets part of the *Aeneid* against one of the poems and then another part against the other. The precise extent and sequencing of these parts may vary, but it is still a kind of poetic double-entry bookkeeping. Each individual reference is recorded as debit from one of the two Homeric accounts and duly entered as a credit in Virgil's account.[40] However, by insisting on a linear, sequential, and binary relationship, the model raises certain objections that it has never addressed–nor ever could possibly address–in a satisfactory manner. By briefly exploring these objections, we can get a more specific sense of the limitations of the model and at the same time consider whether these sorts of questions are ever likely to generate an alternative way of understanding the intertextual relationship.

Any model that states that the first six books of the *Aeneid* are based on the *Odyssey* and the last six on the *Iliad* must answer the following four questions:[41]

1. Why are there Iliadic features in the Odyssean half and vice versa?
2. Why does the Odyssean half come first?
3. Why is the Odyssean half based only on half of the *Odyssey*?
4. Why does the Iliadic half invert key structural patterns in the *Iliad*?

Let us consider each one separately:

1. The presence of "crossover" elements in the alleged halves has been noticed before, but there is little discussion of its implications for the bipartite model. Among the most frequently cited major examples are the funeral games in "Odyssean" Book 5, which appear to be based on those for Patroclus in *Iliad* 23; the early events in Italy (Books 7–8), which draw much from the adventures of Telemachus in *Odyssey* 1–4; the quasi-Iliadic fall of Troy in Book 2; and the conflict between Aeneas and Turnus as "suitors," which suggests the central Odyssean situation.[42] The problem is most naturally answered by pointing out the shared origins of nearly all these examples. Just as Macrobius' ambiguous language suggests the double origin of the *errores* and the *pugnae* in the *Aeneid*, so these structural elements can all be derived from both Homeric poems. The games of Book 5 have the Phaeacian games of *Odyssey* 8 as another model; the arrival in Italy shares many features with the scenes of hospitality in *Iliad* 9 and 24; the flashback of Book 2 corresponds to Demodocus' songs about the post-Iliadic Trojan war; and of course the original epic suitor is Iliadic Paris. In short, there is no reason to privilege one source over the other. But if this is true for these "displaced" elements, then perhaps it is also the case for episodes that are in the "right" half of the poem. There is nothing to prevent us from looking

for a second, Iliadic source for the wanderings of Book 3, or an Odyssean source for the shield of Aeneas except the rigidity of a model that assumes that the correct source is the one that fits the bipartite pattern. I do not mean to suggest that we will necessarily find an Odyssean precursor for the shield, but the mechanical search for sources by its very nature precludes a comprehensive understanding of the intricate intertextual techniques of the poem.

2. By the same token, the question of ordering is an artificial constraint, yet if the bipartite model demands a rigid sequence, it should be forced to explain why that sequence is the reverse of the natural order of the source poems. Macrobius gives the common-sense answer (*Sat.* 5.2.6): "operis ordinem necessario rerum ordo mutavit" ("the order of events necessarily changed the order of the work"), which refers us to the "historical" sequence of Aeneas' wandering and subsequent war in Italy.[43] It would hardly make sense to reverse the traditional account, but this answer does not fully explain why the intertextual models themselves *necessario* are inverted. It is perfectly plausible to imagine a poem about Aeneas in which events at Troy are first recounted in a kind of *Iliad* from the Trojan perspective and then followed by an Odyssean journey and arrival at a new homeland. It might well be argued that the *Aeneid* as we know is, in many ways, that kind of poem, were it not for the assumption that the Odyssean half must come first. If we are determined to take this issue up at all, it would be much more productive to investigate what the sequencing of events in the *Aeneid* reveals about the structures of the *Iliad* and *Odyssey*, rather than trying to impose an absolute notion of those structures onto the *Aeneid*. Once again, the relationship between these texts is constrained only by the external model that has been imposed on it.

3. Even if we tentatively accept the premise that the first half of the poem is a rough approximation of the *Odyssey*, in that it recounts the story of a Trojan war veteran wandering the Mediterranean in a search for his proper home, there is still the problem of the apparent omission of half the source material.[44] A more accurate statement in the terminology of the traditional model would be that the first half of the *Aeneid* corresponds only to Books 5–12 of the *Odyssey*, that is, to the wanderings of Odysseus.[45] The model that forces us to look for the whole *Odyssey* in these first six books cannot adequately explain the discrepancy. From one modern popular perspective that is more accustomed to think of these books of the *Odyssey* as the core of the poem, it is perhaps not surprising that the narrow parameters of the analogy have not been explained away. Still, the natural response should be to search beyond Book 6 for the rest of the *Odyssey*, and, as we have already seen, the wanderings themselves do lap over into the second half of both poems. But once we locate Odyssean elements in the second half of the *Aeneid*, we are driven back into the problem of "displaced" episodes. The bipartite model forces us to violate its own symmetrical logic by

searching in the "wrong" half of the poem, but offers no way to integrate these findings back into the intertextual analysis.

4. The same problem exists to a certain extent in the Iliadic half of the poem, but perhaps because the alleged omissions come from all parts of the poem and include a great many battle scenes, there has been less scholarly anxiety over the discrepancy. The second half of the *Aeneid* has more often been studied in relation to the Achillean paradigm rather than to the whole *Iliad*.[46] Even limiting ourselves to this view, there are at least two types of inversion that require explanation. The first is the role reversal of Aeneas and Turnus. At various moments in the poem, both characters can be connected to three distinct Iliadic models: Achilles, Hector, and Paris. From the Sibyl's initial prophecy about Turnus as a second Achilles (*Aen.* 6.89–90: *alius Latio iam partus Achilles / natus et ipse dea,* "now another Achilles has been born in Latium / he is also the son of a goddess") to his Hectorian death at the hands of an avenging Aeneas, the models are interwoven into an intricate and sometimes contradictory pattern. This pattern has been the subject of most of the aforementioned scholarship,[47] but there is a second inversion that has received no attention. The story of Achilles has often been discussed in terms of wrath and retribution. The anger of Achilles and its consequences occupy the vast majority of the poem, including the books in which he does not appear, but by the end of Book 24, there is a kind of triple resolution to that anger through the funeral of Patroclus, the return of Hector's body to the suppliant Priam, and the burial of Hector. In the second half of the *Aeneid*, this pattern is dramatically inverted. Book 7 begins with the burial of Caieta (*Aen.* 7.1–4) followed immediately by a reference to *pius Aeneas* (7.5), but the poem ends with Aeneas killing Turnus in full rage (described as *ira terribilis* at *Aen.* 12.946–47). We will consider these episodes at the end of Chapter 4, but this kind of elaborate reading of the Homeric model lies outside the boundaries of a traditional bipartite view of the *Aeneid*, which, if it cannot explain why there must be an Iliadic half and why it comes after the Odyssean one, will hardly be able to explain why that half also seems to follow the *Iliad* in reverse.

In raising these questions, I do not mean to suggest that modern Virgilian scholarship has blindly followed a simplistic bipartite model. On the contrary, almost every study of Virgilian allusion or intertextuality at least implicitly rejects the most rigid formulation of the relationship. But in general studies of the poem, it is still quite common to see references to the Odyssean and Iliadic halves of the *Aeneid* without any critical comment; more importantly, many of the studies that do reject the strictures of the model nevertheless find it necessary to offer alternatives that still rely on the fundamental principle of unidirectional, discrete allusions and imitations. As I have suggested, this is due in large part to the fragmenting power of the model itself. There is a massive body of literature on local parallels or allusions,[48] and some serious work on either the alleged Odyssean or Iliadic "half,"[49] but there are almost no comprehensive studies of the systematic relationship between the two poets.[50] The elaborate intertextuality of these poems does not necessarily imply a complicated overall model, but it does demand a method of inquiry that presumes that the intertextuality is active rather than passive–that Virgil is closely reading and rereading Homer in his poem, not silently receiving individual passages and themes.

Donatus' dubious statement about Virgil's own preparations for the composition is hardly reliable evidence for the creative technique of the poet (*Vit. Verg.* 83–85):

> Aeneida prosa prius oratione formatam digestamque in XII libros particulatim componere instituit, prout liberet quidque, et nihil in ordinem arripiens
>
> He first planned the *Aeneid* in prose and divided it into twelve books, and decided to construct it piece by piece, so that he could do each part as he wished, taking up nothing in order.

However, it does embody two conflicting ways of reading the structural principles of the *Aeneid*. The idea of a deliberate overall structure generating enormous poetic freedom on the local level (*particulatim componere*) could suggest the particularized model of intertextuality in which the local contact between the poems is highlighted against a static schematic background. At the same time, however, we can understand it as a concessive statement: *although* he planned it out in prose and divided it into twelve books, Virgil decided to construct the poem piece by piece, taking up nothing in order. This notion of seizing nothing in order (*nihil in ordinem*) chafes against Macrobius' statement about the necessary order of the poem and strongly suggests that the ultimate structure of the poem develops organically out of the local poetic technique. If the latter reading is correct, then in order to understand the relationship between the *Aeneid* and the Homeric poems, we must accept the idea of a fluid intertextuality closely bound up with the whole range of Virgil's poetic activity. In short, we must understand how the goal of *Homerum imitari* is both conceived and executed within the *Aeneid* itself.

ab Homero sibi mutuata est

It has been recognized for a while now by many scholars that the full meaning of *Homerum imitari* is not simply to imitate the actual text of the Homeric poems, but also to read and write epic in a Homeric mode. G.B. Conte's classic distinction between Homer as *modello-esemplare* ("exemplary model") and *modello-codice* ("code model") is an especially insightful way of reorienting the question of local versus systematic contact between the poets.[51] As an exemplary model, Homer serves as the ultimate collection of individual *exempla* for allusion and reference, "ready-made, unsurpassable, complete, needing only to be imitated."[52] This is essentially the passive function that underlies the commentary tradition starting with Macrobius and Servius and culminating in Knauer's exhaustive catalog of references.[53] In this regard, the difference between Homer and every other potential source (Apollonius, Ennius, etc.) seems to be one of degree; they are all fixed entities that supply raw materials for the poetic composition, but Homer supplies a far greater quantity than anyone else. But the more frequent use of this source also contains within it an implicit judgment that the Homeric matter is a *better* source, not necessarily in a purely aesthetic sense, but more specifically in terms of what we might call its imitability. More precisely, the Homeric poems generate widespread imitation, allusion, and reference across vast genres, eras, and languages not simply because they are so widely admired, but because their very essence demands that they be replicated and repeated. This is partly due to certain traditional compositional aspects of the poems (e.g., epithets, formulaic phrases, type scenes), but they are also constructed along thematic lines that constantly reinterpret the same basic actions or motivations in new settings. Thus the anger of Chryses and its consequences in *Iliad* 1 are transformed into the anger of Agamemnon, which begets the anger of Achilles, which in turn becomes the anger of Aeneas, Ariosto's Orlando, Tasso's Rinaldo, and countless other epic heroes.[54] This further argues against the fragmentary model of Homeric allusion. If the imitability is only fully revealed in the intricate way in which the repetitions and elaborations are woven together across the whole of the poem, then a piecemeal selection of particular passages for imitation will obscure the process and consequently be less effective as an intertextual strategy. For Homer to serve as a true exemplary model for the *Aeneid*, the interaction must pervade every aspect of the poetic composition.[55]

One important way in which this is accomplished is through Conte's idea of code-modeling. In addition to serving as repositories of individual passages, the *Iliad* and *Odyssey* provide a framework for processing information Homerically, that is, a system of rules and expectations that define epic poetry. Homer is more than passive text; he is actually a mode of thought: "Homer as the category and genre of epic writing."[56] Not only does this formulation allow us to view Homer as an active participant in the intertextual relationship, but it immediately demonstrates that our study of the interaction with *Aeneid* need not be limited to the readily identifiable "particular passages." If Homer is a generative system of poetics, then his traces should be discernable even in the absence of a specific allusion or imitation. This idea has been used quite effectively to show how even the most common *topos* or formulaic phrase can be part of an active intertextual system,[57] but also to shed light on Virgilian narrative technique as a whole.[58] A crucial implication of these analyses is that the process of code-modeling presumes a critical reading of the original model. The system cannot be activated through slavish imitation; rather, the Homeric poetics must be internalized through a constant dialogue with the source texts. The surest proof of successful code-modeling is the bold revision of obviously Homeric material. The process by which the subject matter of the *Aeneid* is viewed Homerically (i.e., interpreted through Homer) also allows the Homeric poems to be reconfigured within that interpretation.

An excellent example of this effect is in Book 1 when Aeneas is examining the walls of the temple of Juno. Among the scenes that catch his attention is the mistreatment of Hector's body by Achilles and the subsequent ransoming of the corpse (*Aen.* 1.483–84):

> ter circum Iliacos raptaverat Hectora muros
> exanimumque auro corpus vendebat Achilles
>
> Three times Achilles had dragged Hector around the walls of Troy
> and now was selling the lifeless body for gold.

The most obvious model for the first line is the opening of *Iliad* 24, where a grieving Achilles drags the body of Hector around the tomb of Patroclus rather than the walls of Troy (*Il.* 24.14–16):[59]

> ἀλλ' ὅ γ' ἐπεὶ ζεύξειεν ὑφ' ἅρμασιν ὠκέας ἵππους,
> Ἕκτορα δ' ἕλκεσθαι δησάσκετο δίφρου ὄπισθεν,
> τρὶς δ' ἐρύσας περὶ σῆμα Μενοιτιάδαο θανόντος
>
> But when he had yoked up his swift horses under his chariot,
> he would bind Hector behind the chariot in order to drag him,
> and draw him three times around the tomb of the dead son of Menoetius

In Book 22, after he has just killed Hector, he also drags the corpse (*Il.* 22.395–405), but the description of Andromache's view makes it fairly clear that he only parades the body in front of the walls and then takes it off to his camp (*Il.* 22.463–65):

> ἔστη παπτήνασ' ἐπὶ τείχεϊ, τὸν δὲ νόησεν
> ἑλκόμενον πρόσθεν πόλιος· ταχέες δέ μιν ἵπποι
> ἕλκον ἀκηδέστως κοίλας ἐπὶ νῆας Ἀχαιῶν.
>
> She stopped and looked around on the wall, and saw him
> being dragged before the city; and swift horses were dragging
> him pitilessly toward the hollow ships of the Achaeans.

There is an alternative Greek tradition in which Achilles does actually drag the body around the walls of Troy,[60] but the number of times is not mentioned before Virgil.

So far we can see only how Homer provides an exemplary model for the line in question. But the line is also part of a larger system of descriptions of triple attempts generated by the Homeric code model. There are several scenes in the *Iliad* and *Odyssey* in which some activity is attempted three times without success. This is always marked in the text by anaphora of the word *tris*, with the first occurrence coming in line-initial position.[61] Virgil makes use of the same pattern for failed attempts (anaphora of *ter*, the first time in initial position) five times in the *Aeneid*,[62] thus validating the system within his own poem. But at 1.483 the pattern is incomplete; Achilles drags Hector around the walls three times, but there is no responding *ter* to signal the failure of the activity. As we have seen, the Iliadic model for this line also has *tris* without anaphora, a phenomenon that occurs more often in Homer.[63] But the dragging of Hector's body around the tomb of Patroclus three times is clearly a fruitless attempt by Achilles to ease his sorrow over the loss of his companion. The death of Hector by itself has not released him from his suffering, and he continues to be tormented through the ransom scene with Priam. Thus the *tris* here is serving the usual function of the second element in the anaphora, even though there is no first *tris* immediately preceding. Virgil, however, recognizes the responsive function of the line and, furthermore, locates the missing element of the anaphora in the single use of *tris* in Book 22 when Achilles chases Hector around the walls of Troy three times (*Il.* 22.250–52):

οὔ σ' ἔτι Πηλέος υἱὲ φοβήσομαι, ὡς τὸ πάρος περ
τρὶς περὶ ἄστυ μέγα Πριάμου δίον, οὐδέ ποτ' ἔτλην
μεῖναι ἐπερχόμενον·

I will no longer flee you, son of Peleus, as I did before
three times around the great city of Priam, and did not
dare to withstand your approach.

This is the great moment of vengeance that the later triple circling of the tomb shows to be ineffective as a remedy for Achilles' woe. The description on the temple wall is thus both a combination of the two circling episodes and an interpretation of their function within an established Homeric pattern. But in offering this reading of the two Homeric episodes, Virgil makes a choice that demonstrates how adept he is at reconfiguring the code model. Rather than imitating the two lines in the normal *ter/ter* pattern and so signaling his recognition of the pattern through explicit juxtaposition, Virgil combines them into a single line and then sets up his own delayed anaphora. The dragging of Hector three times around the wall of Troy is answered by the procession around the funeral pyres of Pallas and the fallen Trojans in Book 11 (*Aen.* 11.188–90):

> ter circum accensos cincti fulgentibus armis
> decurrere rogos, ter maestum funeris ignem
> lustravere in equis ululatusque ore dedere
>
> Three times they ran around the flaming pyres clad in
> shining armor, three times they went around the sad
> funeral fire on horseback and wailed with their mouths.

These lines already contain the familiar anaphora, but by themselves they do not fit the usual pattern of failed attempts. If, however, we understand them as responding to the earlier dragging of Hector's body, we can see the futility of the cycle of vengeance. The response is explicitly marked by the repetition of the whole line-initial phrase, *ter circum*. Achilles desecrates Hector's corpse in an attempt to avenge Patroclus' death, but the long-term result is the death of another Patroclus figure, Pallas.[64] Aeneas ends up committing himself to the same blind vengeance as Achilles, but this attempt is utterly futile because it is his third time down this road as well. He who was virtually present at the original death of Hector and who literally read it a second time on the wall of the temple finds himself about to repeat the attempt for the third time as a kind of living embodiment of the anaphoric formula. The circling of Pallas' pyre is thus a warning that goes unheeded. Moreover, as a response to the Hector episode, it reinforces the connection between the two Iliadic moments that underlie that scene. Virgil has expanded the scope of the original coding by drawing our attention to the technique of delayed response.

This kind of reading demonstrates some of the ways in which the two types of Homeric modeling reinforce each other. By drawing on multiple source passages and then revising them in light of a larger systematic feature of the poems, Virgil's text requires us to reinterpret the "passive" exemplary model. But this notion of dual modeling fails to make explicit one key aspect of the intertextual relationship. If the idea is that Homer the code model guides Virgil to see things Homerically and to write within the genre or category of epic, then we should also be able to locate within that model the very idea of intertextuality. Earlier we considered how Virgil's systematic use of Homer as an exemplary model is greatly influenced by the ways in which the *Iliad* and *Odyssey* contain frequent imitations and repetitions within themselves. But it makes less sense to talk about, say, *Iliad* 1 serving as a code model for *Iliad* 24 since they are both, by definition, part of a single Homeric system whose function is to provide a kind of consistent generative grammar of the epic genre. But therein lies the problem: unlike the singular *Aeneid*, the Homeric system is not univocal, but rather comprises two distinct texts. The underlying assumption of the Homeric code model view is that the two elements of the Homeric corpus are part of the same primary system. From an oral formulaic perspective, there is some merit to this notion, in that the local compositional techniques of the two poems are based on the same rules and formulaic structures. But from almost any other vantage point, and most importantly from any perspective that, like Virgil's, predates the oral hypothesis, the two texts are distinct entities that are closely intertwined on every level but, nevertheless, often work at cross purposes thematically and structurally. In short, the notion of a single Homeric code does not acknowledge that there is already a working system of exemplary and code modeling between the *Iliad* and *Odyssey*. But it is precisely this Homeric system that, in turn, provides the model for Virgil's own intertextual project.

de Homerici operis speculo

As we have seen, the goal of *Homerum imitari* leads Virgil not simply to imitate the two Homeric poems but to attempt to read and write epic in what he understands as a Homeric mode. Imitating Homer means first and foremost emulating the Greek poet's own habits. For Virgil, this means modeling his intertextual epic on the very first intertextual epic, the *Odyssey*. If the exemplary and code model view does not recognize this fundamental aspect of the relationship because it does not sufficiently distinguish the *Iliad* and *Odyssey*, the traditional bipartite model of the *Aeneid* fails because of the way it excessively segregates the two Homeric poems into equivalent halves of some imaginary whole. But as we noted at the outset of this chapter, the two poems are not completely coordinate; in addition to the explicit temporal and causal ordering, the *Odyssey* is also a repetition of the *Iliad*, or more accurately, a reinterpretation through repetition. Not only are Iliadic characters directly engaged in the first half of the poem, but the second half also contains a repetition of several central Iliadic thematic concerns: a man must reassert his claim to home and wife, regain his honor, and avenge himself after an absence that has led to great devastation.

We will take up the question of Iliadic repetition more thoroughly in subsequent chapters, but it has often been noted that the main narrative events of the *Iliad* are never explicitly mentioned in the *Odyssey*.[65] This fact has sometimes been used to suggest that the *Odyssey* was composed either by a poet who was ignorant of the *Iliad*,[66] or by one who was unwilling to challenge the *Iliad* openly.[67] But from the standard ancient perspective that assumed that the two poems were composed by the same author, these views shed little light on Homeric intertextual technique.[68] A more relevant issue raised by the apparent omission might be the sequence of composition of the two poems, though even here the ancient consensus favored the relative chronology of the stories themselves.[69] Virgil reorients the question of priority by locating his poem on the internal Homeric time line at exactly the same point as the *Odyssey*. In doing so, he is tacitly acknowledging the temporal precedence of the *Iliad* and directing his attention to the ways in which the *Odyssey* manifests its own posteriority. A key aspect of this posteriority is the constant reevaluation of Iliadic concerns, and the marked absence of explicit references to the main Achillean action of the *Iliad* is part of the elaborate intertextual technique that facilitates that reevaluation. In the first half of the *Odyssey*, the effects of the campaign at Troy are considered through the eyes of veterans of the war, the families left behind, and even the casualties of war themselves. In the second half, the results of these explorations are activated in a re-creation of the Iliadic conflict. The *Odyssey* is thus simultaneously a consequence of, a sequel to, and a revision of the *Iliad*. If, then, the *Aeneid* appears to be an "Odyssey" followed by an "Iliad," it is because the *Odyssey* itself contains an "odyssey" followed by an "iliad."

As we have already seen, the notion of discrete halves of the *Aeneid* is undercut by several other structural patterns as well as by the alleged problems of displaced episodes and asymmetrical overlap. But no recalculation of the ratio of influence can obscure the faulty premise of the model. The two Homeric poems are not two separate streams that flow together into an indistinguishable river, nor are they static, segregated repositories of source material; they are a complex intertextual system with which Virgil interacts on every level. It is futile to try to separate the Odyssean material from the Iliadic, because for Virgil there is no *Iliad* that is not already commented on and filtered through the *Odyssey*. This is not to say that the *Odyssey* is necessarily a more important model for the *Aeneid*; on the contrary, Virgil's intense interest in the ways in which the *Odyssey* reads the *Iliad* demonstrates that both poems are constantly in play throughout the *Aeneid*. But for Virgil, the *Odyssey* is the model of intertextuality, the poem whose very essence is to transform and reconfigure the ethical, structural, and thematic world of the *Iliad*. There is simply no way for him to engage the *Iliad* in any kind of meaningful dialogue without using the *Odyssey*.

The notion that the *Odyssey* serves as a master text for the *Aeneid* must be carefully distinguished from the claim that it is merely the primary structural or conceptual model.[70] That view has a great deal to recommend it, but it is not the same thing as saying that the *Odyssey* provides a method of reading and writing intertextually. A very influential idea in the recent study of Latin intertextuality has been the concept of "looking through" one source of an allusion to read its own sources.[71] This technique is also sometimes called "window reference" or "two-tier" allusion, and has primarily been applied to the *Aeneid* in analyzing its relationship to Hellenistic poetry and especially to Apollonius' *Argonautica*.[72] But whatever name we give it, the basic principle is the same: the referring text introduces some element from the source text's own more distant source in order to achieve a kind of serial, rather than parallel, allusion. One limitation of this view is that it tends to privilege one of the two source texts over the other. On the one hand, there is the view that the author bypasses the nearer source in order to get at the original material and then reintroduces that material back into the imitation of the nearer source text, and "in the process the immediate, or chief, model is in some fashion 'corrected.'"[73] That is to say, the author looks through the window in order to identify the ultimate source, but does not actually read that source through the nearer one. On the other hand, there is the idea that the process of looking through one text at another explicitly overrides the effect of any direct reference to the ultimate source.[74] Both approaches can generate quite successful readings of particular allusive moments in Virgil, but they both use a passive model of the source texts. Whether the preexisting relationship between the two sources is used to comment on the farther or nearer one, the actual way in which the one text reads the other is not investigated. A clear window does not significantly alter the rays of light as they pass through it, nor is itself visible if cleaned thoroughly. In short, this method of inquiry is still primarily concerned with exemplary modeling, even if it proposes a very elegant structure for that modeling. It only obliquely acknowledges that the overall system of reference in the source texts might exert an active influence on the referring text, and does not at all broach the possibility that the process of looking through has dramatic effects on the source texts as well.

Even Francis Cairns, who offers the only sustained application of this model to the systematic contact between Virgil and Homer,[75] writes of the intertextuality between the two Homeric poems as a "prerequisite to examination of the *Aeneid* in these terms," and again of a "possible reading of the *Odyssey* as *imitatio cum variatione* of the *Iliad*, which would have allowed Virgil to look through the *Odyssey* to the *Iliad*."[76] The very words *prerequisite* and *allowed* emphasize the passivity of the *imitatio cum variatione* that he has so skillfully demonstrated in the intervening pages. But the relationship between the Homeric poems is not a necessary precondition for Virgil's intertextual project; it is the inspiration for it, the active model for it, its *primum mobile*. My claim is that Virgil's own active reading and reinterpretation of that intertextual relationship does not merely *allow*, but actually demands that we "look through" the *Aeneid* and understand the Homeric model in a new light.

If a window will not bend the light enough to allow for this kind of active interpretation of models, there are still other kinds of glass that can be applied to the reading of intertextual systems. If such metaphors are always heuristic and somewhat outside the poetry itself, in this case there is a long history in Virgilian scholarship.[77] Macrobius himself at one point describes the Virgilian project in optical terms (*Sat.* 5.2.13): "quid quod et omne opus Vergilianum velut de quodam Homerici operis speculo formatum est?" ("In fact, the whole Virgilian work was formed as if from a mirror of the Homeric work"). The notion of composing *de speculo* may only refer to the individual words and phrases that serve as exemplary models throughout the *Aeneid*, or it might imply a full-scale appropriation of Homeric poetics,[78] but either way, the activity of the *speculum* itself is significant. A mirror does not merely reflect an object; it can reverse the image, enlarge, reduce, and distort it in various ways depending on its particular shape and size. Likewise the position of the mirror and the viewer greatly influence the resulting image.[79] Macrobius seems to be saying that the *Aeneid* is like the reflection produced in a mirror that has been directed at the Homeric corpus,[80] a description that recalls both Servius' *ad imaginem* and Donatus' *instar*, but once again his choice of words suggests other possibilities. The *omne opus Vergilianum* is a single, unified work that, properly speaking, reflects two Homeric works; yet here Marcrobius describes a mirror of only one *Homericum opus*. While we might certainly understand this to mean the collection of both poems,[81] we can also read it as a model that defines one of the two poems as a *speculum* that is applied to the other. Moreover, he tells us that Virgil's work is formed *de speculo* "from the mirror," not *in speculo* or *per speculum*, which could mean that it is modeled on the mirror itself in addition to the object being reflected. The *Aeneid*, then, is not simply a reflection of Homer; it is the image produced by reading the *Iliad* in the mirror of the *Odyssey*. Or to put it another way: Virgil's work is not the image in the mirror; it is the image of the Homeric mirroring itself.

In late antiquity and the Middle Ages, the title *speculum* was given to countless encyclopedic collections and learned treatises, from Augustine's *Speculum de Scriptura Sacra* to the *Speculum Majus* of Vincent of Beauvais.[82] In these contexts, the word often simultaneously suggests both a mirror and the image reflected in it. The text is both a mirror through which the world can be examined and the knowledge that results from that investigation. This double meaning echoes Macrobius' ambiguous statement; Virgil is actively engaged in reading the relationship between his chief intertextual looking-glass, the *Odyssey*, and the text to which that glass is applied, the *Iliad*. While it is possible to examine an object in a mirror from an oblique angle so as not to catch a glimpse of oneself, Virgil chooses to engage the optical system in such a way as to leave traces of his own image on the mirror's surface. Virgil is not writing the Roman *Odyssea cum Iliade*, but rather setting his *Aeneid* in direct relation to the transformative power of the *Odyssey* over the *Iliad*. The *Odyssey* thus serves as a master text through which the *Iliad* can be read, but in doing so, it also provides a model for how to read itself. The *Aeneid* makes use of this master text to facilitate a dialogue with both Homeric poems at the same time.

By reading the *Aeneid* as itself containing a reading of an intertextual relationship, we can asymptotically approach, if never actually reach, a bidirectional analysis of the texts. In more restrictive scenarios of one text referring to another, most intertextual interpretations tend to privilege one or the other of the texts.[83] Either the referring text is treated as a unified whole while the model text is broken up into discrete parts (as an exemplary model) or the model text is systematically read against a myriad of fragmentary uses by the referring text. In some cases, this is due to historical circumstances (for example, Callimachus' *Aitia* survives only in fragments, so how can we read it systematically against anything or vice versa?), or to subjective issues of aesthetic taste (Homer is often seen as more interesting and central to the epic tradition so he is usually afforded the systematic reading in relation to discrete references by Apollonius). Stephen Hinds also offers the broader argument that it is actually impossible to read two texts against each other without privileging one or the other at any given moment of interpretation. While there is a great deal of truth in this formulation, the situation is a bit more complex when we are dealing with three texts.[84] If the *Odyssey* and *Iliad* are already engaged in an intertextual dialogue, and Virgil composes his *Aeneid* so that it engages that dialogue in yet another dialogue, then we actually have a pair of nested bidirectional relationships. It is possible to read the internal Homeric relationship from the perspective of the *Aeneid*, and the *Aeneid* itself in relation to the Homeric poems. If we understand the Homeric model as a dynamic system rather than a static object, we can see that it is impossible "to 'freeze' Homer, to *hold him still* for a moment so that he can be contemplated from a Virgilian point of view,"[85] without also contemplating the *Iliad* from an Odyssean point of view. But since this contemplation is motivated by the specific Virgilian context, we are always implicitly feeding Virgil back into the Homeric system. Of course, this does not mean that we can simultaneously analyze the ultimate effects of this bidirectionality on all three texts, nor would we necessarily want to do so. The point is rather that the bidirectionality is built into Virgil's own reading of Homer, and so any analysis of that reading will necessarily reflect its effects on the Homeric dynamic system.

As Hinds points out, this built-in dialogic aspect of the relationship is expressed beautifully in the title of Alessandro Barchiesi's outstanding study of Virgil and Homer, *La traccia del modello*.[86] The *traccia* is both an individual Homeric "trace" in the Virgilian text (a "frozen" moment), and "a Homeric *track* or *trail*, which, once encountered in Virgilian territory, has the potential to lead the reader in directions determined no less by Homer than by Virgil."[87] Following the direction determined by Homer means, among other things, reading him as the *modello-genere*, which fulfills a function similar to Conte's code model; following the Virgilian direction down the trail involves reading his active transformation of that model. In both cases, the act of writing intertextually is modeled by the *Odyssey*. Through a sustained dialogue with that master text, the *Aeneid* reads through the individual moments of the *Iliad* and *Odyssey* and at the same time engages the whole generic code of epic. Nowhere is this notion of engaging the master text in dialogue more clear than in the Dante's own use of various Virgilian *traccie*. Earlier we noted that Dante literally puts words in Virgil's mouth. In fact, he does more that; he explicitly writes *himself* into direct conversation with his master Virgil in a kind of metonymic image of his compositional intertextuality. When he says to Virgil, *tu se' lo mio maestro e 'l mio autore* ("you are my master and my author," *Inferno* 1.85), he is establishing the essential link between Virgil as his guide to writing intertextually and Virgil as the literal source of his character, for the character "Dante" and his journey through *inferno* are modeled

24 *Virgil's Homeric Lens*

on (among other things) Aeneas and his tour of the underworld in Book 6. In this sense, Virgil the poet of the *Aeneid* is the *autore* of the character "Dante," while "Virgil" the character in the *Commedia* is the *maestro* who guides Dante the poet through intertextual dialogue.[88]

We can see the underlying logic even better when we consider that Virgil supplies the model for Dante's conversation specifically in the interaction between Aeneas and Anchises. Virgil does not go so far as to actually put his own master Homer in the underworld episode,[89] but he does base the scene on Odysseus' meeting with the blind seer Tiresias in *Odyssey* 11. This does not prevent the Old English *Meters of Boethius* from offering a Dantesque anachronism:

> Omerus wæs   east mid Crecum
> on ðæm leodscipe   leoða cræftgast,
> Firgilies   freond and lareow,
> þæm mæran sceope   magistra betst.

> Homer lived in the East among the Greeks.
> in that nation he was the most skillful in song.
> He was the friend and teacher of Virgil,
> that great bard, the best of all masters.[90]

Like Dante's *maestro e autore*, the idea of Homer as *freond and lareow* (friend and teacher) to Virgil supplies an excellent metaphor for the dual dialogical and authoritative aspects of the intertextual relationship, while the fact that Virgil himself is called the *magistra betst* (best master) underscores the generative intertextuality that he learned from Homer. The author of these lines may not have any firsthand knowledge of the *Iliad* or the *Odyssey*, but as his own Boethian *translatio* project demonstrates, he is quite familiar with the idea of a subsequent text using a source as a master template while transforming its details in often radical ways.

To return to the classical world, although Virgil is not claiming that the *Aeneid* is a translation of the Homeric poems, the principle is very similar. The successful use of the source involves reading it with a sensitivity to both its imitability and refractibility. But when this double mode of reading is applied to two interrelated sources at once, there must also be an awareness of the ways in which those two texts reflect and refract each other. Virgil accomplishes this by using the *Odyssey* as an intertextual *speculum* or perhaps even a *speculum perspicuum*, a "lens," which can refract, diffract, and, if polished properly, reflect.

In his seminal article on intertextuality in Latin scholarship, Don Fowler suggests that the idea of imposing a hierarchy of reference is problematic because of "the inherently multiple nature of intertextual reference."[91] In the case of the *Aeneid*, however, the hierarchy is built into the original intertextual model. Virgil is not arbitrarily using the *Odyssey* to read the

Iliad; he is doing so because the *Odyssey* does, in fact, read the *Iliad* and, moreover, actively marks that reading as a productive technique of epic composition. Virgil's application of this technique is systematic but not slavish. By establishing an overall method of reading the *Iliad* using the *Odyssey*, he can freely access specific Iliadic material even in the absence of Odyssean analogues and still reap the benefits of the Odyssean lens. At the same time, he positions his text in a way that allows him to challenge the Odyssean reading of an Iliadic moment whenever he wants. By grafting his poem into the Homeric time line at the same point as the *Odyssey*, he can occupy the same relational space as the *Odyssey* vis-à-vis the *Iliad* and thus work out Iliadic consequences in new ways. We have already noted that the *Odyssey* acknowledges the temporal priority of the *Iliad*, but it also recognizes a causal ordering. The action of the *Iliad* leads directly to the action of the *Odyssey* in the basic sense that the latter is a narrative about coming home from the war described in the former, but the actual *Odyssey* is certainly not a necessary consequence of the *Iliad*. While it looks forward in many ways, the *Iliad* does not require Odysseus' particular narrative in the same way that it might entail the subsequent death of Achilles or the fall of Troy. This frees the *Odyssey* to create multiple versions of the Iliadic aftermath as well as multiple readings of the *Iliad* itself. Iliadic characters like Menelaus and Helen can reminisce, Agamemnon and Achilles can reconsider their choices, Odysseus can replay the sack of Troy, all of which reconfigures the entire experience of the *Iliad*.

Virgil is also interested in processing the Iliadic experience, but he recognizes that his narrative is more firmly a consequence of the *Iliad* through Poseidon's prophecy in Book 20, so he turns to the transformative model of the *Odyssey* in order to activate the consequent narrative in more radical ways. Although the *Aeneid* does not offer itself as an explicit replacement for the *Odyssey*, the synchronicity of the two poems nevertheless sets up a healthy rivalry over the claim to the post-Iliadic heritage. By resisting some of Homer's attempts to define that heritage, Virgil brings his own claim into more specific relief. The *Odyssey* offers a thorough investigation of the attitudes of the nominal winning side in the war,[92] and Virgil could not fail to notice the almost total elision of the Trojans from the Odyssean narrative. Odysseus and Telemachus between them encounter most of the major Greek Iliadic figures, living or dead, and various events at Troy are recounted, but there are only a handful of incidental references to actual Trojans, and none at all to the two overarching Iliadic figures, Hector and Paris.[93] This is due in no small part to the fact that Iliadic Greeks control much of the narrative within the poem. The recollections of Nestor, Menelaus, and Helen, as well as Odysseus' own tales are all one level removed from the poet's main narrative, and the reported conversations with other Iliadic figures in the underworld are two levels removed.

Unlike the *Iliad*, which contains many direct descriptions of the Trojans and their conversations, the *Odyssey* relates the experience of the war through these embedded narratives, which allow for the suppression of the Trojan perspective. As we shall see later, this does not mean that the Trojan aspect of the *Iliad* is entirely absent from the poem, but only that there is no explicit treatment of it. As a counterbalance to this suppression, Virgil creates a synchronic Trojan narrative that shadows the Odyssean one and highlights the points of elision through various reworkings of the source text. By presenting a post-Iliadic reality that embraces the Trojan experience while still situating it in the Odyssean framework, Virgil is able to portray the *Aeneid* as the heir to both the Trojan history and the whole Greek epic tradition. Through the Homeric technique of embedded narrative, he allows the Trojans themselves, and especially Aeneas, to lay their own claim to continuity with the *Iliad*. The Odyssean elision certainly underscores the tenuous nature of that claim, but it also provides a powerful model for reorienting Iliadic consequences.

Virgil's simultaneous acceptance and rejection of various aspects of the Odyssean model reflects the sophistication of his intertextual dialogue. The *Aeneid* does not blindly imitate the *Odyssey*, but it also does not displace it from the epic hierarchy. Just as the *Odyssey* reflects the temporal priority of the *Iliad*, so Virgil recognizes the generic priority of the *Odyssey*. It is the first intertextual epic, and consequently it provides both a method of reading and a new poetics of transformation. As a third party to the Homeric dialogue, the *Aeneid* naturally challenges the model in many ways, but it always acknowledges the essential preexisting relationship between the two poems. Virgil uses the Odyssean *speculum* to read the *Iliad* because the *Iliad* demands to be refracted, reflected, and repeated, and because the *Odyssey* already generates a system to meet that need. At the same time, he integrates the results of this reading into his larger poetic project in order to define his own relationship to the epic tradition. The details of this system and some of its specific Virgilian applications will occupy the remaining chapters of this work.

argumentum varium ac multiplex

In his discussion of the imitation of Homer by various poets, Macrobius describes the way in which the primary text holds firm against all manner of intertextual beating (*Sat.* 6.3.1):[94]

> summus Homericae laudis cumulus est quod, cum ita a plurimis adversus
> eum vigilatum sit, coactaeque omnium vires manum contra fecerint,
> *ille velut pelagi rupes immota resistit.* (*Aen.* 7.586)

> It is the highest peak of Homer's glory that, although he is watched
> by so many, and although all join forces to form a band against him,
> *he, like an unmoved rock in the sea, stands firm.*

The fact that he uses a Virgilian simile (*Aen.* 7.586)[95] to describe this resistance already seems to undercut the claim to a certain extent, especially when that simile is directly based on at least one Homeric passage (*Il.* 15.618–21) and possibly others.[96] For anyone who, like Macrobius, is very familiar with both authors, there is no way to read Homer without processing him through Virgil on some level.[97] This reading may not challenge the prestige of Homer, but it does shape many of the questions we ask about the *Iliad* and *Odyssey* as well as influence our attempts to answer them. Furthermore, the very notion of Homer withstanding intertextual attacks presumes that Virgil and other poets are interested in tearing down the rock rather than building upon it. This is another function of the fragmentary view of Homeric reference within the *Aeneid* as well as a denial of the vital productivity of the poems themselves. But in one respect Macrobius is quite right: Homer does resist the many attempts to turn him into a mere quarry for allusions, but he is not *immota*; rather, he actively generates a system of intertextuality that the subsequent epic tradition can use to interact with the Homeric poems.

In order to explore the ramifications of this Homeric system, I propose, in Chapter 2 of this work, to read the intertextual relationship between the *Odyssey* and the *Iliad* independently from the specific context of the *Aeneid*, but still from the general Virgilian perspective. That is to say, Virgil's reading of Homer establishes a temporal and intertextual hierarchy that presumes that the *Iliad* precedes the *Odyssey* and thus filters it through the latter. Furthermore, it treats the poems as written texts, albeit ones with multiple variants, and acknowledges the Alexandrian book divisions as well. I do not mean to exclude the historical possibility of either a reverse sequence (that the *Odyssey* was composed before the *Iliad*) or the idea that the two poems simultaneously emerged from an oral tradition. My purpose is to examine the exclusive relationship from a starting point similar to Virgil's–though obviously not with the same specific tools, apparatus, mind set, or cultural context–in order to see what sorts of readings underlie the notion of the *Odyssey* as an intertextual model. These readings are not offered as actual evidence of the Virgilian intertextual project, but they are certainly motivated and influenced by that project as well as by my own post-Virgilian vantage point.

In Chapter 3, I will then move to the central argument that the *Odyssey* is the master text for the *Aeneid*. This will involve an analysis of the ways in which Virgil models his own intertextual poem on the *Odyssey* while constantly competing with its claim to the Iliadic heritage. By grafting his poem onto the Trojan saga at precisely the same point as the *Odyssey*, Virgil engages his predecessor in a dialogue on the consequences of the *Iliad* and on the poetics of transformation in general. This is especially clear in Book 2, where Aeneas assumes the role of Odyssean storyteller but translates the fall of Troy from a tale of Greek triumph into an elegant assertion of direct continuity with the Iliadic tradition.

Finally, Chapter 4 applies my model of Virgil's Odyssean intertextuality to a series of close readings in *Aeneid* 2 and 3 followed by a broader analysis of the end of the poem, in order to elucidate the value of this interpretation for our deeper understanding of the *Aeneid* as a whole. These explications demonstrate Virgil's thorough engagement with his Homeric sources not merely as repositories of material to be imitated and translated, but as active and productive partners in his own epic project.

2 Iliadic Refraction

Iliados epilogos

If the reputation of the *Aeneid* relative to the Homeric poems has fluctuated greatly in the history of literary criticism, that of the *Odyssey* has consistently suffered by comparison to the *Iliad*.¹ For many centuries, conventional wisdom viewed the *Iliad* as a profound poem about heroism, honor, and death, while the *Odyssey* was often seen as a more disparate collection of character studies and domestic vignettes. In antiquity, the difference between the poems is first described explicitly by Aristotle (*Poet.* 1459b13–15):

καὶ γὰρ τῶν ποιημάτων ἑκάτερον συνέστηκεν
ἡ μὲν Ἰλιὰς ἁπλοῦν καὶ παθητικόν, ἡ δὲ Ὀδύσσεια
πεπλεγμένον ἀναγνώρισις γὰρ διόλου) καὶ ἠθική·

Of his poems, the structure of the *Iliad* is simple
and full of suffering, while the *Odyssey* is complex
(for it is full of recognition) and character-based.

The *pathos* of the *Iliad* is linked to its simple construction, while the complexity of the *Odyssey* is associated with its emphasis on "recognitions" and *êthos*.² On the face of it, this dichotomy does not seem to embody any actual value judgment, only an analytical description of the structure and primary thematic mode of each poem. At a much later stage of the commentary tradition, the twelfth-century Byzantine scholar Eustathius transforms the Aristotelean distinction into a more direct comparison in his discussion of the proem of the *Iliad* (*Comm. ad Il.* 1.7.5–7):

ἀνδρώδης μὲν ἡ Ἰλιὰς καὶ σεμνοτέρα καὶ
ὕψος ἔχουσα, ἐπεὶ καὶ ἡρωϊκωτέρα· ἠθικὴ δὲ
ἡ Ὀδύσσεια, ὡς ἐκεῖ σαφέστερον γέγραπται·

The *Iliad* is manly, more stately, and has more grandeur,
since it is also more heroic, while the *Odyssey* is
character-based, since it is written more clearly.

While this certainly implies that the *Iliad* contains more of the qualities that we commonly associate with epic, there is still a clear attempt to weigh the relative merits of the two poems without explicitly privileging one over the other. The greater solemnity and heroism of the *Iliad* are balanced by the *Odyssey*'s superior clarity and character interest. Furthermore, Eustathius seems to contradict Aristotle directly in describing the *Odyssey* as the clearer (*saphesteron*) of the two poems.

The pithiness of these distinctions somewhat masks the complex principles of aesthetic judgment that underlie them, and it is not entirely clear, for example, whether both Eustathius and Aristotle believe that the *Odyssey* is devoid of all manliness or that the *Iliad* is not interested in character at all. The antithesis between *pathos* and *êthos* is quite common in ancient criticism, but the two terms are not always represented consistently.[3] This is especially true of *êthikê*, which can mean anything from "moral, ethical" to "expressive of character." When set against *pathêtikon*, the term often defines something that is characteristic of everyday life or more realistic, not in terms of plot, but rather in characterization and tone.[4] The implication with respect to Homer seems to be that the *Odyssey* is closer to everyday life in its portrayal of characters, as well as being less serious and grand overall. Even if a correlation between realism and mildness is valid, a large portion of the *Odyssey* is devoted to the fabulous wanderings of the hero, so the alleged lighter tone of the poem cannot be based entirely on its depiction of swineherds, banquets, and other aspects of domestic life. No one would call the Cyclops episode or the descent to the underworld realistic episodes, but they might nevertheless be thought to lack the dramatic intensity and heroic tone of the *Iliad*. This view is most explicit in Longinus' evaluation of the two poems (*Subl.* 9.11–15):

δείκνυσι δ' ὅμως διὰ τῆς Ὀδυσσείας . . . ὅτι μεγάλης φύσεως
ὑποφερομένης ἤδη ἴδιόν ἐστιν ἐν γήρᾳ τὸ φιλόμυθον . . .

δευτέρου δὲ εἵνεκα προσιστορήσθω τὰ κατὰ τὴν Ὀδύσσειαν,
ὅπως ᾖ σοι γνώριμον ὡς ἡ ἀπακμὴ τοῦ πάθους ἐν τοῖς
μεγάλοις συγγραφεῦσι καὶ ποιηταῖς εἰς ἦθος ἐκλύεται.

Yet he shows throughout the *Odyssey* . . . that, when genius declines, the mark of old age is a love of fabulous tales . . .

These things regarding the *Odyssey* should be considered for another reason: so that you may realize how declining emotional power in great writers and poets passes into character study.

Longinus sees the *Odyssey* as the work of a poet who is past his prime and whose own reduced vigor forces him to abandon the emotional power of the *Iliad* in favor of character studies and the fantastic narratives of a geriatric myth-lover (*philomuthos*). This is no mere comparison of the two poems; for Longinus, *êthos* is clearly inferior to *pathos* in the construction of an epic poem, and the *Odyssey*'s additional interest in mythical narratives seals his judgment.

But if this view subordinates the *Odyssey* to the *Iliad* more than Aristotle or Eustathius seems to do, it also attributes that subordination in no small part to the temporal priority of the *Iliad*. Longinus claims that Homer composed the *Iliad* ἐν ἀκμῇ πνεύματος (*Subl.* 9.13),[5] in the prime of his genius, so that the fall from the heights of *pathos* (the *apakme* in the foregoing quote)[6] is an inevitable consequence of the *Odyssey*'s posteriority. The emphasis on the natural decay of genius seems calculated to soften the negative comparison with the *Iliad*, and even in the midst of his litany of criticisms of details in the *Odyssey*, he offers certain moments of reserved praise, which he justifies by saying, ἀλλὰ γῆρας διηγοῦμαι, γῆρας δ' ὅμως Ὁμήρου ("I am describing old age, but it is still Homer's old age," *Subl.* 9.14). The product of Homer's old age still bears the marks of his poetic skill. But embedded within this claim is the implication that the *Iliad* is not simply the fruit of his prime years, but that it actually consumes the bulk of his intensity, so that δίχα τῆς σφοδρότητος παραμένει τὸ μέγεθος ("its greatness remains without its intensity," *Subl.* 9.13). The alleged weaknesses of the *Odyssey* are thus explained not just as a general result of the poet's old age, but as a specific function of the innate temporal relationship between the two poems.

Although there is some evidence for an ancient view that the *Odyssey* was composed first,[7] the general consensus followed the internal chronology of the stories and assigned pride of place to the *Iliad*. As more specific proof of its posteriority, Longinus points to the *Odyssey*'s familiarity with Iliadic characters and its systematic use of λείψανα τῶν Ἰλιακῶν παθημάτων (*Subl.* 9.12), the "left-overs" of the Iliadic events. This notion of the *Odyssey* picking up the remnants of the Trojan saga omitted by the *Iliad* is fairly common in the ancient scholia,[8] but it mostly serves to subordinate the *Odyssey* to the *Iliad* even further, without any discussion of the structural and thematic implications of the specific relationship between the poems. Longinus sums up this whole line of reasoning with a pointed statement (*Subl.* 9.12): οὐ γὰρ ἀλλ' ἢ τῆς Ἰλιάδος ἐπίλογός ἐστιν ἡ Ὀδύσσεια ("for the *Odyssey* is nothing but an epilogue to the *Iliad*"). But what exactly does it mean to be an *Iliados epilogos*, and perhaps more importantly, what does it mean to be "nothing other than an *epilogos*"? While the term is occasionally used to describe the concluding part of a play without any further particular requirements (cf. English "epilogue"),[9] it most commonly has the technical meaning of "peroration" as defined in rhetorical manuals and related discourses, most notably in Aristotle's *Rhetoric*.[10] Longinus, however, seems to mean something more like "sequel" with the primary emphasis placed on the sequential nature of the poem. In light of his earlier statements about the Iliadic left-overs, to say that the *Odyssey* is "nothing but a sequel" implies that its existence is wholly determined by the *Iliad*, while at the same time not actually being required by that *Iliad*.

We will have more to say later on the question of Iliadic necessitation, but it is clear that Longinus sees the posteriority of the *Odyssey* as a mark of its weakness, almost as if it is belated rather than simply coming later. In this regard, he may have inadvertently hit upon a fundamental aspect of the relationship between the two poems. The *Odyssey* is not so much a belated poem as it is a poem about belatedness, and this quality is manifested in its constant engagement with the *Iliad* and its aftermath. The ten years that have passed since the end of the Trojan war may render any hope of Odysseus' homecoming tenuous at best, but they do set up a kind of time-lapse photography system in which to examine the effects of the war in general and of the *Iliad* specifically. One of the immediate consequences of this delayed framework is that it allows the poem to position itself as something more than a mere sequel to the *Iliad*. In Longinus' formulation, there is no attempt to distinguish the *Odyssey* from the Cyclic poems, the *Aethiopis*, *Ilias Parva*, *Ilioupersis*, and *Nostoi*, all of which describe events that come after the *Iliad*.[11] But the *Odyssey* retells many of the episodes contained in those poems, not only in order to summarize the intervening years between itself and the *Iliad*, but also to compare all the possible outcomes of the earlier poem. The ten year gap–the very same length as the war–delays Odysseus long enough to guarantee that he will be the last one home. This facilitates a dual movement throughout the poem: backward through the history of the aftermath, and forward toward the last remaining outcome of the war. That outcome explicitly involves the domestication of the Iliadic experience, an attempt to transform the *pathos* of the battlefield into the *êthos* of home life.

This transformation underlies all the ancient schematic comparisons of the poems, but as Longinus' argument shows, there is no real discussion of the actual intertextual mechanisms that drive it. We have already noticed that the *Odyssey* omits any direct reference to the main narrative of the *Iliad*, and yet it evokes it constantly through its cast of characters, analogous stories, and re-enactment of key events. In this way, the poem can serve as both a definitive sequel encompassing the entire aftermath of the war, and a proper *epilogos* in the rhetorical sense. This does not mean that the *Iliad* is incomplete without the *Odyssey*, but rather that the *Odyssey* makes the *Iliad* the historical starting point of its narrative journey while simultaneously offering a complex, and often unexpected, interpretation of that poem's own narrative and thematic concerns. This dual epilogic function can be understood as a simultaneous superposition and juxtaposition of the *Odyssey* to the *Iliad*; an attempt to construct the aftermath of the poem and to interpret the *Iliad* in light of that aftermath.[12]

Têlemachoio patêr

But if, in the words of Andrew Marvell, "the aftermath seldom or never equals the first herbage,"[13] this is primarily a consequence of defining the new growth as a function of the mowing process rather than in relation to the original source. As a sequel, the *Odyssey* is certainly concerned with the effects of cutting down the Achaean and Trojan flower, but it is not a replacement or substitute for the *Iliad*; rather, it attempts to understand the whole nature of the growth cycle in terms of those effects. There is perhaps a cruel irony in applying Marvell's words to the Homeric poems, in which the mowing down of the Iliadic characters effectively destroys any chance for most of them to generate their own second growth, but the *Odyssey* is still deeply concerned with the relationship between the Iliadic veterans and their children. The whole question of aftermath is first processed through Telemachus' experiences as he wrestles with the domestic consequences of his father's absence and then as he collects information from Nestor and Menelaus.[14] Even before the so-called *Telemachy* properly begins, Zeus relates how another Iliadic son, Orestes, deals with the disastrous return of his own father (*Od.* 1.29–44). As a preface to the *Telemachy*, it establishes a pattern of reading the consequences of the war through the experiences of the subsequent generation, which in turn reinforces the *Odyssey*'s overall method of processing the *Iliad* through its own posterity.

This posterity-posterity equation is a direct response to the *Iliad*'s interest in the parental viewpoint in general, and more specifically in the reactions of parents to their children's peril. The *Iliad* is framed by two episodes in which a concerned parent attempts to ransom his child back from an Achaean captain. In the opening scene of the poem, the priest Chryses is rebuked when he offers a ransom for his live daughter, and turns to Apollo for swift vengeance until Agamemnon reluctantly relents (*Il.* 1.8–120). In contrast, in Book 24 Priam, having already received divine aid, successfully ransoms Hector's corpse from Achilles in his initial attempt. While there are important differences between these two episodes, they both examine the collateral damage of warfare from a parental perspective.[15] Captured prisoners and dead captains are part of the natural course of an extended siege, but by exploring the effects of these events on the parents, the *Iliad* highlights the precarious nature of genealogical succession in times of war. Glaucus' famous words to Diomedes on the battlefield express this idea using another vegetative simile (*Il.* 6.145–49):

Τυδεΐδη μεγάθυμε τί ἤ γενεὴν ἐρεείνεις;
οἵη περ φύλλων γενεὴ τοίη δὲ καὶ ἀνδρῶν.
φύλλα τὰ μέν τ' ἄνεμος χαμάδις χέει, ἄλλα δέ θ' ὕλη
τηλεθόωσα φύει, ἔαρος δ' ἐπιγίγνεται ὥρη·
ὣς ἀνδρῶν γενεὴ ἣ μὲν φύει ἣ δ' ἀπολήγει.

Great-hearted son of Tydeus, why ask about my generation?
As is the generation of leaves, so is that of men.
The wind scatters the leaves on the ground, but the wood
flourishes again in the season when spring returns.
So one generation of men grows and another dies.

In the heat of battle, the lineage of an individual hero who may die shortly seems to matter very little to him, but as it turns out, Glaucus' somewhat reluctant genealogical excursus reveals an ancestral guest-friendship bond that prevents either man from killing the other (*Il.* 6.212–36). Their grandparents have unknowingly interceded in the potentially fatal combat, thereby simultaneously saving their descendants' lives and reinterpreting Glaucus' philosophical statement. The generations of men are like the generations of leaves not simply because they are part of a continuous cycle of birth and death, but rather because they spring from the same source each time and bear the collective legacy of every successive product of that source. Thus the ancestral intercession in this episode may be more indirect than in the case of Chryses or Priam, but it is certainly no less intentional. The relationship entered into by the grandparents involves an expectation that future generations will honor it in perpetuity.

The portability of this kind of intervention is all the more valuable in a war setting where heroes are physically separated from their parents, but it is not especially common in the *Iliad*. As the Chryses and Priam episodes demonstrate, parental success is usually predicated on the involvement of the gods. This becomes tautological when the parents are gods themselves, but even in those cases there is no consistent outcome. Aphrodite only manages to save her son Aeneas from Diomedes in Book 5 because Apollo is there to catch him when she lets him fall from her wounded hands (*Il.* 5.343–45), while in Book 16, Zeus reluctantly allows his son Sarpedon to be killed by Patroclus after Hera warns him about setting a dangerous precedent (*Il.* 16.431–61). In the case of Thetis, the outcome is more complicated since Achilles is the only child in the poem who actually asks his parent for assistance. She helps fulfill her son's desire for vengeance at the expense of her own parental desire for his survival, but even here the consequences of his choices are processed through her point of view. In Book 1, Achilles' tearful complaint to Thetis after he has been wronged by Agamemnon is both a consequence of and an analogue to Chryses' own cry to Apollo, and Achilles emphasizes the close connection between the man and the god in order to draw the parallel more clearly (*Il.* 1.380–82):

χωόμενος δ' ὁ γέρων πάλιν ᾤχετο· τοῖο δ' Ἀπόλλων
εὐξαμένου ἤκουσεν, ἐπεὶ μάλα οἱ φίλος ἦεν,
ἧκε δ' ἐπ' Ἀργείοισι κακὸν βέλος·

The old man went away again in anger, but Apollo
heard his prayer, since he was very dear to him,
and released the evil arrow against the Argives.

In both cases, the intervention of the divinity brings death and destruction to the Achaeans, but while Chryses' violent request is motivated by his parental concern, Achilles is appealing to his own mother, which forces her to choose between his desires and his best interests. As her response shows, she has already accepted his choice and is more concerned with explaining its consequences in terms of the generative cycle (*Il.* 1.415–18):

αἴθ' ὄφελες παρὰ νηυσὶν ἀδάκρυτος καὶ ἀπήμων
ἧσθαι, ἐπεί νύ τοι αἶσα μίνυνθά περ οὔ τι μάλα δήν·
νῦν δ' ἅμα τ' ὠκύμορος καὶ ὀϊζυρὸς περὶ πάντων
ἔπλεο· τώ σε κακῇ αἴσῃ τέκον ἐν μεγάροισι.

Would that you could sit by your ships without weeping, unharmed,
since truly your destiny is to be short, not at all very long.
Now you are both swift-fated and bitter beyond
all men. I bore you to an evil destiny in my hall.

Although Thetis wishes Achilles could sit by the ships untroubled,[16] she acknowledges his brief destiny (*aisa minutha*) and further assumes responsibility for having borne him to this evil destiny (*kakêi aisêi*).[17] Rather than extricate him from a situation that will lead to his early death as Aphrodite does with Aeneas, she prefers to situate his choice in the larger context of human mortality. She will do what he asks because she cannot deny him the chance to acquire his *kleos*,[18] but after the death of Patroclus, she once again interprets his heroic choice as a consequence of her generative function (*Il.* 18.54–56):

ὤ μοι ἐγὼ δειλή, ὤ μοι δυσαριστοτόκεια,
ἥ τ' ἐπεὶ ἄρ τέκον υἱὸν ἀμύμονά τε κρατερόν τε
ἔξοχον ἡρώων·

Alas, woe to me, one who has borne a noble son into misfortune,
since I gave birth to a blameless and powerful son,
standing out among heroes.

The apparent oxymoron *dysaristotokeia* does not mean, as the standard lexicon would have it, "the unhappy mother of a noble son,"[19] but rather, as a reinforcement of her earlier statement in Book 1, "one who has borne a noble son into misfortune."[20] She is certainly unhappy, but her sorrow comes from the knowledge that the very qualities that make Achilles *aristos* have led him to choose an early death.

Glaucus' speech demonstrates that the age-old motif of fleeting life is a concern of any epic hero, but it is particularly relevant to Achilles. While every warrior knows that there is a good chance he will not survive the war, Achilles provides the paradigm for the effects of this knowledge. Because he seems able to choose his destiny more directly than any other character in the poem,[21] he needs to be more acutely aware of the consequences of his choices. Thetis provides this awareness but consistently filters it through the lens of parental concern, thus enabling Achilles to respond appropriately to Priam's own sorrow over Hector in Book 24 and, more specifically, to his request that Achilles think of his own father's potential grief (*Il.* 24.486): μνῆσαι πατρὸς σοῖο ("remember your father"). The parental perspective that is established in the opening book of the poem is thus emphatically reasserted in the final episodes where Priam obtains Hector's body and ordains his burial.

While the poem's main parental interest lies in processing the action of the poem through the concern of the mothers and fathers of the heroes, these Iliadic warriors are also often parents themselves. Even setting aside Nestor, who straddles two generations and whose sons Antilochus and Thrasymedes fight beside him at Troy (*Il.* 5.565, 9.81), Agamemnon names his three daughters, Chrysothemis, Laodice, and Iphianassa (*Il.* 9.145, cf. 9.287), and his son Orestes (9.142, cf. 9.284); Helen mentions her child by Menelaus (*Il.* 3.175); Achilles refers to Neoptolemus once (*Il.* 19.327)[22] and Hermes alludes to him another time (24.467); and of course Hector's son Astyanax-Scamandrius makes an actual appearance in the poem (6.399–484). But it is the poem's striking reference to Odysseus as a parent that serves as the transition to the *Odyssey*'s inversion of the Iliadic pattern. Odysseus twice refers to himself as "father of Telemachus" (*Il.* 2.260: Τηλεμάχοιο πατὴρ; *Il.* 4.354: Τηλεμάχοιο φίλον πατέρα), which the scholia see as evidence of single authorship of the two poems,[23] but there is no ancient discussion of the precise function of this unique construction.[24] The extensive use of patronymics is one of the defining characteristics of Homeric diction,[25] but this is the only certain example of a teknonymic in all of Greek literature.[26] Teknonymy is a common feature of the onomastic systems of many cultures around the world from Arabia to Bali, though its origins have been much debated. One important factor may be a new father's desire to assert his rights within his father-in-law's household,[27] which suggests a very productive interpretation for this specific context. While there is a general impression that Homeric aristocratic society (and by this I mean the society depicted in the Homeric poems rather than any historical reality) is patrilineal, there are significant traces of matrilineal succession or at least succession through daughters.[28] The most apparent example is Menelaus inheriting the throne of Sparta from Tyndareus through his marriage to Helen even though she has brothers. This inheritance is not explicitly described in the poems, but Helen wonders where Castor and Polydeuces are during the *teichoskopia* (*Il.* 3.236–42), which implies they were still alive at some point after Menelaus was already king of Sparta.

The succession conflict in Ithaca presents a more confusing picture. The *Odyssey* offers only vague details about the nature of the kingship, and it is not entirely clear whether Telemachus automatically inherits the throne as the son of Odysseus or whether it can actually be acquired by marriage to Penelope.[29] Further difficulties arise when we consider that Odysseus' own father Laertes is still alive but in retirement (*Od.* 1.188–93) and that Odysseus already ruled Ithaca before the war (*Od.* 2.47).³⁰ Regardless of the exact rewards, both Telemachus and the suitors acknowledge the role of Penelope's father, Icarius, in brokering the remarriage (*Od.* 2.52–54, 113–14), which suggests that she is still somehow considered a part of his household even after a marriage with issue.³¹ It is not surprising, then, that Odysseus might symbolically assert his rights in the father-in-law's home through the use of a teknonymic, particularly since his own name was given to him by his maternal grandfather, Autolycus, in another naming ritual of obscure origin (*Od.* 19.399–412).³²

This symbolic teknonymy also serves to reorient the patronymic world of the *Iliad*, where the heroes are so often examined from their parents' perspective. Whether or not the *Iliad* is actually anticipating the *Odyssey* in this usage, the *Odyssey* itself picks up on this notion of interpreting Odysseus from his son's perspective in the four books of the *Telemachy* that open the poem. In addition to establishing the domestic effects of Odysseus' long absence from Ithaca, these books take us through Telemachus' investigation in painstaking detail and thereby allow us to process the fates of all the Greek commanders through his eyes. In addition to the extended narratives of Nestor and Menelaus, Telemachus hears about the successful return or death of the other six major Iliadic captains before finally learning about Odysseus' detention on Calypso's island (*Od.* 4.555–60).³³ The point is not simply to build suspense about Odysseus' whereabouts or whether he will escape, since we already know from the beginning of the poem that he is with Calypso (*Od.* 1.13–15) and that the gods are planning his return (*Od.* 1.80–87), but rather to allow us to understand the consequences of that belated reintegration into society through the living example of a son who has reached the threshold of manhood without his father. Telemachus' very name emphasizes this belatedness, for while it is usually construed as "fighting from afar" in reference to Odysseus' skill with the bow (cf. *Od.* 8.215–29, 21.393–423, 22.1–7),³⁴ the poem frequently plays on the etymology of the name in order to explore the idea of Odysseus' absence far away at war.³⁵ Thus in Book 15, Athena tells Telemachus that it is time to return home to Ithaca with a subtle reference to the consequences of Odysseus' wanderings (*Od.* 15.10): Τηλέμαχ', οὐκέτι καλὰ δόμων ἄπο τῆλ' ἀλάλησαι ("Telemachus, it is no longer right for you to wander far from home"). If we interpret the vocative *têlemache* as an epithet meaning "he who has fought far away" rather than as a proper name, these words serve equally well as a rebuke to Odysseus. Likewise in Book 17, the goatherd Melanthius hears Eumaeus praying for Odysseus' return and offers up this curse (*Od.* 17.251–53):

αἲ γὰρ Τηλέμαχον βάλοι ἀργυρότοξος Ἀπόλλων
σήμερον ἐν μεγάροις', ἢ ὑπὸ μνηστῆρσι δαμείη,
ὡς Ὀδυσῆΐ γε τηλοῦ ἀπώλετο νόστιμον ἦμαρ.

38 Virgil's Homeric Lens

> If only silver-bowed Apollo would strike down Telemachus
> today in the halls, or if only he were killed by the suitors,
> just as Odysseus, far away, has lost his day of homecoming.

This is an idiomatic form of asseveration in which the destruction of Odysseus is depicted as certain by opposing it to a strong, but less certain or impossible, wish for Telemachus' death,[36] but the implication of the *figura etymologica* is that Telemachus is both the literal and figurative heir to Odysseus' failed homecoming. There are several other examples of this sort of etymological wordplay on the *têle* portion of the name (cf. *Od.* 2.183–85; 3.230–31; 19.26–28, 87–88; 20.338–40), but this example strongly suggests not only the spatial distance between Odysseus and his homeland, but the temporal distance as well. While the word *êmar* is often used with an adjective as a periphrasis for a state or condition (cf. *doulion, eleutheron êmar*), in this particular phrase the literal sense of an actual day of return is still evident, so the day of homecoming (*nostimon êmar*) must have been lost far away in time, i.e., "long ago."[37]

In Book 19, yet another play on *têle* reinforces this notion of the name of the son referring to the span of time separating the war and his father's return. Eumaeus' joyous reunion with Telemachus is described through a surprising simile in which the son is cast as Odysseus who has wandered for ten years, while the father's suffering mirrors Telemachus' own sorrow during the absence (*Od.* 16.17–21):[38]

> ὡς δὲ πατὴρ ὃν παῖδα φίλα φρονέων ἀγαπάζῃ
> ἐλθόντ' ἐξ ἀπίης γαίης δεκάτῳ ἐνιαυτῷ,
> μοῦνον <u>τηλύ</u>γετον, τῷ ἐπ' ἄλγεα πολλὰ μογήσῃ,
> ὡς τότε <u>Τηλέ</u>μαχον θεοειδέα δῖος ὑφορβὸς
> πάντα κύσεν περιφύς, ὡς ἐκ θανάτοιο φυγόντα·

> And just as a father, with loving thoughts, welcomes his son,
> when he returns from a distant land in the tenth year,
> his only and grown son, for whose sake he has undergone many hardships,
> so now the noble swineherd, kissed godlike Telemachos,
> clinging to him, as if he had escaped from death.

The reversal of roles serves as a preview of the imminent reunion between Telemachus and Odysseus and uses the parallels between their respective experiences in the poem to read the father through his son. Just as the entire *Telemachy* establishes a fixed pattern against which to view Odysseus' account of his own wanderings, so this reunion with Eumaeus offers an idealized picture of a father-son meeting. The actual reunion turns out to be less spontaneous since Telemachus first doubts the miraculous transformation of the stranger and only breaks into tears after Odysseus' explanation (*Od.* 16.186–219), but this only underscores the difference between the dreams of the son and the subsequent reality throughout the poem.[39] At the same time, the strong wordplay on *têlugeton/Têlemachon*, which both occupy the same metrical position in their respective lines and rhyme as well, once again defines Telemachus as the supreme consequence of the etymological "fighting far away/long ago." Both the meaning and etymology of the epithet *têlugeton*, which always refers to a dearly loved child in Homer, are uncertain, with conjectures ranging from "only child" to "late born" to "born in a far-off land."[40] In this context, the word seems to mean something more like "grown son" and the play on *têle* further emphasizes the passage of time. The causal relationship between the distant fighter and the grown son is thus defined in terms of the belatedness of Odysseus' return.

If Telemachus is both the literal posterity of the Iliadic hero Odysseus and a figure of the *Odyssey*'s posteriority to the *Iliad*, then Odysseus' use of the teknonymic in the *Iliad* may be a proleptic confirmation of that relationship in light of the delayed homecoming. While Telemachus has certainly not forgotten about his father, their relationship prior to the reunion in Book 19 is based entirely on second-hand information. Not only does his name reflect this distance, but the fact that he is never called by the patronymic *Odysseides* also suggests that he is not yet the true son of Odysseus, but only the product of that distant war and belated homecoming.[41] In Book 1, Athena, disguised as Mentes, an old friend of his father, visits Telemachus and pretends to be uncertain about whether he is actually Odysseus' son (*Od.* 1.206–9):

> ἀλλ' ἄγε μοι τόδε εἰπὲ καὶ ἀτρεκέως κατάλεξον,
> εἰ δὴ ἐξ αὐτοῖο τόσος πάϊς εἰς Ὀδυσῆος.
> αἰνῶς μὲν κεφαλήν τε καὶ ὄμματα καλὰ ἔοικας
> κείνῳ

> But come, tell me this and answer accurately.
> Are you, big as you are, really the son of Odysseus himself?
> You are strangely similar to him in the head and noble eyes.

This pretense allows Athena to comment on the tenuous nature of Telemachus' knowledge about his paternity, while still confirming that patrilineage by emphasizing his physical resemblance to Odysseus.[42] The use of the hesitant patronymic construction *ex autoio . . . pais . . . Odusêos* is partially motivated by her feigned incredulity, but it also confirms that he is not entirely ready to assume the title. The establishment of that identity as Odysseus' son will be one of the key functions of his subsequent journey,[43] and the physical similarity to his father mentioned here will be noted by several other characters,[44] but Telemachus' immediate reply reveals the basis of his doubts (*Od.* 1.215–20):

μήτηρ μέν τέ μέ φησι τοῦ ἔμμεναι, αὐτὰρ ἐγώ γε
οὐκ οἶδ'· οὐ γάρ πώ τις ἑὸν γόνον αὐτὸς ἀνέγνω . . .
. . . νῦν δ' ὃς ἀποτμότατος γένετο θνητῶν ἀνθρώπων,
τοῦ μ' ἔκ φασι γενέσθαι, ἐπεὶ σύ με τοῦτ' ἐρεείνεις.

> My mother says that I am his son, but I do not know.
> For no one really knows his own father . . .
> . . . But that man is the most ill-fated of mortals,
> whose son they say I am, since you ask me about this.

He is not so much denying the truth of his paternity as bitterly lamenting the second-hand nature of its transmission (*phêsi, phasi*). The gnomic *anegnô* is an attempt to generalize his situation, for of course no one in the ancient world can ever be entirely certain of who his own father is, but it also underscores his own dependence on Penelope as both his only certain parent and his most reliable source of information about Odysseus. Athena picks up on this notion in her attempt to reassure him (*Od.* 1.222–23):

οὐ μέν τοι γενεήν γε θεοὶ νώνυμνον ὀπίσσω
θῆκαν, ἐπεὶ σέ γε τοῖον ἐγείνατο Πηνελόπεια.

> The gods have not assigned you a lineage that will be
> nameless hereafter, since Penelope bore such a son as you.

However, the implication of these words actually has little to do with Odysseus' survival. His descendants will have a name even if Odysseus is dead because Penelope bore such an excellent son (which once again may suggest some sort of matrilineal succession), but for the present he must remain nameless (*nônumnon*). If Telemachus is going to secure his identity as son of Odysseus, he will have to make a name for himself. The *Telemachy* is thus defined at the outset in terms of the dual search for his paternal name and his own fame.

At the end of Book 13, Athena reveals herself to Odysseus and instructs him to go to Eumaeus while she brings home Telemachus, who went to Sparta to seek news of his father (*Od.* 13.415: οἴχετο πευσόμενος μετὰ σὸν κλέος, "he went seeking news of you"). Odysseus is concerned that she has not told Telemachus that his father is alive and instead has allowed him to undergo the same wandering and hardship as he did (*Od.* 13.418: ἵνα που καὶ κεῖνος ἀλώμενος ἄλγεα πάσχῃ, "so that, wandering, he should also suffer pains"), but she replies that she set him on this journey so that he might win *kleos* for himself (*Od.* 13.422–23: ἵνα κλέος ἐσθλὸν ἄροιτο κεῖσ' ἐλθών, "so that he might win great glory by going there"). The transfer of meaning of *kleos* from "news" of Odysseus to Telemachus' "glory" in the space of eight lines reflects the double success of the expedition. By making his journey, Telemachus has firmly established his identity as the son of Odysseus both through his diligent inquiries about his father's exploits (*meta son kleos*) and by following in his father's footsteps in acquiring *kleos*. The description of Athena's final departure confirms this new status with the unambiguous patronymic construction (13.440): ἐς Λακεδαίμονα δῖαν ἔβη μετὰ παῖδ' Ὀδυσῆος ("she went to bright Lacedaemon to get the son of Odysseus"). What was a question in Book 1 has become a certainty as the second half of the poem begins.

While Telemachus serves the important function of domesticating the "distant war," he is not the only child to do so in the *Odyssey*. Pisistratus, Nausicaa, and even Odysseus himself act as gateways to their parents. One of the goals of Telemachus' investigation of the Iliadic aftermath is to establish a framework for Odysseus' own specific narrative, and so his own inquiry also begins with the son of a veteran rather than with Nestor himself. Pisistratus appears to be the youngest son of the old king and the only one who is still a bachelor (*Od.* 3.401). Like Telemachus, he is far-removed from the Iliadic space, but his father has returned home in a timely fashion. Although Nestor is present when Telemachus arrives, it is Pisistratus who rises to greet the stranger (*Od.* 3.36), echoing a similar scene described by Nestor in the *Iliad*, where he and Odysseus go to visit Peleus and young Achilles springs up to welcome them (*Il.* 11.765–79). Likewise, Pisistratus accompanies Telemachus to Sparta and speaks to Menelaus first on his behalf (*Od.* 4.155–67), again serving as a bridge to the parental generation.[45]

Once this pattern has been established through both Telemachus and Pisistratus, Odysseus' first step toward reintegration into human society will follow the same lines. In Book 6, his arrival on Scheria involves a three-fold initiation into the household of Alcinous, first through the daughter Nausicaa, then the queen Arete, and finally the king. But it is Nausicaa herself who advises Odysseus on how to reach the palace and what to do when he gets there. Like Pisistratus, she serves as an intermediary between the visitor and the king, but she also provides a counterpoint to Telemachus.[46] As a royal child of an island kingdom, she presents Odysseus with an idyllic picture of an intact single-child ruling family, almost an alternate, idealized version of the disrupted Ithacan reality. Unlike Telemachus, she has a very intimate relationship with her father, whom she even calls *pappa* (*Od.* 6.57) in a marked deviation from standard epic diction, and thus allows Odysseus to see what he has missed as a consequence of his long absence. As we have already noted, the actual reunion between Odysseus and Telemachus is marked by doubt and confusion, but here he gains access to the Phaeacians through Nausicaa's ready acceptance of his supplication.

Furthermore, Odysseus himself also reverses the Iliadic point of view by processing his own parents' experiences during his absence. Both the encounter with the *eidôlon* of Anticleia in Book 11 and the reunion with Laertes in Book 24 are carefully controlled by Odysseus. In the first case,

42 Virgil's Homeric Lens

he sees his mother's ghost immediately after his conversation with Elpenor, but although he is saddened by her death, which took place while he was away, he postpones their reunion a little while longer so that he can converse with Tiresias in accordance with Circe's instructions (*Od.* 11.84–89). This further delay is partly an ironic extension of the overall belated homecoming, which, as he learns when he finally speaks to her, directly caused his mother's death (*Od.* 11.200–3). At the same time, it privileges Odysseus' position in the discourse between the two characters. Unlike Achilles, whose sorrow is consistently viewed through Thetis' concern, which in turn frames all their interactions, Odysseus continues to assert his own perspective. When they do finally converse, he briefly dismisses Anticleia's concern that he himself is dead, and launches into a series of questions about his family and kingdom (*Od.* 11.164–79). In the final part of her answer, Anticleia's fatal longing for Odysseus' return reorients Thetis' own lament about Achilles after the death of Patroclus (*Il.* 18.58–60):[47]

> νηυσὶν ἐπιπροέηκα κορωνίσιν Ἴλιον εἴσω
> Τρωσὶ μαχησόμενον· τὸν δ' οὐχ ὑποδέξομαι αὖτις
> οἴκαδε νοστήσαντα δόμον Πηλήϊον εἴσω.

> I sent him away in the curved ships into Ilium
> to fight with the Trojans; but I will never welcome him again
> returned home into the house of Peleus.

Thetis claims responsibility for having sent Achilles to war and for thus being unable to welcome him home. Earlier we considered how she blames herself for bearing Achilles to a brief and bitter destiny, but here she ties this self-reproach directly to his physical separation from his homeland. The first-person active verbs *epiproeêka* and *hupodexomai* reinforce her belief in her own agency and further motivate her subsequent intervention in the action of the poem.

As a goddess, Thetis can visit Achilles on the battlefield even though she is powerless to prevent his death, but Anticleia must wait until after her own death to see her son finally. She is a passive victim of Odysseus' absence, and the description of her death confirms that even in the underworld she is at the mercy of his decisions and desires (*Od.* 11.202–3):

> ἀλλά με σός τε πόθος σά τε μήδεα, φαίδιμ' Ὀδυσσεῦ,
> σή τ' ἀγανοφροσύνη μελιηδέα θυμὸν ἀπηύρα.

> But, shining Odysseus, it was my longing for you, your counsels,
> and your gentleness, that took away sweet life from me.

Despite the use of the possessive adjective *sos* as an objective genitive and the unusual syntactical shift, the primary sense of the lines seems to be that longing (*pothos*) for Odysseus took away (*apêura*) her sweet life (*meliêdea thumon*, cf. *Il.* 17.17), as well as specific longing for his *mêdea* (counsels, plans, and schemes) and *aganophrosunê* (gentleness).[48] The striking anaphora of the second-person possessive adjectives *sos . . . sa . . . sê* together with the play on *mêdea/meliêdea* firmly assert Odysseus' responsibility for Anticleia's death.[49] The survival of her sweet spirit (*meliêdea*) literally depends on the physical presence of Odysseus' plans (*mêdea*). At the same time, a more natural (if willful) reading of the syntax actually yields an even more accusatory interpretation: "But *your* longing, *your* schemes, *your* [supposed] gentleness, shining Odysseus, took away sweet life from me."[50] Odysseus is, of course, well known for his counsels in the *Iliad* (cf. *Il.* 3.202, 208, 212), but he is also associated with *aganophrosunê*, particularly in regards to his rhetorical abilities. Although this abstract noun is not used elsewhere to describe him,[51] he does make use of gentle (i.e., persuasive) words (*aganois epeessin*) during the marshaling of the troops in Book 2 (*Il.* 2.180, 189), and he also addresses the Naiads with gentle prayers (*eucholêis aganêisi*) upon his arrival in Ithaca (*Od.* 13.357).[52] On the stronger reading, Anticleia's attribution of this quality to her son may be a sarcastic gibe, which provides further contrast with Thetis' position by equating Odysseus with Achilles and stressing the dramatically different outcomes of their choices. Achilles is explicitly described as lacking this gentleness in a pointed comment by the narrator (*Il.* 20.467–68): οὐ γάρ τι γλυκύθυμος ἀνὴρ ἦν οὐδ' ἀγανόφρων, / ἀλλὰ μάλ' ἐμμεμαώς ("for this was a man without sweetness in his soul, and not gentle but furious"). Although it does not directly cause his early death, this lack of *aganophrosunê* is a defining characteristic of Achilles' uncompromising destiny. In contrast, the very fact that Odysseus is so skilled with *aganois* words plays a large part in his continued survival, but it also greatly prolongs his homecoming, which makes him *oud' aganophrôn* to the family that longs for his return.

The contrast with Achilles continues in Odysseus' emotional response to Anticleia's words. In a scene that is modeled on Achilles' moving attempt to embrace the ghost of Patroclus in a dream (*Il.* 23.97–102), Odysseus reaches out to embrace his mother only to have her flutter away like a shadow or a dream (*Od.* 11.206–8):

τρὶς μὲν ἐφωρμήθην, ἑλέειν τέ με θυμὸς ἀνώγει,
τρὶς δέ μοι ἐκ χειρῶν σκιῇ εἴκελον ἢ καὶ ὀνείρῳ
ἔπτατ'· ἐμοὶ δ' ἄχος ὀξὺ γενέσκετο κηρόθι μᾶλλον

Three times I started, and my heart urged me to embrace her,
and three times she flew out of my hands like a shadow
or a dream, and the sorrow grew sharper in my heart.

The threefold repetition recalls the familiar Iliadic pattern of failed attempts, but whereas there is usually a fourth successful try (cf. *Il.* 5.436–37, 16.702–3, 784–85, 20.445–46, 21.176–77), here there is only a corresponding increase

44 Virgil's Homeric Lens

in sorrow (*achos . . . genesketo*). The frustrated desire to make physical contact with his mother causes even greater despair than he felt before (*Od.* 11.87), which once again inverts the Thetis-Achilles paradigm. On four occasions, Thetis visits a sorrowful Achilles and touches him in order to comfort him (*Il.* 1.360–61, 18.70–71, 19.7–8, 24.127). Each time, this physical contact initiates an exchange in which Thetis intervenes in the action of the poem in order to ease Achilles' sorrow: in Book 1 she agrees to ask Zeus to punish the Achaeans for Agamemnon's insult; in Book 18 she promises to acquire new armor; in Book 19 she delivers the armor and volunteers to preserve Patroclus' corpse; and in Book 24 she commands Achilles to return the body of Hector. These interventions correspond to Achilles' four main responses to his own anger and sorrow: the withdrawal from the battle, the killing of Hector, the burial of Patroclus, and the reconciliation with Priam. The sorrow of the son leads the parent to embrace him and then try to help him resolve his anger. In the *Odyssey*, however, we have an attempt to embrace the parent that fails and consequently increases the child's sorrow. In literal terms, an embrace in the underworld can only be an empty gesture, but in contrast to the *Iliad*, both the gesture and its effects are attributed to the child rather than the parent. The inversion of the Iliadic pattern also emphasizes the belatedness of the gesture, which is reinforced by the description of the ghost flying away like a shadow or a dream (*skiêi . . . oneirôi*), images of late afternoon and night respectively, long after the Iliadic heyday. The cruel irony in Odysseus' question after the failed embrace further confirms this belatedness (*Od.* 11.210): μῆτερ ἐμή, τί νύ μ' οὐ μίμνεις ἐλέειν μεμαῶτα ("mother, why do you not wait for me when I yearn to embrace you?"). Anticleia, who spent her final years anxiously waiting for Odysseus' return, can no longer await his embrace now that she is dead. But once again, any responsibility for her death is quickly superseded by Odysseus' own yearning (*memaôta*), as he almost chastises her for causing him sorrow.

Achillêos achos

The sorrow (*achos*) brought on by the failed embrace of Anticleia is further linked to the *Iliad* through a familiar etymological play on Achilles' own name.[53] Regardless of the linguistic realities of this etymology, the *Iliad* supports the notion that Achilles' name means something like "the sorrow (*achos*) of his own people (*lâos*)" through the frequent connection of that name to *achos* and its related verbal forms.[54] Thus, in Book 1 when Achilles promises that Agamemnon will one day regret his outrageous actions, he activates the full potential of his name through a triple wordplay (*Il.* 1.240–42):

ἦ ποτ' <u>Ἀχιλλῆος</u> ποθὴ ἵξεται υἷας Ἀχαιῶν
σύμπαντας· τότε δ' οὔ τι δυνήσεαι <u>ἀχνύμενός</u> περ
χραισμεῖν

> One day longing for Achilles will come to the sons of the Achaeans,
> all of them. Then, even oppressed by sorrow, you will be able to do
> nothing.

Agamemnon's insult and Achilles' subsequent anger will cause not only Agamemnon to be oppressed by sorrow (*achnumenos*), but also all the Achaeans who will desperately long for Achilles' return to battle. The additional wordplay on "Achaeans" (*Achaiôn*) further underscores the strained relationship between Achilles and his *laos* throughout the poem. At the same time, the relationship between *achos* and longing (*pothê*) establishes a paradigm that the *Odyssey* can modify to achieve its own purposes. As we have already seen, it is precisely this sort of longing (*pothos*)[55] for the absent Odysseus that causes Anticleia's death (*Od.* 11.202–3),[56] but her description of Laertes' condition activates the Iliadic connection even more explicitly (*Od.* 11.195–96):

> ἔνθ' ὅ γε κεῖτ' ἀχέων, μέγα δὲ φρεσὶ πένθος ἀέξει
> σὸν νόστον ποθέων·

> He lies there suffering, and the sorrow grows large in his heart
> as he longs for your homecoming.

In Achilles' prophecy, the Achaeans will long for him because of the great hardship caused by his withdrawal from battle, but here Laertes is suffering (*acheôn*) as a consequence of longing (*potheôn*) for his son's return. The *Odyssey* thus transforms the sorrow-induced longing for the warrior into a sorrow-inducing desire for the hero's homecoming. This reconfiguration of the causal relationship between *pothos* and *achos* is perhaps best captured by the English idiom, "to ache for," as in "Laertes aches for your return." Although "ache" is not actually cognate with Greek *achos*,[57] the phonetic similarity suggests the way in which the *Odyssey* views the very act of longing in terms of its physical effects. Both Achilles and Odysseus bring *achos* to their people through their absence, and both cause the death of a loved one, which in turn causes them even greater pain, but Odysseus' reintegration into his society heals this sorrow in various ways, while the *achos* that Achilles has caused consumes him completely, so that his return to battle can only ease the pain of the Achaean army while leaving him in despair for the rest of his life. Odysseus himself predicts this in the embassy scene (*Il.* 9.249–50):

> αὐτῷ τοι μετόπισθ' ἄχος ἔσσεται, οὐδέ τι μῆχος
> ῥεχθέντος κακοῦ ἔστ' ἄκος εὑρεῖν·

> It will be a sorrow to you hereafter, and no cure will be found
> as a remedy for the evil thing once it has been done.

46 *Virgil's Homeric Lens*

The phonetic similarity between *achos* and *akos* in the same metrical position in their respective lines underscores Achilles' own faulty logic: his attempt to heal one wound by withdrawing from battle will actually yield an incurable sorrow through the death of Patroclus.

In contrast, Odysseus will find his own remedy for evil (*kakou . . . akos*) in the slaughter of the suitors and the reunion with Penelope and then Laertes. The only other occurrence of *akos* in the poems makes precisely this point as Odysseus prepares to clean the palace after the slaughter (*Od.* 22.481–82):

οἶσε θέειον, γρηῦ, κακῶν ἄκος, οἶσε δέ μοι πῦρ,
ὄφρα θεειώσω μέγαρον·

Bring me sulphur, old woman, the cure for evils, and bring me fire
so that I can sulphur the hall.

Of course, the palace has already been cleansed of the true evil,[58] but the description of sulphur as a cure for ailments (*kakôn akos*) seals the healing of sorrows with a finality that Achilles can never achieve. Thus Odysseus uses the same medical metaphor to define Achilles' failure and to assert his own mastery of the Iliadic cycle of violence. Furthermore, the metonymic use of the sulphur to define the entire cleansing process strongly aligns the *Odyssey*'s successful outcome with the power of Zeus. Of the five other appearances of sulphur (*theeion*) in the poems,[59] four refer to the effects of a bolt of lightning hurled by Zeus (*Il.* 8.135, 14.415, *Od.* 12.417, 14.307), and one of the most persistent repetitions in the narrative of Odysseus' homeward journey is the destruction of his ship by one of those thunderbolts (*Od.* 5.131, 7.249, 12.387, 12.415–16, 23.330).[60] Indeed, without Zeus' final thunderbolt in Book 24 (*Od.* 24.539), the cycle of violence (and the sorrows of Odysseus) might continue indefinitely. By using the sulphur to cleanse all traces of his own violent retribution, Odysseus engages in a ritual expiation that anticipates Zeus' final resolution to the conflict.

But the sulphur itself also serves to distinguish this successful outcome from Achilles' failure to escape his sorrowful destiny. In *Iliad* 16, when Achilles prays to Zeus for Patroclus' success in battle and safe return, he first cleans the goblet for the libation with sulphur (*Il.* 16.228); unlike his previous request for assistance through Thetis, however, this direct attempt to influence Zeus fails dramatically and the subsequent death of Patroclus fulfills Odysseus' earlier prophecy. From the outset of the poem, the entire chain of events starting with the anger (*mênis*) of Achilles is understood to be fulfilling the will of Zeus (*Il.* 1.5: Διὸς δ' ἐτελείετο βουλή), and just as in the *Odyssey*, Zeus will facilitate the final resolution of the action of the poem through his command to return Hector's body to Priam (cf. *Il.* 24.139–40). Moreover, this denial of Achilles' sulphurous request in Book 16 also closely connects his permanent *achos* with the will of Zeus. There will be no thunderbolt to heal his sorrows, as his mother recognizes quite clearly (*Il.* 18.61–62 = 442–43): ὄφρα δέ μοι ζώει καὶ ὁρᾷ φάος ἠελίοιο / ἄχνυται ("while he lives and sees the sunlight, he has sorrow"). Achilles himself acknowledges this destiny as well (*Il.* 23.46–47):[61]

> ἐπεὶ οὔ μ' ἔτι δεύτερον ὧδε
> ἵξετ' ἄχος κραδίην ὄφρα ζωοῖσι μετείω.
>
> since no second sorrow like this
> will come again to my heart while I am among the living.

Both Thetis and Achilles limit this sorrow to the span of his lifetime, but this is as much an acknowledgment of the brevity of that life as a statement about the magnitude of the grief. As we noted earlier, Thetis tells Achilles at the outset that he has a brief destiny (*Il.* 1.416: ἐπεί νύ τοι αἶσα μίνυνθά περ οὔ τι μάλα δήν), and she repeatedly refers to him as "dying quickly/early" (*ôkumoros*: *Il.* 1.417, 18.95, 18.458, and the superlative *ôkumorôtatos* at 1.505). Likewise, Achilles accepts this fate as the natural consequence of his failure to aid Patroclus (*Il.* 18.98–99):[62]

> αὐτίκα τεθναίην, ἐπεὶ οὐκ ἄρ' ἔμελλον ἑταίρῳ
> κτεινομένῳ ἐπαμῦναι.
>
> May I die at once, since it was not my lot to come
> to the aid of my companion when he was killed.

While this imminent death is itself the supreme cause of Thetis' sorrow, Achilles' own awareness of its proximity is perhaps the only thing that makes his own life-long grief bearable. He is certainly interested in the glory that will accompany his early death (cf. *Il.* 9.412–13, 18.120–21), but the promise of freedom from sorrow is a particularly strong motivation to reenter the war.

The *Odyssey*, however, once again reconfigures these Iliadic views on sorrow and death in order to explore the lasting effects of the Achillean destiny and to position Odysseus in relation to that destiny. The meeting between the two heroes in the underworld (*Od.* 11.467–540) engages the Iliadic tradition through a series of intertextual strategies that allow Odysseus to measure himself against his epic predecessor. Achilles first approaches surrounded by three of his closest companions who also died at Troy: Patroclus, Antilochus, and Ajax (*Od.* 11.467–71):[63]

> ἦλθε δ' ἐπὶ ψυχὴ Πηληϊάδεω Ἀχιλῆος
> καὶ Πατροκλῆος καὶ ἀμύμονος Ἀντιλόχοιο
> Αἴαντός θ', ὃς ἄριστος ἔην εἶδός τε δέμας τε

τῶν ἄλλων Δαναῶν μετ' ἀμύμονα Πηλεΐωνα.
ἔγνω δὲ ψυχή με ποδώκεος Αἰακίδαο

> After this came the soul of Achilles, son of Peleus,
> and the soul of Patroclus and of blameless Antilochus
> and of Ajax, who was the greatest of all the other Danaans
> in beauty and stature after the blameless son of Peleus.
> And the soul of the swift-footed grandson of Aeacus recognized me.

This is precisely the same group of four whose death is described earlier by Nestor (*Od.* 3.109–12) and who will again appear together in the second underworld scene at the end of the poem (*Od.* 24.15–18).[64] In the scene immediately preceding this one, Agamemnon comes to Odysseus surrounded by the anonymous ghosts of the men who died together with him (*Od.* 11.387–89), but here we have something more than a mere collection of Iliadic warriors who fell at Troy: Patroclus is Achilles' best friend, Antilochus is his closest comrade after the death of Patroclus,[65] and Ajax is the best Greek warrior after Achilles (cf. *Il.* 2.768–69).[66] Moreover, they are also all intimately connected to Achilles' sorrow through the death of Patroclus in *Iliad* 16 and its immediate aftermath. In Books 17 and 18, Ajax makes extraordinary efforts to defend Patroclus' body: he covers it with his shield (*Il.* 17.132), protects it from the grasping hands of the Trojans (*Il.* 17.274–318), orders Menelaus and Meriones to carry it from battle while he and the other Ajax provide cover (*Il.* 17.715–21), and wards off Hector's final attempt to carry it away (*Il.* 18.155–60). During this heroic defense, he is also explicitly described as the second-best warrior, using an almost identical phrase to the foregoing one (*Il.* 17.279–80):[67]

Αἴας, ὃς περὶ μὲν εἶδος, περὶ δ' ἔργα τέτυκτο
τῶν ἄλλων Δαναῶν μετ' ἀμύμονα Πηλεΐωνα.

> Ajax, who in beauty and deeds surpassed
> all the other Danaans, after the blameless son of Peleus.

This description establishes Ajax as the most appropriate surrogate for the inactive Achilles and consequently enjoins his full attention in the protection of Achilles' closest companion.

Even in the midst of the furious battle, he is concerned that Achilles has not yet heard about Patroclus' death (whom he calls Achilles' "dear companion" [*philos hetairos*] at 17.642, and then "by far his dearest companion" [*polu philtatos hetairos*] at 17.655) and tells Menelaus to seek out Antilochus, if he is still living (*Il.* 17.652–53: αἴ κεν ἴδηαι / ζωὸν ἔτ' Ἀντίλοχον), so that he might carry the fateful message. The choice of Antilochus is a logical one since he is said to be the preeminent runner among the Achaeans (cf. *Il.*15.570, 23.756, *Od.* 3.112, 4.202), but the uncertainty about whether he is still alive may also hint at his role in the tradition associated with the Cyclic *Aethiopis*, which recounts the events at Troy immediately after the *Iliad*.[68] The surviving summary account of the poem (Proclus *Chr.* 171–204) tells us that Achilles, after killing Thersites, withdraws from battle to Lesbos, sacrifices to Apollo, Artemis, and Leto, and is then purified by Odysseus. Meanwhile, the Ethiopian prince Memnon, son of Eos, arrives to aid the Trojans. Thetis prophesies to Achilles about his future encounter with Memnon, and when the battle begins, Memnon kills Antilochus and is then himself slain by Achilles.[69] The obvious parallels between this Antilochus narrative and the Patroclus story in the *Iliad* have generated a great deal of debate about the relationship between the two poems,[70] and Ajax's uncertainty may foreshadow Antilochus' similar subsequent death at Memnon's hands. Whether or not the *Aethiopis* itself plays a role in this intertextual moment, there is no question that the *Odyssey* knows about this death (*Od.* 4.187–88; cf. also 11.522) as well as about the close relationship between Antilochus and Achilles after the death of Patroclus (*Od.* 24.78–79).[71] The grouping of Antilochus with Achilles and Patroclus in the underworld thus represents a doubling of Achilles' sorrow over withdrawing from battle and losing a close companion.[72]

At the same time, because he is the one who actually brings the news of Patroclus' death to Achilles, Antilochus represents the final link in the transmission of sorrow, which begins with the death itself, passes through Ajax's valiant defense of the body, and finally reaches Achilles. When Menelaus finds him on the far side of the battle, he has not yet heard about Patroclus' death and his reaction is particularly intense (*Il.* 17.694–96):

Ὣς ἔφατ', Ἀντίλοχος δὲ κατέστυγε μῦθον ἀκούσας·
δὴν δέ μιν ἀμφασίη ἐπέων λάβε, τὼ δέ οἱ ὄσσε
δακρυόφι πλῆσθεν, θαλερὴ δέ οἱ ἔσχετο φωνή.

Thus he spoke, and Antilochus heard the word and was horrified at it.
Speechlessness held him for a long time, and his eyes
filled with tears, and his strong voice was held back.

Antilochus' response to the command to deliver the news to Achilles is a triple crescendoing renunciation of the speaking role of a messenger. He is horrified at Menelaus' words (*katestuge muthon*), he is seized by a sudden inability to form words (*amphasiê epeôn*), and finally his entire voice is held back (*thalerê . . . escheto phône*). While the first expression is unique in the poems,[73] the second two lines are also used to describe Penelope's reaction to the herald Medon's news that Telemachus has gone in search of information about Odysseus (*Od.* 4.704–5). This outpouring of emotion is particularly strong but certainly justified since she is the person closest to Telemachus, and the same response from Achilles upon hearing of Patroclus' death might be expected,[74] but Antilochus anticipates that reaction of an intimate or relative and thus transforms himself from a mere messenger like Medon into an attendant co-mourner.[75] But who is actually being mourned? There is no prior connection between Antilochus and Patroclus,[76] but as I have already noted, subsequent events in the Trojan saga will position Antilochus as a surrogate Patroclus whose death motivates Achilles' last great deed in the war, and Antilochus' explicit laying aside of his armor before running off to report Patroclus' death to Achilles (*Il.* 17.698–99) may suggest a kind of proleptic identification with the recently spoiled Patroclus (*Il.* 17.125).[77] But more importantly, Achilles' vengeance against Memnon is closely followed by his own death at the hands of Paris and Apollo in front of the Scaean gates (cf. Proclus *Chr.* 191–92), which is already explicitly predicted in Hector's dying words (*Il.* 22.358–60) and, with less specificity, by the ghost of Patroclus (*Il.* 23.80–81) and by his own horse Xanthus (*Il.* 19.416–17).[78] Moreover, the battle that swirls around the body of Patroclus in *Iliad* 17 and 18 prefigures the furious struggle for Achilles' corpse, which is mentioned in the *Odyssey* by Odysseus himself, when he wishes he had died there (*Od.* 5.308–10), and described in more detail by the ghost of Agamemnon, who tells Achilles about the events that followed his death (*Od.* 24.36–42).[79] Agamemnon describes the death itself with a memorable image that sheds further light on the mourning of Antilochus (*Od.* 24.39–40):

σὺ δ' ἐν στροφάλιγγι κονίης
κεῖσο μέγας μεγαλωστί, λελασμένος ἱπποσυνάων.

And you lay in the whirl of dust,
great in your greatness, having forgotten all your horsemanship.

These words, and especially the phrase "great in your greatness" (*megas megalôsti*), closely echo Achilles' reaction when Antilochus informs him of Patroclus' death (*Il.* 18.26–27): αὐτὸς δ' ἐν κονίῃσι μέγας μεγαλωστὶ τανυσθεὶς / κεῖτο ("and he himself, great in his greatness, lay stretched out in the dust").[80] But while Antilochus responded to the news by appropriating the mourner's role properly belonging to Achilles, the latter appears to assume the role of the dead man himself.[81] The phrase *tanustheis keito*, "lay stretched out," (or more precisely, the opposite word order: *keito tanustheis*) is otherwise only used to describe figures who are actually dead (all Trojans: Asius, *Il.* 13.392; Sarpedon, *Il.* 16.485; Deucalion, *Il.* 20.483). Likewise, the detailed account of the mourning of Thetis and the Nereids that follows (*Il.* 18.35–51) again resembles Agamemnon's description of the same group mourning Achilles' death (*Od.* 24.47–59). Finally, Antilochus himself stands beside the grieving hero and holds his hands to prevent him from transforming this figurative death into an actual one by cutting his own throat (*Il.* 18.34): δείδιε

Iliadic Refraction 51

γὰρ μὴ λαιμὸν ἀπαμήσειε σιδήρῳ ("for he feared that [Achilles] might cut his throat with iron").[82] But in preventing his physical death here, he both deprives Achilles of that immediate relief from sorrow that, as we have already noted, the latter believes can only come with the end of life, and at the same time sets the hero up for the potential doubling of that sorrow through his own death later in the Trojan story. The reunion of these figures in the Odyssean underworld thus focuses attention on the causal chain between the deaths of Patroclus and Achilles. By recalling Antilochus' double role as the herald of the first death and a proximate cause of the second, the *Odyssey* reinterprets the long-term consequences of Achilles' attempts to ease his own sorrow in order to define Odysseus' own struggle. Achilles is unquestionably dead now, but that death has its symbolic origin in the moment when this group surrounding him in the underworld first effected the transmission of his great sorrow. On the other hand, Odysseus is not yet dead, despite his presence in the underworld, but he has an opportunity to learn from the experiences of his epic predecessor both through this reconfiguration of a key Iliadic moment and through direct discourse.

eidôla kamontôn

The actual conversation between Odysseus and Achilles deploys the intersection of the two intertextual themes of sorrow and parent-child perspectives to further the Odyssean revision of Iliadic paradigms and, at the same time, to view that revision through the overarching theme of belatedness that permeates the whole poem. We have just examined how the description of Achilles' entourage generates a specific reading of his sorrow in the *Iliad*, but this same scene also sets up a framework in which to read Odysseus' own complicated relationship with Achilles and the heroic ideal he represents. The account of Achilles' approach uses three different patronymic epithets in the space of five lines to establish the pedigree of the hero (*Od.* 11.467–71):

> ἦλθε δ' ἐπὶ ψυχὴ <u>Πηληϊάδεω Ἀχιλῆος</u>
> καὶ Πατροκλῆος καὶ ἀμύμονος Ἀντιλόχοιο
> Αἴαντός θ', ὃς ἄριστος ἔην εἶδός τε δέμας τε
> τῶν ἄλλων Δαναῶν μετ' <u>ἀμύμονα Πηλεΐωνα</u>.
> ἔγνω δὲ ψυχή με <u>ποδώκεος Αἰακίδαο</u>

> After this came the soul of Achilles, son of Peleus,
> and the soul of Patroclus and of blameless Antilochus
> and of Ajax, who was the greatest of all the other Danaans
> in beauty and stature after the blameless son of Peleus.
> And the soul of the swift-footed grandson of Aeacus recognized me.

Although these traditional phrases are all familiar from the *Iliad*, the triple juxtaposition is a unique phenomenon.[83] Furthermore, the triplet moves up the family tree so that he is called first "Achilles, son of Peleus" (*Pêlêiadeô Achilêos*), then "son of Peleus" (*Pêleiôna*), and finally "grandson of Aeacus" (*Aiakidao*). Thus between Achilles' arrival and his recognition of Odysseus, his soul (*psuchê*) has been situated among his fallen comrades and his ancestors, in short, in its place among the dead. At the same time, the setting is unmistakably Iliadic, albeit filtered through an Odyssean lens. The opening line ends in the familiar formula *Pêlêiadeô Achilêos*, which echoes the first line of the *Iliad*,[84] and the fact that Achilles has not yet recognized Odysseus allows us to catch one last glimpse of that Iliadic heroic ideal before the two epic worlds collide explicitly. His comrades represent the defining moment in his Iliadic destiny while the patronymics reassert the Iliadic parental viewpoint.

Similarly, the assertion of Ajax's position second only to Achilles in form and stature (cf. *Il.* 2.768–69, 17.279–80, *Od.* 11.550–51, 24.17–18) reflects the Iliadic hierarchy in which wily Odysseus is no match for the two most physical warriors. This particular subordination of Odysseus' cleverness to Ajax's plain strength manifests itself most clearly in three episodes in the *Iliad*. In the embassy scene in Book 9, Ajax attempts to open the negotiations by signaling to Phoenix to begin, only to have Odysseus cut in and deliver the first speech (*Il.* 9.222–24).[85] Odysseus' great rhetorical ability is of no avail, and his speech not only seems to strengthen Achilles' resolve to depart for home the next morning, but also earns a scathing rebuke from the hero (*Il.* 9.312–13):

ἐχθρὸς γάρ μοι κεῖνος ὁμῶς Ἀΐδαο πύλῃσιν
ὅς χ' ἕτερον μὲν κεύθῃ ἐνὶ φρεσίν, ἄλλο δὲ εἴπῃ.

For hateful to me as the gates of Death is that man
who hides one thing in his heart and says another.

Achilles clearly rejects Odysseus' plea on the grounds that it is not presented in good faith, and while his comment can be read as an attack on Agamemnon as the ultimate source of the deceit, it is nevertheless a criticism of Odysseus' particular capacity for duplicity. In contrast, Ajax's brief, but heartfelt address (*Il.* 9.624–42) manages to keep Achilles at Troy, even though he still refuses to return to battle, and at the same time elicits explicit praise (*Il.* 9.644–45):

Αἶαν διογενὲς Τελαμώνιε, κοίρανε λαῶν,
πάντά τί μοι κατὰ θυμὸν ἐείσαο μυθήσασθαι·

Ajax, sprung from Zeus, son of Telamon, lord of the people,
all that you have said is spoken after my own heart.

Ajax's straightforward strength triumphs again in Book 11, where Odysseus has been wounded by the Trojan Socus and calls for help. Menelaus and Ajax respond, and the ensuing rescue is described in a disturbing simile (*Il.* 11.473–86):[86]

      ἀμφὶ δ' ἄρ' αὐτὸν
Τρῶες ἕπονθ' ὥς εἴ τε δαφοινοὶ θῶες ὄρεσφιν
ἀμφ' ἔλαφον κεραὸν βεβλημένον, . . .
. . . ὠμοφάγοι μιν θῶες ἐν οὔρεσι δαρδάπτουσιν
ἐν νέμεϊ σκιερῷ· ἐπί τε λῖν ἤγαγε δαίμων
σίντην· θῶες μέν τε διέτρεσαν, αὐτὰρ ὃ δάπτει·
ὥς ῥα τότ' ἀμφ' Ὀδυσῆα δαΐφρονα ποικιλομήτην
Τρῶες ἕπον πολλοί τε καὶ ἄλκιμοι, . . .
. . . Αἴας δ' ἐγγύθεν ἦλθε φέρων σάκος ἠΰτε πύργον,
στῆ δὲ παρέξ· Τρῶες δὲ διέτρεσαν ἄλλυδις ἄλλος.

The Trojans pressed around him
just as tawny jackals in the mountains
press around a horned stag who is stricken, . . .
then the flesh-eating jackals devour him in the mountains
and the shaded glen. But a spirit led a ravenous lion there;
the jackals scatter and the lion feasts.
So around intelligent, much-devising Odysseus
The Trojans pressed, numerous and bold . . .
Now Ajax came near him, carrying his tower-like shield,
and stood beside him, and the Trojans scattered one way and another.

The comparison of Odysseus to a wounded deer at the mercy of a pack of ravenous jackals is by itself quite unfavorable (cf. Achilles' insult of Agamemnon at *Il.* 1.225), but the contrast with the representation of Ajax as a lion further asserts his physical superiority over the wounded Odysseus.[87] This is made more explicit in the shocking conclusion to the simile, where the Ajax-lion drives off the jackals and then proceeds to devour the Odysseus-deer. Although this feast can be understood as a representation of Ajax's facilitation of Odysseus' removal from the battlefield, it is nevertheless another strong assertion of Ajax's greater share of the Achillean heroic ideal. The helpless Odysseus is described as "intelligent and much-devising" (*daiphrona poikilomêtên*),[88] a double epithet that occurs five times in the *Odyssey* (*Od.* 3.163, 7.168, 22.115, 202, 282) but only this once in the *Iliad*. By applying an expression that is unique to Odysseus and that also highlights his particular un-Achillean heroic characteristics, his extreme vulnerability and subsequent rescue by Ajax become another assertion of the Achillean heroic paradigm over the Odyssean one.

In both the embassy scene and the rescue from battle, Ajax gets the better of Odysseus in significant but oblique ways. The simmering conflict

54 Virgil's Homeric Lens

between the two heroes finally emerges as direct confrontation in the wrestling match during Patroclus' funeral games in Book 23 (*Il.* 23.707–39). At first glance, it may seem strange that Odysseus rises to challenge Ajax when the latter has such an obvious advantage in size and strength, but from the outset the match is framed as another clash between the two heroic paradigms. When Achilles announces the contest, Ajax leaps up first and is quickly followed by Odysseus (*Il.* 23.708–9):

> ὣς ἔφατ', ὦρτο δ' ἔπειτα μέγας Τελαμώνιος Αἴας,
> ἂν δ' Ὀδυσεὺς πολύμητις ἀνίστατο κέρδεα εἰδώς.
>
> Thus he spoke, and right away huge Telamonian Ajax arose,
> and Odysseus of many counsels stood up, versed in craftiness.

In addition to the contrast between standard epithets of the two heroes,[89] the phrase *kerdea eidôs* in this context means something like "versed in craftiness or guile," which makes reference to Odysseus' usual *modus operandi* and explains how he can hope to defeat *megas* Ajax.[90] As the grappling match proceeds, neither wrestler is able to gain a clear advantage and the spectators grow impatient, which leads Ajax to propose that each should alternately allow the other to try to get a throw by lifting him (*Il.* 23.724: ἤ μ' ἀνάειρ', ἢ ἐγὼ σέ, "lift me, or I will lift you").[91] Such an arrangement clearly favors the heavier and stronger Ajax, who immediately lifts his opponent from the ground, but Odysseus responds with a trick (*Il.* 23.725: δόλου δ' οὐ λήθετ' Ὀδυσσεύς, "but Odysseus did not forget his craft") and strikes him in the hollow behind the knee causing him to buckle. In the next round, Odysseus unsuccessfully attempts to lift Ajax and finally hooks him with a knee so that they tumble to the ground together (*Il.* 23.729–32). In spite of (or perhaps because of) Odysseus' dubious methods, Achilles declares the match a draw and distributes the prizes equally. Although Odysseus' craftiness defeats Ajax's brute strength, his reliance on a trick (*dolos*) once again casts Ajax in the nobler light. In the scene that induces the rescue by Ajax in Book 11, Socus addresses Odysseus before wounding him by making specific reference to his reliance on *doloi* (*Il.* 11.430): ὦ Ὀδυσεῦ πολύαινε δόλων ἆτ' ἠδὲ πόνοιο ("much-praised Odysseus, insatiable of tricks and toil").[92]

This wrestling match also prefigures the famous contest over Achilles' arms where Odysseus once again triumphs, and it may hint at a questionable victory there as well.[93] The *Odyssey* takes up the matter in the underworld encounter with Ajax, which immediately follows the dialogue with Achilles (*Od.* 11.541–67). Through a masterful display of the kind of rhetorical manipulation that won him the arms in the first place, Odysseus literally rewrites that contest as a metaphor for the Iliadic conflict between heroic types alluded to by Ajax's presence in Achilles' entourage and asserts his own claim to the mantle of heroic paradigm.[94] He says that he won the arms through disputation (*dikazomenos*) in a contest that was judged (*dikasan*) by the sons of the Trojans (*Od.* 11.545–48),[95] but the exact details of that contest are left vague.[96] Given that the only other time these two heroes delivered persuasive speeches alternately (in the embassy scene in *Iliad* 9) Ajax's concise, sincere approach was more successful, it is perhaps not surprising that Odysseus denies his audience the opportunity to judge the contest for themselves. But he takes this rhetorical suppression one step further in actually rendering Ajax silent throughout this alleged attempt at reconciliation, thereby allowing him complete control over the reinterpretation of the Iliadic conflict. On the one hand, Odysseus appears to reassert the Iliadic viewpoint: he expresses regret at the victory since it led to Ajax's death (*Od.* 11.548–49), he again describes him as unsurpassed in *eidos* and *erga* save only for Achilles (*Od.* 11.550–51), and he claims that the Achaeans grieved for his death as continuously as for Achilles (*Od.* 11.556–58).[97] Furthermore, his description of Ajax's anger over the loss of the arms recalls the *primum mobile* of the whole *Iliad* (*Od.* 11.554–55): οὐδὲ θανὼν λήσεσθαι ἐμοὶ χόλου εἵνεκα τευχέων / οὐλομένων; ("not even in death can you forget your anger toward me because of that cursed armor?"). The enjambed adjective *oulomenôn*, which grammatically describes the armor (*teucheôn*) but which makes as much, if not more, sense as a transferred epithet properly referring to Ajax's anger (*cholou*), recalls the similarly positioned form *oulomenên* in the proem to the *Iliad* (*Il.* 1.2), where it describes the wrath (*mênis*) of Achilles. There, too, the anger is engendered by a dispute between two captains, and the results are equally calamitous.

At the same time, while Odysseus never claims that he did not deserve the victory, he attempts to absolve himself of responsibility by explicitly blaming the situation on Zeus (*Od.* 11.558–59: οὐδέ τις ἄλλος / αἴτιος, ἀλλὰ Ζεὺς, "no one else is to blame but Zeus"), and he impatiently asks Ajax to tame his *agênora thumon*, "headstrong spirit" (*Od.* 11.562). Likewise there is a double meaning in his claim that he addressed him with "gentle words" (*Od.* 11.552: *epeessi . . . meilichioisin*), since this phrase can also mean something like "beguiling words" (cf. *Il.* 6.342, *Od.* 9.33, 18.283). Finally, having depicted Ajax as stubbornly silent throughout the encounter, Odysseus closes his narrative of the episode with the astonishing suggestion that as Ajax departed, he still might have been willing to converse and be reconciled, but he, Odysseus, was now distracted by the desire to see the souls of other heroes (*Od.* 11.565–67).[98] After strategically undercutting his own attempt at reconciliation, Odysseus implies that Ajax would have come around to see it his way, but that the offer had expired. Whether Ajax would actually have spoken and what he would have said are, of course, impossible to determine, but Odysseus the storyteller resolutely refuses to allow the possibility of a rebuttal. The victory of the arms of Achilles must be total in order to ensure the triumph of the Odyssean heroic paradigm. Moreover, that victory is sealed in a way that reinforces the *Odyssey*'s constant attention to the consequences of its own belatedness. Ajax and the

56   Virgil's Homeric Lens

Iliadic world view he represents might have made their case, but it is too late now as Odysseus moves on to the next revision of the past.

Odysseus may not allow Ajax to state his case, but he does recount his conversation with Achilles in some detail. I will consider the question of Odysseus' reliability as a narrator in more detail in the next chapter, but it is important to recognize that, whether the conversation actually took place or not, Odysseus is the sole authority for both sides of the exchange. This in itself is an assertion of the power of rhetoric over physical strength, and his specific representation of Achilles is calculated to distinguish between the two heroic paradigms just as much as his earlier account of Ajax. In this regard, Achilles' opening remarks are far from a defense of the Iliadic ideal (*Od.* 11.473–76):

> διογενὲς Λαερτιάδη, πολυμήχαν' Ὀδυσσεῦ,
> σχέτλιε, τίπτ' ἔτι μεῖζον ἐνὶ φρεσὶ μήσεαι ἔργον;
> πῶς ἔτλης Ἄϊδόσδε κατελθέμεν, ἔνθα τε νεκροὶ
> ἀφραδέες ναίουσι, βροτῶν εἴδωλα καμόντων;

> Son of Laertes sprung from Zeus, resourceful Odysseus,
> unyielding man, what still greater deed will you contrive in your mind?
> How did you endure to come down to Hades' place, where the
> senseless dead dwell, mere images of worn-out mortals.

The line-length epithetic address is fairly common in the poems (seven occurrences in the *Iliad*, fifteen in the *Odyssey*) given that it can only be uttered in the second person, but it is nevertheless almost always used in contexts involving trickery or cunning action by Odysseus.[99] Thus, in the *Iliad*, Ajax uses it when he proposes the alternate lifting in the wrestling match (*Il.* 23.723), and more significantly, Achilles himself uses it in his scathing reply in the embassy scene (*Il.* 9.308). Here, it is an appropriate expression of amazement and perhaps even praise for Odysseus' daring journey to the realm of the dead, but the old tension between the two heroes quickly surfaces in the next vocative, *schetlie*, which both compliments him on his ruthlessness and expresses frustration at his stubborn pursuit of impossible goals.[100] But there is also a strong sense of bitterness in his description of the residents of the underworld. The "senseless dead" (*nekroi aphradees*) may be a literal description for the disembodied ghosts who populate Hades, but the phrase can be translated equally well as "reckless corpses." The adjective *aphradês* and its related forms are otherwise always used in the poems to describe something or someone as "reckless" or "careless," while *nekros* refers to an actual corpse throughout the *Iliad* and in every case in the *Odyssey* except for a handful of references to the underworld.[101] Thus, in calling them the "senseless dead," Achilles is referring to the "reckless" heroes who became "corpses" at Troy, of which he and his immediate entourage are conspicuous examples.

This commentary on the Iliadic past is further extended in the final description of the ghosts as *eidôla kamontôn*, literally, "images of worn-out men" or possibly "of men who have labored," that is, "phantoms of the dead." The exact meaning of this phrase, which occurs again in the second underworld scene (*Od.* 24.14), is difficult to determine, but it is already familiar to Achilles from the speech of Patroclus' ghost on the beach at Troy (*Il.* 23.72): τῆλέ με εἴργουσι ψυχαί, εἴδωλα καμόντων ("the souls, the images of worn-out men, keep me at a distance").[102] The image of the dead as those who have completed all their labors or who are completely worn out by them once again perfectly fits the Iliadic veterans. The great toil of the Trojan war has long since passed, and they are all only *eidôla* of their former selves.[103] Achilles' judgment here confirms his own hypothesis in the *Iliad* after he fails to embrace the ghost of Patroclus (*Il.* 23.103–4):[104]

ὢ πόποι, ἦ ῥά τίς ἐστι καὶ εἰν Ἀΐδαο δόμοισι
ψυχὴ καὶ εἴδωλον, ἀτὰρ φρένες οὐκ ἔνι πάμπαν·

Oh, there is something left even in the house of Hades,
a soul and an image, but there is no life in it at all.

The *eidôlon* is thus a hollow facsimile rather than the essence of the man,[105] and so Achilles, who begins his speech "lamenting for himself" (*Od.* 11.472: *r' olophuromenê*), is also mourning his own death as the death of the Iliadic heroic paradigm in no uncertain terms.

Just as Achilles addresses Odysseus with the same extended epithetic phrase he had used in the embassy scene, Odysseus in turn replies with a similar Iliadic line (*Od.* 11.478): ὢ Ἀχιλεῦ, Πηλῆος υἱέ, μέγα φέρτατ' Ἀχαιῶν ("o Achilles, son of Peleus, far best of the Achaeans"). These same words open his previous attempt to change Achilles' mood after the death of Patroclus (*Il.* 19.216).[106] More specifically, Odysseus tries to persuade the grieving Achilles to partake of food and drink before assaulting the Trojans. On a practical level, this is sound advice since Achilles has vowed to abstain from eating until he has completed his revenge (*Il.* 16.205–14), but Odysseus' entire approach is badly miscalculated.[107] He begins with the epithetic line and then proceeds to delimit the praise contained in the phrase "best of the Achaeans" (*phertat' Achaiôn*) (*Il.* 19.216–19):[108]

ὢ Ἀχιλεῦ Πηλῆος υἱὲ μέγα φέρτατ' Ἀχαιῶν,
κρείσσων εἰς ἐμέθεν καὶ φέρτερος οὐκ ὀλίγον περ
ἔγχει, ἐγὼ δέ κε σεῖο νοήματί γε προβαλοίμην
πολλόν, ἐπεὶ πρότερος γενόμην καὶ πλείονα οἶδα.

O Achilles, son of Peleus, far best of the Achaeans,
you are stronger than I am and greater by not a little

with a spear, but I might surpass you in understanding
by far, since I was born earlier and know more things.

Achilles is *phertatos* only in so far as he is physically stronger (*kreissôn*) and better with a spear (*pherteros . . . enchei*). The shift from the superlative *phertatos* to the comparative *pherteros* underscores the narrowing scope of Odysseus' praise and prepares us for the antithesis that follows. Odysseus presents his own credentials with the unusual verb *probaloimên*, which elsewhere in the poems means physically "throw down" or "hurl together."[109] The required sense here is clearly "excel" or "surpass" (cf. *periballein Il.* 23.276, *Od.* 15.17) but the idea seems to be that he "throws further" than Achilles in understanding or thought, which cleverly plays on Achilles' skill with the spear. Finally, Odysseus attributes this superiority to his older age (*proteros genomên*) and, quite bluntly, to the fact that he simply knows more than Achilles (*pleiona oida*). These same phrases are used by Poseidon to declare his superiority over Apollo (*Il.* 21.440) and again in the third person to declare Zeus' authority over Poseidon (*Il.* 13.355).[110] Odysseus thus brashly asserts his own claim in the rivalry between heroic types by likening himself to the eldest gods, and at same time belittles the very physicality that will bring Achilles his desired revenge.

This insulting preamble can hardly be expected to persuade Achilles to heed Odysseus' advice, but the advice itself displays an even more callous insensitivity to his specific situation (*Il.* 19.225–29):[111]

> γαστέρι δ' οὔ πως ἔστι νέκυν πενθῆσαι Ἀχαιούς·
> λίην γὰρ πολλοὶ καὶ ἐπήτριμοι ἤματα πάντα
> πίπτουσιν· πότε κέν τις ἀναπνεύσειε πόνοιο;
> ἀλλὰ χρὴ τὸν μὲν καταθάπτειν ὅς κε θάνῃσι,
> νηλέα θυμὸν ἔχοντας, ἐπ' ἤματι δακρύσαντας·

> It is not possible for the Achaeans to mourn a dead man with the belly.
> For too many fall, one after the other, every day.
> How could anyone get breathing room from this toil?
> But with pitiless heart we must bury the man who dies
> after we have wept for him for a day.

In general, Odysseus' point is quite sound; with so many soldiers dying every day, it hardly makes sense to mourn each one "with the belly" (*gasteri*), that is, through fasting.[112] But Patroclus can scarcely be counted among the nameless *polloi*, and just as in the embassy scene, Odysseus' attempt to appeal to Achilles' sense of loyalty to the greater community completely ignores the hero's personal motives. Moreover, the suggestion that it is necessary to bury the dead with "pitiless heart" (*nêlea thumon*) after only one day of weeping contains another subtle jibe, since, among living things in the *Iliad*, the adjective *nêlês* is only applied to Achilles in three attempts to persuade him to rejoin the war (Phoenix, *Il.* 9.497; Ajax, *Il.* 9.632; Patroclus, *Il.* 16.33).[113] It was precisely his earlier *nēlēs thumos* that indirectly caused the very death that he is now mourning. For Odysseus to suggest that he should resume that pitiless disposition and bury Patroclus is both ironic and insensitive.

Odysseus' response to Achilles' opening remarks in the underworld reflects a similar attempt to comfort Achilles, albeit without the Hesiodic advice concerning fighting on an empty stomach.[114] After beginning with the same epithetic phrase and answering the practical question about why he has come to the underworld, Odysseus tries to console Achilles by contrasting his own perpetual troubles with the dead hero's perpetual glory (*Od.* 11.482–86):

> ἀλλ' αἰὲν ἔχω κακά. σεῖο δ', Ἀχιλλεῦ,
> οὔ τις ἀνὴρ προπάροιθε μακάρτερος οὔτ' ἄρ' ὀπίσσω·
> πρὶν μὲν γάρ σε ζωὸν ἐτίομεν ἶσα θεοῖσιν
> Ἀργεῖοι, νῦν αὖτε μέγα κρατέεις νεκύεσσιν
> ἐνθάδ' ἐών· τῷ μή τι θανὼν ἀκαχίζευ, Ἀχιλλεῦ.

> I always have troubles. But, Achilles, no man
> before was ever more blessed than you, nor ever will be.
> For before, while you were alive, we Argives honored you
> as we did the gods, and now that you are here,
> you have great authority over the dead
> Therefore, do not grieve, though you are dead, Achilles.

Whereas he, Odysseus, is weighed down with troubles (*kaka*), no man has ever been, or will ever be, more blessed (*makartatos*) than Achilles. As in *Iliad* 19, Odysseus resorts to a superlative statement of praise and highlights a specific quality as consolation. He then attempts to show that Achilles' good fortune persists even in death: just as when he was alive the Argives honored him like the gods (*isa theoisin*), so now he exercises great authority (*mega krateeis*) among the dead. The greater effect of this comparison, however, is to emphasize the contrast between life and death.[115] Achilles has just disparaged the senseless phantoms who populate the underworld, and yet here Odysseus claims that being lord of the dead is equivalent to the honor that was heaped upon the living Achilles. The absurdity of this assertion underscores the true comparison: he may be best of the Achaeans, but the unavoidable fact is that blessed Achilles is dead, while Odysseus, with all his troubles, lives on. In suggesting that Achilles should not continue to mourn since his troubles are all behind him, Odysseus is also implying that even with all his own troubles, he does not mourn, and that this is why he has survived.

This is not so far removed from his meaning in *Iliad* 19, where the essential point is that mourning for the dead should not consume the living.

60 Virgil's Homeric Lens

Achilles, the ideal physical hero, has allowed his sorrow to waste away his life, and, as we have seen, he is at least symbolically dead from the time he hears the news of Patroclus' death.[116] Odysseus takes up this fundamental aspect of Achilles' nature in his final statement of consolation (*Od*. 11.486): τῷ μή τι θανὼν ἀκαχίζευ, Ἀχιλλεῦ. ("therefore, do not grieve, though you are dead, Achilles"). This is the only explicit Odyssean instance of the familiar Iliadic play on *achos* and Achilles' name,[117] but as we have already seen, the *Odyssey* is constantly engaged in reinterpreting the Iliadic view on sorrow. Here the effect is twofold: it once again identifies the causal link between Achilles' Iliadic sorrow and his subsequent death, and it draws attention to the fact that both Thetis and Achilles are mistaken when they optimistically suggest that his sorrow will only last his lifetime.[118]

The Achilles of *Iliad* 19 is too absorbed in his sorrow and bloodlust and also perhaps too angry at Odysseus' insensitivity to make any reply at all,[119] but here in the underworld his frustration generates what appears to be a startling renunciation of his famous Iliadic choice (*Od*. 11.488–91):

> μὴ δή μοι θάνατόν γε παραύδα, φαίδιμ' Ὀδυσσεῦ.
> βουλοίμην κ' ἐπάρουρος ἐὼν θητευέμεν ἄλλῳ,
> ἀνδρὶ παρ' ἀκλήρῳ, ᾧ μὴ βίοτος πολὺς εἴη,
> ἢ πᾶσιν νεκύεσσι καταφθιμένοισιν ἀνάσσειν.
>
> Do not persuade me about my death, shining Odysseus.
> I would rather be on the earth as a serf to another,
> to some poor man without much livelihood,
> than be lord over all the perished dead

Achilles' abrupt retort is usually taken to mean something like "don't console me about my death," but the precise meaning of the verb *parauda* is difficult to determine.[120] The only other occurrences of the verb all suggest something more along the lines of "persuade" (*Od*. 15.53, 16.279, 18.178), which also suits this context since Odysseus has not strictly been consoling Achilles as much as laying out an argument for why he should not lament his death. To demonstrate his total rejection of Odysseus' logic, he offers his own assessment of the relative merits of life and death. It has often been argued that Achilles here is rejecting his own Iliadic choice of a short life with great honor (*kleos*) instead of a long, insignificant life with a safe return home (*nostos*) (cf. *Il*. 9.410–16),[121] but his key point is simply that any kind of life on earth (*eparouros*)[122] would be preferable even to lordship over the dead (*nekuessi*). His optative statement is not a real wish, but a hypothetical possibility: Achilles is no more lord of the dead now than he ever served a man without possessions (*andri aklêrôi*).[123] Odysseus' claim that Achilles rules over the dead is hyperbole, or even flattery, calculated to reinforce the argument that he is honored as much in death as he was in life. But as we have seen, Odysseus has specifically not said that death is better

Iliadic Refraction 61

than life; on the contrary, his entire speech is structured to contrast his own ongoing life with the worn-out death of Achilles. On the other hand, he does suggest that Achilles' death is much like his life, which can be taken as a compliment or an insult depending on whether one understands him as referring to his honor or his sorrow. Achilles, however, in expressing his hypothetical wish, is not rejecting the actual life he led, but rather confirming that death has not released him from sorrow as he had hoped. Thus the triumph of the Odyssean heroic paradigm is defined not so much in terms of the innate superiority of *nostos* to *kleos* as abstract goals, but rather as a function of how well Odysseus himself can process the Iliadic past through his belated *nostos*, and more specifically, how well he can transform the all-consuming Achillean sorrow and master the Iliadic cycle of violence as he draws ever closer to the conflict that awaits him at home.

In a final reconfiguration of the Iliadic perspective, Achilles turns from lamenting his own condition to inquiring about his loved ones, specifically his son Neoptolemus and his father Peleus (Od. 11.492–94):

ἀλλ' ἄγε μοι τοῦ παιδὸς ἀγαυοῦ μῦθον ἐνίσπες,
ἢ ἕπετ' ἐς πόλεμον πρόμος ἔμμεναι ἦε καὶ οὐκί.
εἰπὲ δέ μοι Πηλῆος ἀμύμονος εἴ τι πέπυσσαι

But come now, tell me news of my noble son,
whether he was a front-rank fighter in battle or not.
And tell me if you have heard anything about blameless Peleus.

As an Iliadic figure, Achilles naturally asks about his son first and then his father, but Odysseus will focus entirely on the son in his response, again signaling the *Odyssey*'s shift from a parental perspective to the child's perspective. His specific question about whether Neoptolemus was a front-rank fighter in battle (*es polemon promos*) makes use of two fundamentally Iliadic phrases that occur nowhere else in the *Odyssey*,[124] but since Neoptolemus does not actually appear in the *Iliad*, this vocabulary is an attempt by Achilles to perpetuate his own Iliadic existence through his post-Iliadic son. Furthermore, Achilles' interrogation of Odysseus for details about his son's military career inverts the earlier pattern of the *Telemachy* in which Telemachus collects stories about his own father's adventures. Not only does the underworld setting underscore the belatedness of Achilles' inquiry and of the parental perspective in general, but in making the request in the first place, he is ceding control over his son's narrative, and thus his own posterity, to Odysseus.

Odysseus responds by defining Neoptolemus' excellence almost entirely in relation to his own post-Iliadic successes.[125] He relates how he himself brought Neoptolemus from Scyros to join the Achaeans at Troy (*Od.* 11.508–9); he states that the young man was third-best in oratory after Odysseus and Nestor (*Od.* 11.512); and he describes in some detail how

Neoptolemus was the calmest and most eager soldier in the belly of the wooden horse, of which Odysseus himself was, of course, in charge (*Od.* 11.523–32). In addition to this explicit subordination of Neoptolemus to the Odyssean paradigm, he closes his description by recounting how after the city was sacked, the young man boarded his ship unscathed (*askathês*), unlike so many others who were wounded in fighting (*Od.* 11.532–37). This final assessment strongly distinguishes Neoptolemus' successful *nostos* from his father's early death, and thus asserts the Odyssean heroic paradigm through the lens of the Odyssean interest in the child's perspective.

Just as in the Ajax episode that immediately follows, Odysseus has the last word. Achilles departs in silence, rejoicing in his son's great achievements (*Od.* 11.538–40):

ὣς ἐφάμην, ψυχὴ δὲ ποδώκεος Αἰακίδαο
φοίτα μακρὰ βιβᾶσα κατ' ἀσφοδελὸν λειμῶνα,
γηθοσύνη, ὅ οἱ υἱὸν ἔφην ἀριδείκετον εἶναι.

Thus I spoke, and the soul of the swift-footed grandson of Aeacus
walked off in long strides across the field of asphodel,
happy because I had said that his son was famous.

Once again, his interlocutor's silence allows Odysseus to interpret the encounter on his own terms. He depicts the soul of Achilles as happily striding off in sharp contrast to his mourning, and he attributes this change in mood to what he himself had told him (*ho ephên*) about his son. Thus Odysseus takes credit both for the achievements of the son and the triumph over the father's everlasting sorrow, thereby bringing together two of the central intertextual themes of the poem. But he also encapsulates the careful strategy of reading the *Iliad* through the *Odyssey*'s own belatedness. Odysseus is the last man standing, and his story is both a continuation of that Iliadic past and a revisionist commentary on it. It is both a sequel to the earlier poem and its rhetorical summation; in short, a complete *Iliados epilogos*.

3 Odyssean Diffraction

degenerem Neoptolemum

One of the key structural features of the *Aeneid*'s dialogue with the *Odyssey* is the tension between each poem's attempt to portray itself as the definitive account of the aftermath of the Trojan war and, by extension, of the *Iliad* itself. In Chapter 1, we briefly considered the role of Poseidon's prophecy (*Il.* 20.302–8) in necessitating a particular destiny for the Homeric character Aeneas. Although Virgil acknowledges this necessity in various ways, the *Aeneid* nevertheless undertakes the *Odyssey*'s program of exploring multiple outcomes of the war. Moreover, it uses the *Odyssey* itself to provide a context for this exploration. This is the heart of what I have referred to as the Odyssean lens: Virgil positions the *Aeneid* in relation to the *Iliad* through the *Odyssey*'s own manipulations of the post-Iliadic experience.

The marked absence of nearly any reference to Trojan characters in the *Odyssey* does not merely reflect the natural viewpoint of the victorious side in a war; it is an active part of an elaborate reading of the negative experiences of those victors.[1] By eliding the ostensible losers of the war from its narrative, the *Odyssey* can refocus our attention (and sympathy) onto the considerable losses of the "winners": the deaths at Troy of Achilles and Ajax; the failed homecomings of Little Ajax, Idomeneus, Diomedes, and especially Agamemnon; and the shipwrecks of Menelaus and Odysseus himself. Having spent the first half of the poem rehearsing these losses, the second part of the *Odyssey* attempts to redeem them by representing Odysseus' negotiation of his homecoming from war as a kind of revised *Iliad*, a repetition of the basic pattern of absence, return, and retribution that lies at the heart of Achilles' story.[2] Inherent in this repetition is a thorough understanding of the original paradigm. Since Odysseus has the advantage of both having experienced the *Iliad* for himself and having directly investigated its long term effects on Achilles, his specific choices in this repetition are a key part of the overall project of defining Odysseus as a successful replacement for Achilles in the epic hierarchy.

For all its preoccupation with the Iliadic past as well as its own belatedness, the *Odyssey* also looks to its own future and establishes itself as a type of self-replicating narrative. In the end, Odysseus does return to Ithaca and reclaim his home, family, and kingdom, but only after a series of cyclical adventures framed by a miniature version of the sack of Troy among the Cicones and an idealized homecoming among the Phaeacians.[3] Even the resounding finality of the killing of the suitors and treacherous servants does not prevent him from almost immediately becoming embroiled in another, potentially larger, battle with the suitors' kinsmen.[4] Likewise, the constant testing of his household and family that begins immediately upon his arrival in Ithaca further reflects the tenuousness of the reintegration process. The harshness of Odysseus' treatment of Laertes has often been noted,[5] but when viewed in the context of the long series of stratagems and acts of violence, it is perhaps not surprising that he saves the cruelest trick for last.[6] Of course, this is only a temporary ending to the story: Zeus' thunderbolt prevents Odysseus from enacting a second slaughter on Ithacan soil (cf. *Od.* 24.528), but it does not seal his return. Tiresias has already told the hero (and he, in turn, has reported to Penelope) that he must once again leave Ithaca and travel to a land whose inhabitants know nothing about the sea and mistake an oar for a winnowing fan, and there offer a sacrifice to Poseidon. Only then can he make his way home to enjoy prosperity and old age before his death (*Od.* 11.119–37; 23.264–84).

Tiresias' prophecy entails a repetition of the pattern of wanderings in the manner of the first half of the *Odyssey*, followed by yet another homecoming narrative as in the second half of the poem. This prophecy and other related legends seem to have inspired the Cyclical *Telegony*, which, according to Proclus' summary (*Chr.* 305–30) and the scholia (Schol. HQV ad *Od.* 11.134), related Odysseus' further adventures away from Ithaca and his eventual death at the hands of Telegonus, his son by Circe.[7] However, the reliability of Odysseus as a narrator in *Odyssey* 9–12 raises some doubts about the function of this prophecy.[8] The clear implication of Tiresias' words is that Odysseus will return home without properly propitiating Poseidon and only then embark on a further mission to repay that specific debt. In this sense, while the *Odyssey* itself is only one out of many possible outcomes of the *Iliad*, the Odyssean aftermath is specifically determined by a prophecy. But since we only have Odysseus' word for this prophecy, he may not so much be determining his post-Odyssean destiny as he is liberating himself from the finality of the Iliadic experience. Achilles' actual death lies beyond the boundaries of the *Iliad*, but, as we have already seen, that death looms large throughout the poem and is even explicitly predicted by Hector (*Il.* 22.358–60) and, as noted earlier, in vaguer terms by the ghost of Patroclus (*Il.* 23.80–81) and Achilles' horse Xanthus (*Il.* 19.416–17). Although his cycle of return and retribution is not quite as laden with the imminence of his own death, Odysseus among the Phaeacians has no way of knowing whether he will actually avoid the Achillean fate when he attempts his own vengeance, and so he protects himself with a prophecy that requires him to survive the homecoming and sail away victorious again.

Even after he successfully regains his home and the danger appears to be over, he repeats the prophecy to Penelope almost immediately upon revealing his true identity to her (*Od.* 23.264–84), both to ward off any lingering perils and to confirm his control over his own narrative. What was perhaps only a hopeful vision of living to fight another day while Odysseus was still laboring to get home becomes an affirmation of the poem's own afterlife. In short, Tiresias' prophecy is an attempt to guarantee that the *Odyssey* will be a victor's epic despite the constant reminder of the losses incurred by the victorious Iliadic Greeks, which is to say that Odysseus' Iliadic aftermath will be the most successful one.

By using the term "victor's epic" I am engaging a dichotomy described by David Quint in his important study of the *Aeneid* and post-Virgilian epic, entitled *Epic and Empire*.[9] For Quint, the distinction between victors' and losers' epics is embodied in the opposition (first defined explicitly in the Renaissance) between epic and romance: "To the victors belongs epic, with its linear teleology; to the losers belongs romance, with its random or circular wandering."[10] My claim here is that the *Odyssey*, which has a long history of being assimilated to the category of romance,[11] moves from a loser's perspective in the first half to that of a winner at the end of the poem both by asserting itself as the fulfillment of the linear Iliadic narrative and by establishing its own improved teleology through a repetition *cum variatione* of key narrative and thematic elements of its predecessor. This is very close to what Quint believes takes place in the *Aeneid* as the poem moves from the "Odyssean" romance of Books 1–6 to the revisionist "Iliadic" epic of the second half.[12] However, since the *Odyssey* already contains this movement within itself, I would argue that the bipartite model of the *Aeneid* fails to acknowledge the fundamental role of the Odyssean revision in shaping Virgil's own "repetition-as-reversal" of the Iliadic war.[13] If, as Quint says, "[t]he epic victors both project their present power prophetically into the future and trace its legitimating origins back into the past,"[14] then the *Aeneid* uses the *Odyssey*'s simultaneous cyclical and forward motion, the path traced by the curve known in mathematics as the cycloid, to mediate its own aetiological glance back to an Iliadic past as well as to the inversion of that past in defining its own teleology.

This cycloidal design is enabled in part by the inherent indeterminacy of the *Odyssey* itself in relation to the *Iliad*. Its careful omission of any explicit reference to the events of the *Iliad* proper, as well as its selective accounts of the Cyclical material, allow the *Odyssey* to establish a strong claim to the Iliadic heritage that cannot be refuted precisely because the *Iliad* does not appear to require it. Thus a post-Iliadic episode such as the stratagem of the wooden horse is told, in varying degrees of detail, multiple times in the *Odyssey* in order to transform the *Iliad*'s implication of a fall of Troy at least initiated by Achilles into a clear Odyssean triumph.[15] The Iliadic figure Menelaus recalls the tale in conversation with Helen and Telemachus (*Od.* 4.266–89), Odysseus himself incorporates it into his description of

Neoptolemus to Achilles (*Od.* 11.523–32), and finally, in a metonymic figure of the *Odyssey*'s constant redirection of the Iliadic narrative, the Phaeacian singer Demodocus tells the fullest version at Odysseus' specific request (*Od.* 8.499–520). Just as in the Neoptolemus narrative, the implicit claim of these repetitions is that Odysseus finishes what Achilles sets in motion but can never accomplish himself: the upbringing of even Achilles' son, the victory over Troy, and the survival after the war. This determination of the *Odyssey* as the completion of an open-ended *Iliad* reinforces its function as the definitive interpretation of that *Iliad*. While the prophecy of the post-Odyssean future necessitates a victorious outcome for the *Odyssey* itself, the notion of Odysseus as a kind of fulfillment of Achilles determines the *Iliad*'s posterity just as well.

To return to Virgil's subsequent reading of this interpretive process, the *Aeneid* does not reject the *Odyssey*'s strategic self-definition, but instead draws inspiration from that strategy to challenge the very foundations of the *Odyssey*'s claim to the Iliadic heritage. And like Odysseus, Aeneas uses a story about Neoptolemus to epitomize his own version of the Iliadic aftermath. Just as Odysseus' carefully crafted account of Neoptolemus summarizes the *Odyssey*'s revision of the Iliadic hierarchies concerning parental perspective, sorrow, and the Achillean heroic ideal, so Aeneas uses his own description of a Neoptolemus episode to establish a competing revision that makes use of the thematic orientation of the Odyssean narrative while simultaneously undermining its authority. Neoptolemus is an ideal figure of the Iliadic afterlife since he can represent his father both genetically and typologically after Achilles' death. As we have already seen, Odysseus chooses to suppress this ideality, or at least subordinate it to his own excellence. By virtually adopting Neoptolemus and molding him into his own reflexive ideal of the eponymous "new warrior," Odysseus represents himself as definitively replacing Achilles in the epic hierarchy. At the same time, he provides himself with a surrogate child on the battlefield in the absence of Telemachus, the "far-off fighter" who will eventually assume his rightful role beside his father in the battle with the suitors.

If the simultaneous glorification and subordination of Neoptolemus is designed to establish Odysseus' ascension over Achilles, Aeneas' extended account of the young man's rampage through Troy and slaughter of Priam at the altar (*Aen.* 2.469–558) confronts both Achilles and Odysseus at once. By appropriating the *Odyssey*'s technique of using a post-Iliadic episode to reinterpret the Iliadic narrative, Virgil challenges the Odyssean description of Neoptolemus' bravery in the sack of Troy while also offering a very different reading of Achilles' own violence and its consequences. At the same time, his account sets up the comparisons of Aeneas to Achilles in the later books of the poem, by demonstrating how Aeneas' inversions of the *Iliad* in his storytelling can adversely affect his own actions.

The first appearance of Neoptolemus in the list of Greek warriors hidden in the horse already establishes an identity between the father and the son that will control the later episode. Of the nine names mentioned, his is the only one accompanied by a parental epithet (*Aen.* 2.263): *Pelidesque Neoptolemus* ("and Neoptolemus, grandson of Peleus"). While this naturally draws attention to Achilles, the use of *Pelides* as a papponymic in reference to Neoptolemus' grandfather Peleus rather than the expected patronymic is unique to this passage and suggests an even stronger interpretation. Elsewhere Virgil only uses *Pelides* to refer to Achilles (*Aen.* 2.548, 5.808, 12.350),[16] and there appears to be no extant Greek example of this name applying to Neoptolemus. On a formal level, papponymics are rare in the Homeric poems except in the prominent case of the name *Aiakidês* for Achilles, and Virgil's use of an analogous form here is perhaps an acknowledgment of this tradition.[17] However, the patronymic *Pêleidês* is so commonly applied to Achilles in the Homeric poems[18] that it seems naturally to serve here as a synonym for Achilles, as it does in the other three passages in the *Aeneid* where it stands alone. Thus while *Pelides Neoptolemus* appears to be a standard proper noun + patronymic phrase, the terms can also be reversed so that *Pelides* serves as the proper noun modified by *Neoptolemus* as an epithet. In this inverted form, Achilles, son of Peleus, will be reborn from the belly of the horse as the "new warrior" defined by his own son's name.[19]

When the young avatar reappears some two hundred lines later, he has a new name, Pyrrhus, and is immediately described in terms that suggest that this is another apt epithet for Achilles (*Aen.* 2.469–70): *Pyrrhus / exsultat telis et luce coruscus aëna* ("Pyrrhus leaps forth glittering in armor and bronze light"). As has been noted by scholars,[20] the phrase *telis et luce coruscus aëna* recalls the Iliadic line αὐγὴ χαλκείη κορύθων ἄπο λαμπομενάων ("the bronze light from the glittering helmets," *Il.* 13.341), which refers to the blinding gleam of the armed men fighting by the Achaean ships. While this is a likely source for the overall image and the phrase *luce aëna* in particular, Virgil's version also strongly resonates with the light imagery used to describe Achilles in his final duel with Hector.[21] Achilles is likened to the evening star when shaking his spear at Hector (*Il.* 22.317–21); his bronze armor shines all around him like the light of a blazing fire or the rising sun (*Il.* 22.134–35: ἀμφὶ δὲ χαλκὸς ἐλάμπετο εἴκελος αὐγῇ / ἢ πυρὸς αἰθομένου ἢ ἠελίου ἀνιόντος); and again the gleam of his armor (*Il.* 22.32: χαλκὸς ἐλάμπε) is compared to the Dog Star, which is the brightest (*lamprotatos*) and brings fever to wretched mortals (*Il.* 22.31: καί τε φέρει πολλὸν πυρετὸν δειλοῖσι βροτοῖσιν). In these last two cases, the gleaming bronze is specifically linked to words derived from the root *pur* ("fire"), which also yields Neoptolemus' alternate name, *Pyrrhos*, or "flame-colored, red-haired."[22] In the simile that immediately follows Pyrrhus' entrance onto the scene (*Aen.* 2.471–75), he is compared to a glittering (*nitidus*) snake emerging from its dark hiding place into the light (*in lucem*), rearing up toward the sun (*arduus in solem*), and flashing (*micat*) its tongue, which further underscores the connection between the fiery son and his shining father. In this regard, the description of the snake sloughing off its skin (*Aen.* 2.473: *positis novus exuviis nitidusque iuventa*, "with his skin cast off, made new and bright with youth") has often been interpreted as an image of rebirth, both in the personal sense (Achilles reborn as Pyrrhus) and in the larger framework of the poem (the Trojan war renewed in Italy), and Bernard Knox, in his classic discussion of this passage, points out that the word *novus* here alludes to Pyrrhus' other name, Neoptolemus, which can mean both "new warrior" and "new war."[23]

While the conversation between Neoptolemus and Priam will challenge the identity between father and son established here,[24] the specific connection to the glimmering imagery of Achilles fighting Hector frames the subsequent scene, which culminates in Priam's death, as a revision of the Iliadic climax. Neoptolemus pursues and kills Polites before his father Priam's eyes and then converses with the Trojan king before slaughtering him at the altar (*Aen.* 2.526–58). This corresponds to Achilles' combat with Hector in full view of the Trojans on the walls above (*Il.* 22) and the later ransom scene with Priam (*Il.* 24.468–676), but Virgil transforms the model in crucial ways: Polites is no Hector to begin with in respect to fighting ability,[25] nor is there an indication that he put up any kind of fight before being wounded and fleeing; Neoptolemus does not kill Polites in the open field of battle, but rather pursues him into the innermost courtyard of the palace (*Aen.* 2.526–30); instead of dragging the body away so that Priam must come to him to retrieve it, he drives Polites to expire at Priam's feet (*Aen.* 2.530–32); and with the need for any reconciliation removed, their exchange of words culminates in a violation of the sanctity of Jupiter's altar (*Aen.* 2.550–53) as opposed to the respect for Zeus' decree, which prevents Achilles from striking Priam down in the midst of their encounter (*Il.* 24.560–70). In short, where the *Iliad* contextualizes Achilles' violence within a framework of vengeance and reconciliation, here unremitting violence against weaker parties is portrayed as both a means and an end in itself. Neoptolemus, then, is not so much Achilles reborn as Achilles revised for the specific task of completing the annihilation of Troy, a task that is embodied in his second functional name, Pyrrhus.[26]

This revision is a direct response to the *Odyssey*'s reevaluation of the Achillean paradigm. At first glance, Aeneas' disapproving account of Neoptolemus' actions seems to challenge the authority of Odysseus' description of the young man's heroism that pleases Achilles so much (*Od.* 11.539–40).[27] Priam explicitly contrasts Neoptolemus' cruelty in killing his son Polites at the altar with Achilles' mercy in returning the body of another son, Hector (*Aen.* 2.540–43):

> at non ille, satum quo te mentiris, Achilles
> talis in hoste fuit Priamo; sed iura fidemque
> supplicis erubuit corpusque exsangue sepulcro
> reddidit Hectoreum meque in mea regna remisit.

> But that Achilles, from whom you falsely claim to be born,
> did not behave this way toward Priam his enemy;
> but he respected the claims and the trust of a suppliant
> and returned the bloodless body of Hector for burial
> and sent me back to my realm.

Priam distinguishes between the respectful behavior of "that (*ille*) Achilles" in *Iliad* 24 and the gross impiety of *this* new "Achilles" who lies (*mentiris*) when he claims to be the former's offspring (*satum*). By directing Neoptolemus' attention to his father's behavior in one particular instance, Priam downplays the violent similarities between Achilles and his heir. Achilles' rampage after the death of Patroclus, his brutal treatment of Hector's corpse, his human sacrifice on Patroclus' altar (*Il.* 23.175–77), and his flashing anger when meeting with the suppliant Priam are not far removed from Neoptolemus' behavior in this scene. Moreover, our narrator Aeneas has already seen the temple of Juno, which depicts Achilles dragging Hector's body around the walls and ransoming the corpse for gold (*Aen.* 1.147–48).[28] But whereas Priam was able to soften Achilles by asking him to imagine his own father Peleus' grief at losing his only son (*Il.* 24.485–512), here he tries to shame Neoptolemus by claiming that he is not worthy of being called Achilles' offspring. Priam's specific account of Achilles' actions only serves to demonstrate how much the circumstances of the war have changed since the *Iliad*. Although Priam is nominally a suppliant at an altar (*Aen.* 2.524–25), he is fully armed (*Aen.* 2.509–11) and even attempts to attack Neoptolemus after this speech (*Aen.* 2.544–46).[29] Moreover, Neoptolemus has already brought Polites back to Priam bloodless (*exsangue*, cf. *Aen.* 2.532: *multo vitam cum sanguine fudit*, "he poured out his life with much blood"), and he cannot send Priam back into his realm (*in mea regna*) because they are already deep within the palace while the city is being destroyed around them.

The "new warrior" is a product of the new circumstances of the war, and those circumstances have been determined by the machinations of Odysseus himself. We have already seen how Odysseus reclassifies Neoptolemus' bravery as a species of his own heroic genus (and genius) rather than Achilles', and to a certain extent the contrast between Aeneas' negative portrayal of the youth and Odysseus' lavish praise is designed to question the reliability of the Homeric narrative. But Virgil recognizes that Odysseus' duplicity lies not in the actual facts of Neoptolemus' story but in their presentation as an extension of his own excellence, and so he uses his own account to challenge the *Odyssey*'s revision of the Iliadic climax. Virgil acknowledges that Odysseus has already assimilated Neoptolemus to his own ruthlessness, but he locates the paradigm for that ruthlessness in the return to Ithaca and the "new war" that Odysseus wages there rather than in the Trojan war itself. Neoptolemus is deceitful, sharp-tongued, and utterly merciless; he is the model of the "new warrior" as defined by Odysseus in his own replay of the Iliadic retribution: Odysseus penetrates the palace, slaughters suitors who are no match for him (as well as defenseless maidservants), and when confronted by their kinsmen, defiantly prepares for further bloodshed. Although he is nominally taking a kind of vengeance, his actions are quite literally overkill and, moreover, we do not see the same kind of reconciliation that marks the end of Achilles' cycle of violence. Athena and Zeus must directly intervene to restrain Odysseus as he leaps at the suitors' kinsmen at the very end of the poem (*Od.* 24.537–40); while they manage to impose a peace agreement on both sides, Odysseus still comes dangerously close to annihilating a great portion of his own Ithacan subjects.

Furthermore, the last man killed is Eupeithes, the father of the leading suitor Antinous (*Od.* 24.520–25), an event that ironically alludes to the successful mission of Priam in *Iliad* 24. The fact that it is Laertes, not Odysseus, who kills Eupeithes reinforces the departure from the Iliadic pattern. Whereas suppliant Priam persuaded Achilles to ransom the body of his son Hector by asking the younger man to think of his own father Peleus, here Eupeithes, the etymological "good persuader,"[30] attempts to avenge his son's death on Odysseus and is instead slain by Odysseus' father, Laertes.[31] The inversion is underscored by Penelope's earlier attempt to save Telemachus from Antinous' murderous scheme by reminding him of the protection that Odysseus once gave Eupeithes when he was a suppliant fugitive (*Od.* 16.420–33). Her Priamic appeal to the memory of a father falls on deaf ears, and Antinous' stubborn rejection of the Achillean model is reflected in Eupeithes' failure to negotiate the appropriate Iliadic settlement for his dead son and the subsequent inadvertent payment of his own debt to Odysseus with his life.[32]

This manifold Odyssean reconfiguration of the settlement between Achilles and Priam provides the context for Virgil's presentation of Neoptolemus. The violent nature inherited from Achilles is honed into a pitiless cruelty under Odysseus' tutelage, and the young protégé plays his own scene with Priam accordingly. Faced with a similar situation as his father, he chooses to follow the *Odyssey*'s rejection of the Iliadic type of settlement, and Aeneas' negative portrayal of this choice foregrounds the tension between heroic paradigms inherent in Odysseus' self-serving account of Neoptolemus in *Odyssey* 11. Thus when Priam accuses Neoptolemus of falsely claiming to be Achilles' son, he is marking Odysseus' virtual adoption of the boy as a type of perversion of the Iliadic balance between extreme violence and deliberate reconciliation.

Given this portrayal of Neoptolemus as a subverted Achilles, we can better understand the surprising fact that the snake simile that introduces him in this episode is based on the Homeric simile that describes Hector as he prepares to meet Achilles in battle (*Il.* 22.93–95).[33] Neoptolemus is first established as an avatar of his father when he emerges from the belly of the horse as the "new warrior"; this identification is confirmed when he enters Priam's palace as the "fiery" destroyer with glittering armor; finally, through the simile, he also becomes an inverted Hector who will triumph in his slaughter. The transference of this simile from the victim to the conqueror allows Neoptolemus to represent the breakdown of Hector, whose name literally means "keeper" or "defender,"[34] and so it is no accident that his final acts here involve first killing the son of Priam named Polites, "citizen," a metonymic figure for the Trojan people,[35] and then Priam himself, who regularly stands for the city in both the Homeric poems and the *Aeneid*.[36] Neoptolemus thus destroys the citizenry and city itself in consecutive blows while recalling the victimization of the last true "defender" of the city by Achilles. At the same time the image of a "keeper" of the home wreaking havoc inside the home itself echoes Odysseus' slaughter in his own palace, further confirming the essential Odyssean transformation of Neoptolemus. In this regard, Neoptolemus is very much a precursor of Aeneas in the later books of the poem, where he shifts between representing Hector and Achilles in his conflict with Turnus.[37] We will consider the ramifications of this relationship in the next chapter, but for now we may note that the specific realization in Aeneas of the roles of defender of the home and private avenger represented by the conflation of Hector and Achilles is informed both by this episode in Book 2 and by the *Odyssey*'s own portrait of Odysseus as simultaneous defender and avenger.

By the end of the encounter, Neoptolemus himself seems to acknowledge that he embodies a fundamental transformation of the Iliadic paradigm in his sarcastic reply to Priam's charge that he is a false son of Achilles (*Aen.* 2.547–50):

> cui Pyrrhus: 'referes ergo haec et nuntius ibis
> Pelidae genitori. illi mea tristia facta
> degeneremque Neoptolemum narrare memento.
> nunc morere.'

> To whom Pyrrhus replied: "Therefore you shall carry back
> these words and you shall go as a messenger to my father Achilles.
> Remember to tell him of my sorrowful deeds and how degenerate
> Neoptolemus was. Now die."

These are the only words Neoptolemus speaks in the *Aeneid*, and given Odysseus' claim that the young man was especially skilled in oratory (*Od.* 11.511: αἰεὶ πρῶτος ἔβαζε καὶ οὐχ ἡμάρτανε μύθων, "he always spoke first and never made a mistake with in words"), it is not surprising that he answers Priam's taunt with a witty riposte.[38] But there is more to this brief speech than mere verbal sparring. Neoptolemus is trapped between his Achillean genetics and his Odyssean training, and while he accepts that he is in some way *degener*, literally "falling away from his ancestry/forebears,"[39] he still attempts to prove himself a worthy heir to Achilles. By referring to his father as *Pelidae*, he is laying claim to the lineage of Peleus even if the awareness of that lineage does not sway him as it did Achilles when faced with Priam's request for mercy. Instead, Neoptolemus chooses to emulate Achilles' pitiless killing of Hector in *Iliad* 22, and he tries to send the actual victim of his own cruelty as proof of his successful imitation of his father. His final exhortation, *nunc morere*, echoes Achilles' own command to dying Hector, *tethnathi*, ("die," *Il.* 22.365),[40] but with the cruel twist that it precedes the actual blow that kills Priam rather than following it. Even in this imitation, the Odyssean rhetoric frames the Achillean deed itself.

Although Neoptolemus charges Priam with the double task of delivering this message (*refers . . . et nuntius ibis*) and serving as the physical evidence of it,[41] there is a savage irony in the fact that the last image of Priam depicts him as quite unsuitable for either task (*Aen.* 2.557–58): *iacet ingens litore truncus, / avulsumque umeris caput et sine nomine corpus* ("he lies on the shore, a giant trunk, his head torn from his shoulders, and a corpse without a name"). A headless, nameless corpse can neither give voice to the message nor serve as a renowned trophy from the war.[42] Neoptolemus is trying to establish his own heroic credentials in the eyes of his father, but he uses the wrong messenger.[43] Priam has already had his chance to speak to Achilles in a kind of katabasis in *Iliad* 24, and he has just now described that visit in terms that whitewash the primal violence of the father in order to enhance the contrast with the savage young son. Neoptolemus' ironic commission to Priam is ripe with the knowledge that in the internal Homeric narrative of the war, the proper messenger turns out to be Odysseus, who gives a favorable, if ambiguous, account of Neoptolemus' heroic success to Achilles. As we have already seen, that positive account omits any explicit reference to Neoptolemus' brutality, but here the *Aeneid* uses our awareness that it is Odysseus, another figure explicitly associated with cruelty by Virgil,[44] who actually delivers the message to raise doubts about the authority of the *Odyssey*'s version. Aeneas, then, appears to provide a corrective to Odysseus' manipulation of the message by not only describing the actions of Neoptolemus but also quoting his actual words.

Aeneas' account of Priam's last stand has been compared to a messenger's speech in Greek tragedy,[45] and one of the most striking aspects of the episode is Aeneas' passive observance without any attempt to intervene on Priam's behalf.[46] Given his tortured debate about whether to take action in the case of Helen in the scene that immediately follows (*Aen.* 2.567–88),[47] it is strange that here, in a situation that he presents as an unambiguous violation of *pietas* and sanctity, he can only report. But of course his very report constantly intervenes in the action by presenting such a negative picture of Neoptolemus. If he cannot physically avenge the death of Priam, he can at least excoriate the man responsible for that death. This condemnation involves the refutation, or at least the ironizing, of Odysseus' praise of Neoptolemus, but Virgil makes the intervention more explicit by inserting this description into the internal Homeric timeline at a point earlier than the *Odyssey*'s own narrative. Thus, although Aeneas and Odysseus describe events that take place at the same time in the Trojan war, the explicit quotation of Priam's criticism and Neoptolemus' cruel speech undermines Odysseus' repetition of his own eyewitness testimony delivered to Achilles almost three years after the fall of Troy.[48] Aeneas' third-person account of the scene, complete with dialogue, thus creates an impression of greater authenticity than Odysseus' first-person reminiscence of an ambiguous description that he himself once gave.[49]

Nevertheless, by challenging the accuracy of Odysseus' characterization of Neoptolemus, Virgil inevitably raises doubts about Aeneas' own reliability as a narrator. There is no objective reason to privilege Aeneas' representation of Neoptolemus over Odysseus': Aeneas may be fabricating the content or the tone of the quoted speeches, his memory of the events may be confused, or his original observation might have been compromised in some way. At various points in Book 2, Aeneas draws attention to the limitations of his sensory perceptions and his resulting states of confusion and bewilderment,[50] and even more tellingly, his overall program of laying the foundations for the transformation from loser's to victor's epic requires a highly selective account of the action. As I have already suggested, this transformation is patterned on a similar movement in the *Odyssey* itself, and Virgil underscores the connection by having his hero present the loser's perspective in a carefully wrought first-person narrative to the Carthaginians, just as Odysseus narrates his numerous trials to the Phaeacians.

Aeneas' narrative is self-serving and, at times, intentionally obfuscating, but this is also in keeping with his Odyssean model and its practical goal of inspiring pity in the hero's Phaeacian audience and securing their hospitality.[51] But whereas Odysseus must use increasingly fantastic stories of his postwar wanderings to break himself down in the eyes of his hosts after the great victory sung by Demodocus, Aeneas' narration dwells on the waning moments of the war and pays special attention to the treacherous nature of the Greeks and the brutal victimization of the Trojans. It is a dangerous strategy because it exposes the Trojans' folly and Aeneas' failure in particular, but this, too, mirrors Odysseus' technique of obliquely blaming his comrades for his own inability to avert disaster. In the mishap with Aeolus' bag of winds, the sojourn with Circe, and most significantly, the Thrinacia episode, which leads to his final shipwreck, Odysseus forestalls any critique of his effectiveness as a captain by blaming the rashness of his companions for the ensuing trouble. Aeneas similarly attributes the fall of the city to the recklessness of the Trojan populace (cf. *Aen.* 2.54–56, 228–339, 244–45), shifting uneasily between first- and third-person plural forms; he does not describe any of his own individual actions until after the horse is brought into the city and he is visited in a dream by Hector (*Aen.* 2.270–71). In the case of Priam's death, where Aeneas' failure to act is especially conspicuous, he manages to deflect criticism by assuming the perspective of an omniscient narrator and only explicitly describing his own emotions after the literary flourish of Priam's epitaph (*Aen.* 2.559–60): *at me tum primum saevus circumstetit horror. / obstipui* ("this was the first time savage horror took me. I was dumbstruck"). The adverbial *tum primum* reinforces the idea that, until this moment, Aeneas has only been an observer, and that now the full implications of Priam's death for his own situation become clear to him.[52]

But there is an irony in his claim that this new fear caused him to become dumbstruck or numb (*obstipui*), since he had been quite paralyzed throughout the whole preceding episode. Aeneas uses the same verb of physical immobility, *obstupescere*, on three subsequent occasions to describe his own surprise at encountering children of Priam: when he sees the ghost of his wife Creusa, who was also a daughter of Priam (*Aen.* 2.774);[53] when he hears the ghostly voice of Polydorus in Thrace (*Aen.* 3.48); and most significantly, when he learns that Helenus is ruling over part of Neoptolemus' kingdom and is married to Andromache (*Aen.* 3.298). The physical helplessness produced by his proximity to Priam's blood is a recurring symbol of Aeneas' failure to prevent the destruction of Troy. Even amidst all the considerable physical difficulties on his long journey, the memory of that failure is perhaps his greatest obstacle. The successful movement from loser's to victor's epic is predicated on Aeneas' constructive response to that memory. Immediately after Priam's death, his immobility gives way to concern for his family, starting with his father (*Aen.* 2.560–62): *subiit cari genitoris imago, / ut regem aequaevum crudeli vulnere vidi / vitam exhalantem* ("the image of my dear father rose before me when I saw the king, his equal in age, breathing out his life beneath a cruel wound"). In a clear reference to the Iliadic antecedent of the preceding scene, Priam has made Aeneas think of his own father, Anchises, in words that recall the king's famous plea to Achilles (*Il.* 24.487: τηλίκου ὥς περ ἐγών, ὀλοῷ ἐπὶ γήραος οὐδῷ, "one who is as old as I am, on the destructive doorstep of old age"),[54] which further reinforces the contrast with Neoptolemus' disdain for the conciliatory gesture of his father in *Iliad* 24.[55]

Aeneas' response reflects a major shift in his heroic priorities. Although Anchises' name occurs in two oblique instances earlier in the poem (*Aen.* 1.617, 2.300), this is the first meaningful reference to the hero's father. Now that Priam has been killed before his very eyes, the fate of the kingdom is sealed, and so Aeneas is violently forced to turn his attention to the preservation of his immediate family and the fulfillment of his personal destiny. Whereas at the beginning of the assault he was eager to meet his death in battle (*Aen.* 2.316–17: *furor iraque mentem / praecipitat, pulchrumque mori succurrit in armis*, "rage and anger drive my mind, and I am seized by the thought that it is a fine thing to die in arms"), he now begins to acknowledge his greater responsibilities.[56] Priam, once the living symbol of old Troy, is replaced by his age-mate (*aequaevum*) Anchises, the progenitor of the family that will found the new civilization. Ensuring the safety of Anchises, which is already his filial duty, becomes an essential symbolic task for Aeneas. Later, when he tries to persuade his stubborn father to leave the city, he explicitly warns that young Pyrrhus is on his way fresh with the blood of another father and son pair (*Aen.* 2.662–63): *iamque aderit multo Priami de sanguine Pyrrhus, / natum ante ora patris, patrem qui obtruncat ad aras* ("soon Pyrrhus will be here, fresh from Priam's copious blood, he who massacres the son before his father's eyes, and then the father at the altar"). The brutal verb *obtruncat* vividly recalls the resulting *truncus* of Priam on the shore (*Aen.* 2.557), while the polyptoton of *patris/ patrem* emphasizes Aeneas' primary concern for Anchises.

Although Aeneas manages to rescue both his father and himself from the burning city, the subsequent reminders of his inability to save Priam produce the same paralysis that led to his failure in the first place. It is only once he actually hears the account of Pyrrhus' death from Andromache, and then receives an extensive prophecy from Helenus, that he is able to begin transforming the shame of his earlier impotence into a steely resolve to found the new Troy by any means necessary. As we will see in the next chapter, this closely mirrors Odysseus' own approach to his homecoming, but one of the key elements of that process is the appropriation and novel application of character traits exhibited by Neoptolemus. Just as Neoptolemus represents a kind of Odyssean modification of Achilles, so Aeneas will make further changes to the pattern as he goes deeper into his new war. Even though he has no hand in it, the death of Neoptolemus is a crucial step in burying his past failure, especially because it appears to be an act of divine retribution (*Aen.* 3.331–32): *Orestes / excipit incautum patriasque obtruncat ad aras* ("Orestes surprises Pyrrhus and massacres him at his father's altar"). The repetition of *obtruncat ad aras* and his victimization at the hands of another son of a prominent Greek veteran establish Pyrrhus' death as an exact reprisal for his treatment of Polites and Priam.[57] Given the strong influence of Odysseus on Neoptolemus, this condemnation of the young man's actions also calls into question the overall Odyssean heroic paradigm. The intersection with Agamemnon's unsuccessful homecoming and its dire consequences, a story that serves as a crucial counterpoint to Odysseus' own *nostos* throughout the *Odyssey*, may even be designed to suggest that Odysseus will eventually suffer a similar fate for his own crimes.[58] Finally, the account of Neoptolemus' death seals Aeneas' challenge to Odysseus' authority by extending the time frame of the narrative beyond the scope of the Homeric hero's underworld account. Not only can Aeneas quote the young man's cruel speech at Troy, but he can also confirm that his negative characterization was accurate by describing Pyrrhus' retributive death.

pendetque iterum narrantis ab oris

Aeneas' attempt to undermine Odysseus' authority is successful precisely because he is able to manipulate the formal relationships between their two narratives. Virgil has the benefit of a complete *Odyssey* as a temporal and spatial framework into which he can interject his own version of post-Iliadic events. As we will see in the next chapter, during his journey around the Mediterranean in Book 3, Aeneas can get as close to or as far from Odysseus as he likes without ever meeting him, because Virgil already "knows" where Odysseus is at any given time. But this strategy extends to the narrative technique of the poem as well. Virgil repeatedly blurs the line between his own narration and Aeneas' reported speech in Book 2.[59] Although he narrates the entire book without break, Aeneas is virtually absent as a player in the long story of the horse and then again during the Neoptolemus episode. These are the same stories that the *Odyssey* uses to demonstrate Odysseus' fulfillment of the incomplete Achillean projects of capturing the city and raising Neoptolemus as a great warrior. In the case of the horse, Odysseus' brief version is only the last in a sequence of accounts that reinforce one another, while we only have Odysseus' own tendentious report to Achilles as a source for Neoptolemus. Virgil presents both stories through the voice of his hero, but by nearly eliding the distinction between his own point of view and Aeneas', he moves very close to the kind of authority provided by *Odyssey*'s multiple accounts of the horse, and then pulls away from Odysseus' personal account to question his authority in the description of Neoptolemus. That is to say, he positions Aeneas at several distinct vantage points with respect to Odysseus' storytelling technique in order to create tension between the two separate accounts of the post-Iliadic world, while still using that technique as the primary model for his own narrative.

This is especially apparent in the specific circumstances surrounding their respective storytelling sessions. As an anonymous guest in a remote land, Odysseus is in a peculiar position regarding the Phaeacians. His primary aim is to secure safe passage back to Ithaca, but he is not entirely sure of his standing in this strange community. When he first supplicates Nausicaa, her comments to her maids reveal how isolated from other humans the Phaeacians are (*Od.* 6.204–5): οἰκέομεν δ' ἀπάνευθε πολυκλύστῳ ἐνὶ πόντῳ, / ἔσχατοι, οὐδέ τις ἄμμι βροτῶν ἐπιμίσγεται ἄλλος ("and we live far away in the much-dashing sea, at the very end, nor does any other mortal mix with us").[60] If they do not mingle with other men very often, then they may be wary of his request for assistance. But perhaps more important than concern for his physical safety is his anxiety about his heroic identity. Odysseus may suspect that the Phaeacians are unfamiliar with his exploits at Troy and that a bold announcement of his name and lineage in the usual manner of an Iliadic hero would produce no reaction. This fear of obscurity contributes a great deal to Odysseus' reticence throughout the subsequent episode.[61] Nausicaa does not ask for his name, but when he arrives at the palace and supplicates Arete, Alcinous uses his speech to the Phaeacian leaders to inquire obliquely about Odysseus's identity (*Od.* 7.186–206). Like Nausicaa earlier (*Od.* 6.243, 280–81), Alcinous wonders whether the stranger is a god (*Od.* 7.199: εἰ δέ τις ἀθανάτων γε κατ' οὐρανοῦ εἰλήλουθεν, "but if one of the immortals has come down from heaven"), but his comment is clearly designed to elicit a response from Odysseus himself.[62] Odysseus answers this query by asserting his status as a long-suffering mortal, but he does not identify himself any further. The gradual process by which he reveals himself to the Phaeacians continues when Arete directly asks him his name and how he came to Scheria (*Od.* 7.237–39). He replies with an account of his sojourn with Calypso and his subsequent escape, but deftly sidesteps the matter of his name. Despite this caginess on Odysseus' part, Alcinous is clearly swayed by his rhetoric and agrees to convey the hero to his still unnamed homeland and even suggests a marriage with Nausicaa. This is either a display of extraordinary naiveté on the king's part or an intentional ruse. On the one hand, he claims that the furthest his people have ever sailed is Euboea (*Od.* 7.321–23), so they hardly could have any direct knowledge of Troy, but his willingness to give his daughter in marriage suggests that he at least has some suspicions about the status of his guest.

Moreover, there is at least one member of the Phaeacian court who demonstrates great familiarity with Odysseus' achievements in the Trojan war. During the entertainment on the following day, the blind bard Demodocus sings three songs, two of which feature Odysseus prominently. By telling these stories about Odysseus, Demodocus proves to be a key ally in the stranger's campaign of gradual self-revelation.[63] After each song, Odysseus weeps and tries to hide his tears, which Alcinous nevertheless notices (*Od.* 8.83–95, 521–34). After the third song, Alcinous finally asks for the stranger's name (*Od.* 8.550–86) and Odysseus embarks on his long tale with his heroic pedigree already established. But at the same time, the contents of the songs, and their presentation of Odysseus in particular, do not necessarily paint the precise heroic picture that Odysseus himself desires. When Odysseus finally takes up his own story, he has to reckon with the challenge put forth by Demodocus' representation of him. This provides a key motivation for the particular kind of story Odysseus chooses to tell. These circumstances strongly suggest a kind of singing competition. Odysseus' earlier response to Arete's queries in Book 7 (*Od.* 7.240–97) is a very effective recapitulation of the events described by the Homeric narrator in *Odyssey* 5–6 recast from the point of view of Odysseus himself and with certain rhetorical moves designed to elicit maximum sympathy.[64] While Odysseus is obviously not competing with Homer in the literal sense, the poem does use this retelling of the story to establish a distinct narrative point of view for Odysseus that must be taken into account in Books 9 through 13, where the voice of Odysseus and the Homeric narrator appear to merge completely.

However, as I have been arguing throughout, Odysseus does compete in various ways with the Homeric narrator of the *Iliad*; Demodocus both highlights that competition and acts as a surrogate for the Iliadic poet in it.[65] The notion of poetic competition is not unprecedented in the Homeric poems: in the Catalogue of the Ships, the *Iliad* tells the story of the Thracian singer Thamyrus, who is stripped of his voice after challenging the Muses (*Il.* 2.594–600).[66] Like his Ithacan doublet Phemius, who entertains the suitors with a song about the return of the Achaeans from Troy (*Od.* 1.325–27), Demodocus possesses a body of song material that defines the limits of the pre-Odyssean world.[67] Phemius can sing the bitter homecoming of the Achaeans (*Od.* 1.326–27: *Achaiôn noston . . . lugron*), but this obviously cannot include Odysseus' *nostos*, even if Telemachus' assertion that the audience always prefers the "latest song" (*Od.* 1.351–52) suggests that this is fresh material. It will be the *Odyssey* itself that will tell the latest homecoming story, once again establishing its claim as the superior narrative.

Demodocus' first song (*Od.* 8.73–82) tells the story of a quarrel between Achilles and Odysseus. This story is not known from any other source, and since Demodocus' narrative is only described in general terms, we do not have any clear sense of the actual circumstances of the quarrel.[68] Nevertheless, the song makes explicit the conflict between the two heroic paradigms represented by Achilles and Odysseus, while still situating that competition in an Iliadic context. The theme of a quarrel between two generals, the occurrence of the epithetic phrases *Peleideô Achilêos* (*Od.* 8.75) and *anax andrôn* (*Od.* 8.77), the involvement of Apollo, as well as the description of the woe brought down upon the Greeks and Trojans through the plans of Zeus (*Od.* 8.82: *Dios . . . boulas*) all strongly allude to the opening of the *Iliad* itself (cf. *Il.* 1.5: *Dios . . . boulê*).[69] By casting Odysseus in the role of Agamemnon, Demodocus elevates Odysseus above his Iliadic status, but obliquely suggests that Achillean physical strength is still superior to Odyssean cleverness.

Throughout the song, Odysseus manages to conceal his tears from everyone but Alcinous, who may have deduced the stranger's identity from his sorrow. In light of Demodocus' implicit assessment of the relative strengths of the two heroes, Alcinous' proposal of athletic games (*Od.* 8.97–103) may be designed to test Odysseus' physical prowess. At first, Odysseus refuses to compete, but the increasingly heated exchange with the two Phaeacian youths (*Od.* 8.132–85) yet again recalls the escalation of tensions between Achilles and Agamemnon in *Iliad* 1, and thus represents another attempt to cast him in the role of Achilles' subordinate. Odysseus has no choice but to demonstrate his abilities with a superhuman discus throw followed by a bold assertion of his skill with a bow. Here he comes very close to revealing his identity when he ranks himself among the Achaean archers at Troy (*Od.* 8.219–20): οἷος δή με Φιλοκτήτης ἀπεκαίνυτο τόξῳ / δήμῳ ἔνι Τρώων, ὅτε τοξαζοίμεθ᾽ Ἀχαιοί ("Philoctetes alone surpassed me with the bow in the land of the Trojans, when we Achaeans shot with bows"). If Demodocus and the Phaeacians insist on comparing him to Achilles, then he will shift the terms of that comparison away from the specific context of the *Iliad* toward aspects of the Trojan war that present his own excellence more clearly.

This also involves moving from the early history of the war, exemplified by the first song's reference to the beginning of the suffering (*Od.* 8.81: *pêmatos archê*), to its latest stages. Thus, after the interlude provided by Demodocus' second song about Ares and Aphrodite, Odysseus explicitly asks the bard to sing about the wooden horse (*Od.* 8.494–95): ὅν ποτ' ἐς ἀκρόπολιν δόλον ἤγαγε δῖος Ὀδυσσεύς, / ἀνδρῶν ἐμπλήσας οἳ Ἴλιον ἐξαλάπαξαν ("the trick that godlike Odysseus led to the citadel, after filling it with the men who then sacked Ilium"). This request is clearly aimed at establishing his identity once and for all, and given his earlier claims about his archery skills, no Phaeacian who was familiar with the war could miss the import of his song selection. But so far, only Demodocus has displayed such familiarity, and if the bard does know that this stranger is Odysseus, he is only partially willing to grant him the full honor he desires.[70] Demodocus does not begin with Odysseus' *dolos*, the planning for his stratagem of the horse, but rather at the moment when the Trojans have already brought the horse into the city and are deliberating over it (*Od.* 8.499–514). After describing the sack of the city by the Achaeans, he ends with an account of how Odysseus went with Menelaus to fetch Helen from the house of Deiphobus, where he triumphs in the "grimmest fighting" (*ainotaton polemon*) with the help of Athena (*Od.* 8.515–20). Although the song eventually comes around to a specific account of Odysseus actions, he is hardly depicted as the master of cunning implied in his initial request to Demodocus. Moreover, even in his physical triumph he is both portrayed as a supporting character to Menelaus and given a backhanded compliment for receiving Athena's aid. Demodocus establishes the stranger's heroic credentials, but he does not explicitly support Odysseus' claim to a superior heroic paradigm based on intellect.

Having been foiled in his attempt to use Demodocus' song as a definitive introduction, Odysseus weeps again, only to have Alcinous finally demand that he reveal himself.[71] Whether the Phaeacian king has truly missed all the hints as to the identity of his guest or is play-acting for some unknown reason, Odysseus is faced with an audience that has not acknowledged any awareness that he has come from Troy. This may reflect a lack of interest in the Trojan war or, as Demodocus' songs suggest, a strongly Iliadic view of it, but either way, Odysseus is in a difficult position as he embarks on his narrative. In order to meet the challenge, he picks up the story after the end of the war, which has essentially just been narrated by Demodocus, and resumes the theme of his misfortune with which he began his earlier response to Arete. Rather than rushing headlong into his own explicit version of the war, Odysseus tells the Phaeacians a tale they could not possibly have heard already, and in the course of that story, revises various elements of the Trojan war in order to secure a more favorable position for himself. This strategy is especially clear in the movement from the first major episode, the story of the Cyclops, to the last, the descent to the Underworld. The latter is his most elaborate opportunity to engage the *Iliad* directly and set the record straight from his perspective, while the former is designed both to appeal to the particular interests of his Phaeacian hosts, whose own ancestors fled the Cyclopes (cf. *Od.* 6.4–6), and to remind them of the perils of bad hospitality.[72]

By the time his story is complete, Odysseus has artfully demonstrated that the mere victory at Troy was insufficient to guarantee a victorious epic tale, and that surviving the war and returning home without getting killed is the supreme heroic achievement. By offering the Phaeacians the chance to play a crucial role in his homecoming, he suggests that they, too, can partake of the glory associated with his brand of heroism. Thus, when he first supplicates the king, Odysseus explicitly refers to the *asbeton kleos*, "imperishable glory," which Alcinous will obtain when Odysseus returns to Ithaca (*Od.* 7.330–33), and thereafter, Alcinous makes four explicit attempts to ensure that Odysseus praises the Phaeacians when he returns to his native land (*Od.* 8.100–3, 241–45, 250–53, 431–32).[73] Although he does eventually mention the Phaeacians briefly to Telemachus and Penelope (16.227–31, 19.278–82, 23.338–41), he never explicitly refers to Alcinous, thus denying him any specific *kleos*. Moreover, Odysseus' most detailed account of his passage to Ithaca comes in his first lying tale to disguised Athena, where he substitutes the Phoenicians for the Phaeacians (*Od.* 13.253–86).[74] Among the magical Phaeacians, who seem so unreal, his allegedly true tales are full of unbelievable elements; back home in the "real" world of Ithaca, his lies must be more credible, and so even the Phaeacians are translated into a more familiar analogue. Odysseus' rhetorical excellence lies in his ability to adapt the narrative to his particular audience in order to inspire the desired reaction. The lying tales at home are no more true or false than the long story of his wanderings as told to the Phaeacians; they are simply two versions of a basic story pattern that have been elaborated in different ways.[75]

While Virgil's interaction with the *Odyssey* is considerably more than a rendition of his Homeric model, he does acknowledge the fluidity of this kind of Odyssean transformation. If Odysseus substitutes the Phoenicians because they are more believable than Phaeacians, then Virgil plays on that substitution in order to assert the greater authority of Aeneas' own tale. Just as Nausicaa informs Odysseus that he is in the land of Phaeacians (*Od.* 6.195: Φαίηκες μὲν τήνδε πόλιν καὶ γαῖαν ἔχουσιν, "the Phaeacians possess this city and land"), the first thing Aeneas learns when he questions Venus in disguise is that he has arrived at a Phoenician kingdom (*Aen.* 1.338: *Punica regna vides*, "you see a Punic realm"). The reader has already learned that the residents are Phoenicians a few lines earlier, when Mercury is sent to ensure that *ponuntque ferocia Poeni / corda* ("the Phoenicians set aside their fierce spirits," *Aen.* 1.302–3), but more importantly, this description firmly associates these *Poeni* with the historical Carthaginians so familiar to the Romans. Virgil has transformed the magical Phaeacians into the concrete ancestors of Hannibal and his menacing armies, and thereby provides a kind of external authentication for his story. But Virgil's audience knows quite well that the Carthaginians will not "set aside their fierce spirits" until they are physically subdued, so there is an expectation that Aeneas will not receive passage "home" to Italy from his hosts without some sort of violence.

There is, in fact, already a great deal of uncertainty about what kind of place Aeneas has discovered even before we learn that the inhabitants are Phoenicians. As Servius says about the description of the Libyan harbor (Serv. ad *Aen.* 1.159): "topothesia est, id est, fictus secundum poeticam licentiam locus" ("it is an imaginary description of a place, that is, a place invented according to poetic license").[76] In this case, Virgil's *poetica licentia* leads him to combine elements from the *Odyssey*'s descriptions of the harbor at Ithaca (*Od.* 13.96–104),[77] the port of the Laestrygonians (*Od.* 10.87–94), and the Goat island off the coast of the Cyclopes' land (*Od.* 9.116–41).[78] This elaborate design sets up a great deal of suspense about Carthage: it may prove to be a kind of homecoming or a source of further dangers. But the juxtaposition of these diverse sources also serves as a strong reminder that there is less of a difference between Odysseus' experiences with the Cyclops and the Laestrygonians on the one hand, and in his own home at Ithaca on the other, than we might imagine. In each case, an arrival in a peaceful harbor misrepresents the dangers that lie within, and all three encounters involve a perversion of the rules of hospitality: the Cyclops and the Laestrygonians literally eat their guests, while the suitors in Ithaca are eating their host out of house and home.

At the same time, the entry into the harbor follows a storm scene (*Aen.* 1.81–123) that is generally understood to be modeled on the account of the storm that washes Odysseus ashore on Scheria (*Od.* 5.282–312),[79] but which also recalls the shipwreck that deposits Odysseus on Calypso's island (*Od.* 13.403–49; cf. 7.244–55). These two sources suggest that Carthage will occupy an intermediate position between the supernatural hazards of the Cyclops or Laestrygonians and the final homecoming in Ithaca. As we have seen, Venus' explanation of Aeneas' whereabouts suggests Nausicaa as a model, but her subsequent account of Dido's history more closely resembles the genealogical excursus given by Athena disguised as a young girl while Odysseus makes his way to Alcinous' palace (*Od.* 7.18–77).[80] This conflation of a mortal and an immortal model sets up the subsequent double representation of Dido as both Nausicaa and Calypso. When Dido first appears on the scene, she is described in a simile likening her to Diana (*Aen.* 1.498–505), which is based on the comparison of Nausicaa playing with her handmaids to Artemis enjoying the hunt (*Od.* 6.102–9).[81] At the same time, Mercury's earlier intervention to soften the Carthaginians recalls Hermes' mission to Calypso (*Od.* 5.28–115),[82] a connection confirmed by Mercury's second visit in *Aeneid* 4.219–78, where Jupiter's command to his messenger is a very close adaptation of Zeus' orders to Hermes.[83] Once again, it is unclear whether Aeneas is facing a short layover before arriving at his final destination or a lengthy imprisonment.

82 *Virgil's Homeric Lens*

Aeneas himself demonstrates this uncertainty in his first exploration of the new land.[84] Like Odysseus when he first awakens on Scheria (*Od.* 6.119–21) and when he sets off to explore the Cyclops' land (*Od.* 9.173–76), Aeneas is unsure whether there is even any civilization to be found here (*Aen.* 1.308): *qui teneant (nam inculta videt), hominesne feraene* ("who owns [the land] (for he sees that it is uncultivated), whether men or beasts"). But in marked contrast to his Homeric predecessor, Aeneas does not show any reluctance to identify himself to the inhabitants of this unknown country. When Venus in disguise asks him directly to identify himself, his origins, and his destination (*Aen.* 1.369–70), he launches into a full account of his misfortunes that Venus is forced to interrupt (*Aen.* 1.385–86): *nec plura querentem / passa Venus medio sic interfata dolore est* ("Venus did not endure further complaint and broke into the middle of his lament like so"). Although (or, perhaps, because) her question clearly mirrors Alcinous' direct interrogation of Odysseus (*Od.* 8.550, 555, 573–75), Venus knows that Aeneas must tell his full tale to Dido, and so she resumes her guiding function and directs him toward the city.[85] Like Odysseus, Aeneas is unsure both about the reception he will receive and about his heroic status, but rather than clinging to anonymity as long as possible, he meets the challenge head-on. In response to the question about the origin of his journey, he shows concern that she may not have heard of Troy (*Aen.* 1.375–76): *si vestras forte per auris / Troiae nomen iit* ("if by chance the name of Troy has ever come to your ears"); and in identifying himself, he strongly asserts the fame of his name (*Aen.* 1.378–79): *sum pius Aeneas, raptos qui ex hoste penatis / classe veho mecum, fama super aethera notus* ("I am pious Aeneas, who carries my household gods in my ship with me, having snatched them from my enemies, and whose fame is known beyond the heavens"). The phrase *fama super aethera notus* is based on a similar phrase in Odysseus' answer to Alcinous, which begins his long tale (*Od.* 9.20: καί μευ κλέος οὐρανὸν ἵκει, "and my fame reaches heaven"), but in a bold challenge to his predecessor, Odysseus' fame only reaches the heavens, while Aeneas' goes beyond them.

This may be wishful thinking, for by the time Venus interrupts him, he has gone from declaring his eternal fame to claiming that he is *ipse ignotus, egens* ("myself unknown and needy," *Aen.* 1.384). The force of *ignotus* is simultaneously passive and active: Aeneas is unknown in this land and he knows no one;[86] though, as he soon finds out, the passive half of that equation is not quite true. His claim of being *egens*, "needy," is repeated again when he describes the Trojans to Dido as *omnium egenos*, ("lacking everything," *Aen.* 1.599), and Dido herself repeats his characterization when she chastises Aeneas for leaving her: (*Aen.* 4.373–74): *eiectum litore, egentem / excepi* ("I took him in as a castaway on the shore, needy"). This is clearly a key component of Aeneas' strategy to inspire pity in his hosts, but it is not entirely consistent with Virgil's narration. We are told that the Trojans had treasure with them, a portion of which is lost with Orontes' ship (*Aen.* 1.113–19), yet Aeneas can present Helen's wedding regalia, as well as Ilione's scepter, crown, and necklace, to Dido (*Aen.* 1.647–56) and still have Priam's regalia left over to give to Latinus (*Aen.* 7.246–48).[87] As with his fame, Aeneas wants to have it both ways: to be unknown and destitute enough to obtain a generous welcome, yet renowned and wealthy enough to dazzle his hosts.

The true extent of the Carthaginians' knowledge of Aeneas and the Trojan war only begins to reveal itself when Aeneas arrives at the temple of Juno amid the bustle of the ongoing construction of the city. Even before we are told exactly what he sees, we learn that Aeneas grows calmer and allows himself to hope for safety (*Aen.* 1.450–52: *hoc primum in luco nova res oblata timorem / leniit, hic primum Aeneas sperare salutem / ausus*, "here for the first time something new appeared in the grove that calmed his fears, here for the first time Aeneas dared to hope for safety"), and once he has actually begun to examine the panels, he can even comfort Achates aloud (*Aen.* 1.463): *solve metus; feret haec aliquam tibi fama salutem* ("release your fear; this fame will bring you some safety").[88] The images on temple walls present Aeneas with definitive proof that the Trojan war is known in Carthage, but they depict a knowledge that is not necessarily beneficial to Aeneas' cause.[89] As I noted in Chapter 1, Aeneas is described as seeing *Iliacas ex ordine pugnas* ("the battles at Troy in order," *Aen.* 1.456), and his decipherment of the images is a reading of the *Iliad* into the text of the *Aeneid*. However, that reading is clearly not an objective process. Virgil claims that Aeneas sees the battles *ex ordine*, but the actual episodes that draw his attention are not described in chronological order, nor are they all battle scenes.[90] In general, the images depict the cruelty of the Greeks and the tragic losses of the Trojans and their allies, but the dominant figure throughout is Achilles. He is seen routing the Trojans (*Aen.* 1.468), killing Troilus (*Aen.* 1.474–78), and dragging and ransoming Hector's corpse (*Aen.* 1.483–87). Although only the third of these episodes is explicitly Iliadic (and even there, the dragging of the body has been relocated from Patroclus' pyre to the walls of Troy), Aeneas is clearly reading Achilles' experience in the *Iliad* as the definitive background for his own present condition. Thus when he first approaches the temple, he sees *Atridas Priamumque et saevum ambobus Achillem* ("the sons of Atreus and Priam, and Achilles fierce toward both of them," *Aen.* 1.458), a compact summary of the events that frame the *Iliad*.[91]

At the same time as he establishes the dominance of Achilles, Aeneas is also forced to acknowledge his own dubious role in the *Iliad*. The image of Diomedes killing Rhesus and stealing his horses (*Aen.* 1.469–73) clearly recalls how Diomedes won Aeneas' horses and nearly killed him in *Iliad* 5, only to be thwarted by divine intervention. Likewise, the various images of Achilles must also remind Aeneas of his own failed encounter with the Greek champion in *Iliad* 20. In this regard, the temple ecphrasis serves a similar function to Demodocus' first song in *Odyssey* 8.[92] The story of the quarrel between Achilles and Odysseus places the conflict between the two heroic types in an Iliadic context, which draws attention to Achilles' clear superiority in that poem, but the salient detail in the song is that the dispute between the captains gave Agamemnon pleasure because it predicted a Greek victory in the Trojan war (*Od.* 8.77–82). Despite the differences between their heroic types, the Greeks are ultimately only successful in the war through the efforts of both Achilles and Odysseus in two distinct stages of the conflict. The story thus lays the foundation for the third song, which describes the actual sack of the city by the Greeks. In the same way, the temple ecphrasis draws attention to Aeneas' failures in the *Iliad* and implicitly links them to the fall of Troy, though it, too, stops short of actually describing the city's destruction.

It is not surprising, then, that immediately after examining the panel that depicts the dragging and ransoming of Hector's body, essentially a summary of *Iliad* 22–24, Aeneas briefly spies himself amid the Greek leaders (*Aen.* 1.488): *se quoque principibus permixtum agnovit Achivis* ("he recognized himself as well, mixed up with the Achaean leaders"). The description is too vague to determine what actually inspires this moment of self-recognition. Either the craftsmanship he so admires from the outset (*Aen.* 1.455–56: *artificumque manus inter se operumque laborem / miratur*, "he marvels at the handiwork of the rival craftsmen and the product of their labor") has managed to create an actual physical likeness of Aeneas, or more likely, he recognizes himself from the particular activity depicted.[93] The phrase *principibus permixtum Achivis* ("mixed up with the Greek leaders") has a clear Homeric model in *promachoisi migenta*, which is used to describe Odysseus on two occasions (*Il.* 4.354; *Od.* 18.379), but the precise context is unclear.[94] Just as in Demodocus' first song, there is a vague allusion to a conflict between captains, but in this case, the implication is that Aeneas is engaged in open combat. Given the emphasis on Diomedes and Achilles in the previous panels, it seems quite likely that Aeneas sees one of his unflattering Iliadic encounters with the two Greek heroes, but the ambiguous language allows him to suggest a more positive representation. After Poseidon rescues Aeneas from Achilles, he tells him that once Achilles is dead, Aeneas can fight with the foremost men, since no other Achaean will be able to kill him (*Il.* 20.338–39): θαρσήσας δὴ ἔπειτα μετὰ πρώτοισι μάχεσθαι· / οὐ μὲν γάρ τίς σ' ἄλλος Ἀχαιῶν ἐξεναρίξει ("then have courage and fight with their foremost men, for no other Achaean will be able to kill you").[95] By alluding to this prophecy in the phrase *principibus permixtum*, Aeneas' Iliadic failures are contrasted with his post-Iliadic destiny. That destiny can only be fulfilled once Troy has fallen, and so Aeneas moves immediately from his own image to two post-Iliadic scenes, the armies of Memnon and Penthesilea (*Aen.* 1.489–93), as if to advance the story as quickly as possible toward its inevitable conclusion.

The temple of Juno, like every other building in Carthage, is still under construction when Aeneas arrives (*Aen.* 1.446–47: *hic templum Iunoni ingens Sidonia Dido / condebat*, "here Sidonian Dido was establishing a huge temple to Juno"), which suggests both that the story told on its walls is still incomplete and that Aeneas himself has arrived in time to help determine the direction of that story.[96] Several critics have explored the ways in which the scenes depicted on the temple walls anticipate episodes in *Aeneid* 7–12,[97] but before that more distant resolution to the Trojan story begun in the ecphrasis, Aeneas must describe the immediate aftermath of the scenes he has just examined, and more importantly, he must "correct" the negative representation of the Trojans and himself in particular. His predicament is similar to Odysseus' after Demodocus' first song in that he wants to be recognized, but not exactly in the manner that has just been put forth by the work of art, and like Odysseus his first response is to cry. But whereas Odysseus' tears are at least partly designed to orient the first half of the *Odyssey* as a loser's epic despite the Achaean victory at Troy, Aeneas needs no such motivation. The scenes on the panels leave little doubt about the status of the Trojans, and Aeneas does not require an Alcinous to witness his tears in order to identify himself.[98] In the scene immediately following, Aeneas watches as Ilioneus, the etymological "man of Ilium,"[99] gives an account of the Trojan refugees and praises Aeneas extensively (*Aen.* 1.522–60). Dido's reply confirms that she knows even more of the story than is depicted on the temple walls (*Aen.* 1.565–66): *quis genus Aeneadum, quis Troiae nesciat urbem, / virtutesque virosque aut tanti incendia belli?* ("who doesn't know the race of Aeneas, who doesn't know the city Troy, its bravery and its men, or the blaze of such great war?"). The pointed reference to the *incendia* reveals that even the latest stage of the war is familiar territory, and her subsequent offer of hospitality, and even the possibility of a union between the Trojan and Phoenician peoples (*Aen.* 1.567–78), reflect her deep sympathy for the plight of the defeated *Aeneades*.

Similarly, when Aeneas reveals himself to be the very man Dido has been discussing (*Aen.* 1.595–96: *coram, quem quaeritis, adsum, / Troius Aeneas*, "I am here in person, him whom you seek, Aeneas the Trojan"), she replies in disbelief (*Aen.* 1.617: *tune ille Aeneas. . .?* "are you that Aeneas?") and proceeds to explain how she learned of Aeneas and the Trojans from the Greek Teucer when he was in exile from Salamis.[100] Although her question *tune ille Aeneas* is sometimes understood as a combination of surprise and admiration,[101] the tone is not so readily apparent.[102] Given that she has the temple panels within her sight, it seems quite possible that the *ille* has a deictic force as she physically points to the very picture of Aeneas that caught the hero's eye earlier. If this is a negative or ambiguous representation, then her tone may reflect some surprise at the discrepancy between that picture and the man before her, in addition to the obvious shock at finding him alive at all. There is a similar ambiguity in her explanation of how she came to know of Aeneas. Although she claims that Teucer himself *Teucros insigni laude ferebat* ("greatly praised the Trojans," *Aen.* 1.625), her only reference to Aeneas in this story juxtaposes him to the fall of Troy

(*Aen.* 1.623–24): *tempore iam ex illo casus mihi cognitus urbis / Troianae nomenque tuum* ("the misfortune of the Trojan city was already known to me from that time, and your name"). This may simply reflect his status as the preeminent Trojan survivor of the war, but by linking Aeneas' name to the destruction of the city, she is at least hinting at the possibility that he did not do enough to prevent it. There is, in fact, an alternate ancient tradition in which Aeneas is actually implicated, along with Antenor, in the betrayal of the city to the Greeks,[103] but even his failure to take advantage of Poseidon's assurance that he cannot be killed by any other Greek after Achilles is a strong enough condemnation of his performance in the war.

For Aeneas, who has feared all along that he would be *ignotus* in this land, Dido's ambiguous recognition of him demonstrates the challenges facing him as he attempts to carve out a new role for himself vis-à-vis the Iliadic tradition. Like Odysseus, his first encounter with an artistic representation of the Iliadic past leaves him in an awkward position. His fame is acknowledged, but so is his inferiority to the Greek champions. The parallel between the two heroes' situations is strengthened by the appearance of the Phoenician bard Iopas, whose Lucretian interlude between the intense sorrows of the temple ecphrasis and Aeneas' own story in Book 2 corresponds to Demodocus' second song about Ares and Aphrodite.[104] But while Odysseus attempts once more to persuade Demodocus to sing an account of the Trojan war that favors the Odyssean paradigm, Dido cuts off any similar attempt from Aeneas by asking him pointed questions about his experience in the war (*Aen.* 1.752): *nunc quales Diomedis equi, nunc quantus Achilles* ("now what were Diomedes' horses like, now how big was Achilles?"). Odysseus also asks Demodocus to tell about a famous horse (*Od.* 8.493), but his goal is to move as far away from the *Iliad* story as possible. Here, Dido's questions dwell not only on the Iliadic material, but more specifically on Aeneas' poor showing in that story. Aeneas would know quite well what sort of horses Diomedes had, since they are the very ones he takes from Aeneas in *Iliad* 5, which he then uses to win the chariot race in Patroclus' funeral games in *Iliad* 23.[105] Likewise, as we have already noted, Aeneas has a very good vantage point from which to determine Achilles' size when he is nearly killed by him in *Iliad* 20. Later in the poem, Liger uses the same double reference to taunt Aeneas in battle (*Aen.* 10.581): *non Diomedis equos, nec currum cernis Achilli* ("these aren't Diomedes' horses that you see, nor Achilles' chariot").

By asking these questions, Dido reveals that she knows Aeneas' Iliadic persona as well as Virgil's readers do. Aeneas does not seem to respond, and perhaps out of an awareness that she has touched a raw nerve, she changes directions and asks him to tell the whole tale in order (*Aen.* 1.753–55):

> "immo age et a prima dic, hospes, origine nobis
> insidias" inquit "Danaum casusque tuorum
> erroresque tuos"

"But come, guest," she said, "and from the very beginning tell us
the snares of the Danaans, and your people's misfortunes,
and your own wanderings."

In calling him *hospes* here for the first time, she is marking this moment of information exchange as a crucial reciprocation for the aid she has given him.[106] Like Alcinous, she has already displayed the usual desire of a host to be remembered for her hospitality (*Aen.* 1.733), and Aeneas promises this remembrance when he first appears to her out of the cloud (*Aen.* 1.609–10: *semper honos nomenque tuum laudesque manebunt, / quae me cumque vocant terrae*, "your honor, your name, and your praise will always remain"), a sentiment he repeats at *Aen.* 4.335–36.[107] But at the same time, the specific starting point she requests for the tale, the *insidias Danaum*, is precisely the same as the *dolos* Odysseus asks Demodocus to sing (*Od.* 8.494).[108] Once again, she highlights a moment of glory for the Greeks and links it to the downfall of the Trojans. The *insidias* lead directly to the *casus*, and most ominously of all, to Aeneas' *errores*. The double meaning of this word as both "wanderings" and "mistakes" posits a clear causal relationship between Aeneas' own actions during the final stages of the war and his subsequent years of wandering.[109]

Faced with an audience that knows his Iliadic failures, is familiar with the story of the Greek victory won through the schemes of Odysseus, and suspects that he failed the city in its time of need (and possibly even betrayed it), Aeneas cannot afford to put off his account of the fall of Troy. Dido has asked him point-blank to begin at that moment, and unlike Odysseus, he does not have to luxury of delaying his revisionist account. He must offer a definitive Trojan perspective on the war to give voice to the losers and to inspire pity, but also to undermine the Odyssean account of the postwar experience. Odysseus begins his story after the Greek victory, which Demodocus has just described, in order to focus on his own suffering and thereby present himself from a loser's perspective. Once that perspective is established, he carefully revisits the Iliadic experience to promote his own heroic image. But since Odysseus does not give his own direct account of the end of the war, Aeneas has an opportunity to preempt his rival, and throughout Book 2, he uses every opening to attack Odysseus. By laying the blame for the fall of the city on Odysseus' treachery and cruelty, Aeneas simultaneously undermines the *Odyssey*'s own claims for its heroic paradigm and absolves himself from responsibility.

As we saw earlier, Aeneas regularly deflects any criticism of his own individual failings by merging himself into the Trojan populace or by stepping outside of the action and assuming the perspective of an omniscient narrator. Aeneas begins his performance by claiming that the story is too sorrowful be told (*Aen.* 2.3: *infandum, regina, iubes renovare dolorem*, "you command me to renew unspeakable sorrow"),[110] and then follows that claim with a rhetorical question (*Aen.* 2.6–8): *quis talia fando / Myrmidonum*

Dolopumve aut duri miles Ulixi / temperet a lacrimis? ("what Myrmidon or Dolopian or soldier of harsh Ulysses could keep from tears in telling such things?). In the movement from *infandum* to *fando*, Aeneas takes up the challenge of delivering a virtuoso performance. At the same time, he sets up the three primary targets in his project to claim the definitive Iliadic aftermath: the Myrmidons and Dolopes are the troops of Achilles and Neoptolemus respectively, while *durus Ulixes* describes his chief narrative rival in no uncertain terms. Odysseus is not only unable (or unwilling) to tell this story, but he cannot even listen to Demodocus tell it without shedding tears. Throughout Book 2, Aeneas dwells on Ulixes' deceit both in his own narrative voice and also in the character of Sinon who assumes a Trojan attitude toward Ulixes.[111] This reflects yet another motive for Aeneas to begin with his own greatest failure. Odysseus clearly defines himself in terms of his rhetorical power,[112] but he is constantly using that power for deception, rendering his wandering narrative unreliable. This is why, among other things, he must substitute the more believable Phoenicians for the Phaeacians in his lying tales on Ithaca. By starting with a story that is already known to his hosts, one that is almost carved onto their walls,[113] Aeneas can win credibility for his version of the Iliadic aftermath and undermine the *Odyssey*'s clever funneling of the multiple aftermaths into the definitive story of Odysseus.

When Neoptolemus kills Priam at the altar, he sends him as a messenger to his father, Achilles, and tells him to *narrare* all of his wretched deeds and his degeneracy (*Aen.* 2.549). The word *narrare*, like its English derivative "narrate," suggests a storytelling session rather than a plain report of facts,[114] and we have already discussed how Aeneas preempts Odysseus' function as the definitive narrator of these events by giving an elaborate account of both the actions and words. On a larger scale, Aeneas' entire performance in Books 2–3 is an assertion of this narrative supremacy. Thus when Aeneas finally ends his tale in Book 3, Virgil summarizes his activity by saying (*Aen.* 3.717): *sic pater Aeneas intentis omnibus unus / fata <u>renarrabat</u> divum* ("thus father Aeneas alone recounted his god-given destiny to everyone listening intently"), which emphasizes that he alone (*unus*) controlled the definitive tale of his destiny (*fata*).[115] Similarly, in the throes of her madness, Dido craves his storytelling like a drug (4.78–79): *Iliacosque iterum demens audire labores / exposcit pendetque iterum <u>narrantis</u> ab ore.* ("out of her mind, she demands to hear the Trojan labors again, and hangs again on the storyteller's lips").[116] The vivid image of Dido almost physically hanging on his narration demonstrates the sheer power of his performance, and more specifically, his great success in portraying the victimization of the Trojans at the hands of the Greeks.

Aeneas the character thus emerges from the flames of Troy as the definitive epic loser, but Aeneas the narrator has achieved a triumph of storytelling. And while Odysseus gets the credit for the actual events of the sack of Troy, it is Aeneas who gets the glory for the account of that destruction.

Having secured a Trojan version of the end of the war and preempted Odysseus' own claims to the status of sorriest survivor, he can proceed to a different kind of narrative challenge in Book 3, where he directly engages the tale that Odysseus actually tells to the Phaeacians, rather than the one he omits. But just as he replaces the fantasy world of the Phaeacians with the realities of the struggling new city being built by exiled Phoenicians, Virgil has Aeneas deliver his sorrowful tale of the fall of Troy first, which further resists the *Odyssey*'s authority. Similarly, the death of Priam, which lies at the heart of his story, demonstrates just how effectively Virgil uses the *Odyssey*'s narrative techniques to comment on the *Iliad* and to establish a different view of Achilles and Neoptolemus (and by extension the *Iliad* and the post-Iliadic tradition) that he can apply in the later books of the *Aeneid*.

4 Virgilian Reflection

met' Odusseôs

In his account of the origins of Rome, Dionysius of Halicarnassus reports the following curious story about Aeneas and Odysseus (*Ant. Rom.* 1.72.2):

> ὁ δὲ τὰς ἱερείας τὰς ἐν Ἄργει καὶ τὰ καθ'
> ἑκάστην πραχθέντα συναγαγὼν Αἰνείαν φησὶν
> ἐκ Μολοττῶν εἰς Ἰταλίαν ἐλθόντα μετ' Ὀδυσσέως
> οἰκιστὴν γενέσθαι τῆς πόλεως, ὀνομάσαι δ' αὐτὴν
> ἀπὸ μιᾶς τῶν Ἰλιάδων Ῥώμης.

> But the author of the history of the priestesses at Argos,
> and of what happened under each of them, says that
> Aeneas came into Italy from the land of the Molossians
> and became the founder of the city with Odysseus,
> which he named after Romê, one of the Trojan women.

The source Dionysius is referring to is the fourth-century BCE historian Hellanicus of Lesbos' *Priestesses of Hera in Argos* (*FGrHist* 4 F 84). Later on, Dionysius says that Damastes of Sigeum and others agree with Hellanicus' account (*Ant. Rom.* 1.72.3). If the attribution is correct, then this represents the earliest known version of the founding of Rome. Whether the precise details of this story make any sense within the morass of fragmentary information that constitutes the pre-Virgilian Aeneas legend has been discussed in detail by scholars,[1] but the central idea that Aeneas founded the city "with Odysseus" (*met' Odusseôs*) has a particular figurative resonance with my own argument. The notion of the *Odyssey* as a crucial partner in Virgil's intertextual project is central to my thesis, but in the previous chapter, I attempted to demonstrate how this partnership is as much a rivalry as it is an alliance of narrative techniques. By navigating a middle path between slavish imitation and outright rejection of his Homeric model, Virgil establishes a system that mirrors the *Odyssey*'s own attitude toward the *Iliad*. The rivalry between Aeneas and Odysseus as narrators of their own postwar experiences takes its cue from Odysseus' figurative competition with Demodocus' quasi-Iliadic songs. Like both of those competitors, Aeneas tells a story that engages key moments in the *Iliad* without actually narrating any of the events from the poem. Even his earlier decipherment of the murals on the temple of Juno presents only an allusive account of key Iliadic moments and contains much that stands outside that tradition as well. Virgil reads the *Iliad* with the help of the *Odyssey*, and consequently, Aeneas defines the post-Iliadic experience together with Odysseus (*met' Odusseôs*).

However, there is a variant in one of the older and better manuscripts of Dionysius that reads μετ' Ὀδυσσέα with the accusative instead of genitive.[2] Apart from the intriguing literal interpretation that Aeneas was only the second founder of Rome after Odysseus had already established the city (*met' Odussea*), this alternative reflects another aspect of the Virgilian intertextual system. Both Aeneas and Odysseus are hurled into the Iliadic aftermath at the same point in fictive history, but they do not occupy the same place in the causal hierarchy. While the Iliadic prophecy of Poseidon requires the basic narrative of Aeneas' survival, the *Odyssey* provides an even more immediate motivation by attributing the actual destruction of Troy to Odysseus. Although the triumph of the Odyssean heroic paradigm over the Achillean one is not complete until Odysseus can apply his wartime lessons to the domestic situation on Ithaca, the Odyssean sack of Troy, so prominently mentioned in the proem (*Od.* 1.2: ἐπεὶ Τροίης ἱερὸν πτολίεθρον ἔπερσε, "after he had sacked the sacred citadel of Troy"), is the proximate cause of Aeneas' exile and wandering.[3] The *Aeneid* obviously does not tell the story of what happens after (*meta*) the *Odyssey*,[4] a function apparently fulfilled by the Cyclical *Telegony*, but it is nevertheless a kind of meta-Odyssey. It ostensibly describes the same post-Iliadic world as the *Odyssey*, and it follows the same basic plot of wandering followed by a violent homecoming, but it also stands several ages removed from that *Odyssey* and thus brings to bear a decidedly first-century Roman perspective on the model. We may recall that Servius defines Virgil's *intentio* in the poem as *Homerum imitari et Augustum laudare* ("to imitate Homer and praise Augustus," Serv. *praef.*); the *Aeneid* acknowledges the *Odyssey* as its master text, but it also reflects its Augustan context. Thus in Jupiter's famous promise to Venus about the Roman people, another *meta* is activated as well (*Aen.* 1.278): *his ego nec metas rerum nec tempora pono* ("I place no limits or duration on their possessions"). In promising the absence of any Latin *meta*, meaning "end" or "limit," to their dominion, Jupiter is projecting the Augustan ideal for the Roman people.

Going beyond (*meta*) any limit (*meta*) imposed by the Homeric tradition is an integral part of Virgil's poetics, but it is important to keep the two variant readings in Dionysius in play simultaneously. As a meta-Odyssey, the *Aeneid* follows the *Odyssey*'s essential structural and intertextual model, but it also inserts itself into the Odyssean world in unexpected ways in order to draw out innovative readings of the Iliadic and post-Iliadic experience. In this chapter, I will examine scenes from *Aeneid* 2 and 3 that especially demonstrate the operation of the (meta-) Odyssean lens in the text, and then turn to some of the broader implications of this intervention into the *Odyssey* for the interpretation of the ending of the *Aeneid*.

insidias Danaum erroresque tuos

As I argued in the previous chapter, Aeneas' virtuoso storytelling performance in Book 2 is in large part an attempt to rehabilitate, or at least redirect, an Iliadic image that appears to be as familiar to Dido as it is to Virgil's readers. The implication that Dido herself might be a reader of Homer underscores the urgency of Aeneas' plan to preempt Odysseus' own poetic reclamation project. If Dido knows an *Iliad*, then there is at least a symbolic danger that she might stumble upon an *Odyssey* as well and therein encounter a competing account of the postwar experience. The tension between the two accounts of the Iliadic aftermath is partly generated by the synchronicity of the two heroes' wanderings or, to activate Dido's ambiguous Latin usage (*Aen.* 1.755), their *errores*. In addition to physical wandering, *error* can mean a "mistake" or even the cause of a mistake, i.e., "deception" or "derangement."[5] As Odysseus and Aeneas drift away from the Trojan war, and from the *Iliad* in particular, their various *errores* help to shape their physical and psychological itineraries. At the beginning of *Aeneid* 2, Virgil defines the Trojans' credulousness regarding the horse as their ultimate mistake. When Laocoon begs the mob not to accept the gift, he reminds them of Odysseus' reputation for deceit (*Aen.* 2.44: *sic notus Ulixes?* "Is that how you know Ulysses?"), and then a few lines later, makes the direct link to the horse (*Aen.* 2.48): *aliquis latet error* ("some deception lies hidden"). Once the attack is unleashed, Trojan mothers are seen roaming the halls in terror (*Aen.* 2.489: *tum pavidae tectis matres ingentibus errant*), and the Greek troops range everywhere (*Aen.* 2.598–99: *undique Graiae / circum errant acies*). At the same time, Aeneas is personally involved in both a deception and a mistake (a double *error*) when he and his band are almost killed by their fellow-Trojans after they follow Coroebus' suggestion and put on the armor of the Greek Androgeos and his men (*Aen.* 2.411–12): *oriturque miserrima caedes / armorum facie et Graiarum errore iubarum* ("and wretched slaughter arises because of the look of our armor and the *error* of our Greek crests").[6] Finally, at the end of the book, Aeneas wonders if Creusa was torn from him by fate, or if she lost her way (*Aen.* 2.739: *erravitne via*), though he is at least partly responsible for neglecting her as they fled.

Odysseus' initial deception thus engenders Aeneas' own *errores*, but the two heroes are also literally wandering the streets of Troy at the same time. From Aeneas' opening statement that not even a *duri miles Ulixi* ("soldier of harsh Ulysses," *Aen.* 2.7) could tell this tale without tears, through Laocoon's sinister reference to *notus Ulixes* ("notorious Ulysses"), and then finally the multiple references in Sinon's deceitful account, the anticipation of Aeneas actually seeing Odysseus in person grows steadily. Virgil playfully inserts a false encounter in the account of the Greeks exiting the horse. Although Aeneas says that *dirus Ulixes* ("terrible Ulysses," *Aen.* 2.261) was the third man to emerge, he could not actually have witnessed this event, since nine lines later we are told that he was asleep at the time (*Aen.* 2.270). As I argued earlier, part of Aeneas' strategy to absolve himself from blame is to assume an omniscient narrative stance. By making Aeneas' first direct description of himself reveal that he was literally asleep while the Greeks crept in, Virgil undermines that tactic with a clear demonstration of Aeneas' failure to prevent the assault. At the same time, he implies that Aeneas' "source" for the account is the *Odyssey* itself, which describes the Achaeans in the horse on three separate occasions (*Od.* 4.265–89, 8.499–520; 11.523–32).[7] But since, from the perspective of the Homeric timeline, Odysseus' tale has not yet been told,[8] Virgil is attributing his own reading habits to Aeneas. The use of the adjective *laeti* ("happy," *Aen.* 2.260) to describe their mood as they descend from the horse seems to confirm that the episode is seen from the point of view of the Greeks, but Virgil complicates this perspective by having Aeneas describe Odysseus as *dirus*. If Aeneas is "reading" from the *Odyssey* to a certain extent here, he nevertheless maintains his own voice by characterizing Odysseus in his usual negative manner.

Aeneas first learns that the Greeks have penetrated the city when Hector visits him in a dream and reports the disaster (*Aen.* 2.290): *hostis habet muros; ruit alto a culmine Troia* ("the enemy holds the walls; Troy falls from her high peak"). This scene recalls Achilles' dream vision of Patroclus (*Il.* 23.65–107),[9] though the significance is somewhat inverted. Patroclus accuses Achilles of having forgotten him and asks for a swift burial, but he also tells him that his own destiny is to die under the walls of Troy (*Il.* 23.80–81): καὶ δὲ σοὶ αὐτῷ μοῖρα, θεοῖς ἐπιείκελ' Ἀχιλλεῦ, / τείχει ὕπο Τρώων εὐηφενέων ἀπολέσθαι ("and you, godlike Achilles, have your own destiny: to die under the wall of the wealthy Trojans"). Although Hector does not accuse him of it, Aeneas nevertheless appears to have forgotten that Hector is dead (*Aen.* 2.285–86: *quae causa indigna serenos / foedavit vultus? aut cur haec vulnera cerno?* "what shameful cause has defiled your bright features? And why do I see these wounds?").[10] More importantly, Hector describes a scenario that is the opposite of Patroclus' prediction: Troy is dying around Aeneas (*ruit alto a culmine Troia*) but he will live to find new walls (*Aen.* 2.294–95): *moenia quaere / magna pererrato statues quae denique ponto* ("seek out the great walls that you will establish at last, after wandering the sea"). Virgil secures the authority of the Iliadic figure Hector for Aeneas' claim to a definitive Trojan aftermath of the war (elaborating Poseidon's prophecy in the process), and he activates the Odyssean trope of asserting the hero's survival as a clear mark of superiority over the Achillean paradigm. Aeneas thus establishes himself as an heir to both Hector and Achilles, a dyad that will feature prominently in the later stages of the poem.

In referencing the wandering (*pererrato*) that will precede the foundation of the new city, Hector introduces another familiar Odyssean element into the interpretation of the underlying Iliadic material. Aeneas will certainly roam widely across the Mediterranean in order to fulfill Hector's prophecy, but his present condition is an *error* as well. Aeneas, after all, is still asleep in his father's secluded house (*Aen.* 2.299–300: *secreta parentis / Anchisae domus*), and he is only finally awakened by the increasing noise of the attack (*Aen.* 2.301–2): *clarescunt sonitus, armorumque ingruit horror. / excutior somno* ("the sound grows louder and the horror of arms approaches. I am shaken from sleep"). The image of the hero sleeping while disaster strikes echoes Odysseus' situation in the Aeolus episode (*Od.* 10.31–55) and on Thrinacia (*Od.* 12.338–73). In both cases, the actions of his crew postpone his homecoming, while the latter episode also costs him their lives. Later he even accuses Zeus of lulling him to sleep *eis atên*, "to his folly" or perhaps even "to his ruin." (*Od.* 12.372).[11] The destruction of the city, already set in motion by one kind of Odyssean *error*, is now compounded by Aeneas' imitation of Odysseus' own mistakes. The juxtaposition of Odysseus' emergence from the horse with Aeneas' Odyssean emergence from sleep once again uses the physical proximity of the heroes to define their rivalry. Having just positioned Aeneas in a favorable relation to the *Iliad* using an Odyssean trope, he now reasserts the dangers of following too closely in Odysseus' footsteps.

Aeneas does finally catch up with Odysseus in person at the very end of Book 2. After realizing his mistake in losing Creusa (but attributing that *error* to her), Aeneas rushes back into the burning city and revisits the various scenes of his earlier inaction: first, the walls and the gates through which the horse had been brought into the city (*Aen.* 2.752: *muros obscuraque limina portae*, "the walls and the dark threshold of the gate"); then his own home where he slept as the Greeks attacked (*Aen.* 2.756: *domum*); finally, Priam's palace, where he watched Pyrrhus slaughter the king (*Aen.* 2.760: *Priami sedes arcemque*, "Priam's palace and citadel"). This second tour through the contents of Book 2 is marked explicitly by the verbs Aeneas uses to describe his actions. He resolves to go through the disasters again (*Aen.* 2.750: *stat casus renovare omnis*), to turn back to the city (*Aen.* 2.750: *reverti*); he seeks out the walls again (*Aen.* 2.753: *repeto*), takes himself back home (*Aen.* 2.757: *refero*), and sees the palace once more (*Aen.* 2.760: *reviso*). The verb *renovare* is the same word Aeneas uses to describe his *infandum dolorem* as he begins his story to Dido (*Aen.* 2.3).[12] While this re-narration clearly highlights Aeneas' *dolor*, as well as his own earlier *errores*, it is neither a precise backward movement nor an exact repetition of his own route. Aeneas retraces the motion of the Greeks themselves as they penetrated the walls, came ever closer to his home, and finally descended on Priam's palace. The final destination suggests that he might even be following Neoptolemus' steps, as if to replay the horror of Priam's death from the other side.

We might even expect to find Neoptolemus waiting at the palace as Aeneas arrives, but instead, Aeneas catches that long-awaited glimpse of Odysseus. The "new warrior" is replaced by his teacher, but the image of Odysseus seems strongly Iliadic. Aeneas spots him standing guard over the plunder in front of Juno's sanctuary within the palace precinct (*Aen.* 2.761–63):

> et iam porticibus vacuis Iunonis asylo
> custodes lecti Phoenix et dirus Ulixes
> praedam adservabant
>
> and now, in the empty colonnades of Juno's sanctuary,
> the chosen guards, Phoenix and terrible Ulysses,
> watch over the plunder

The use of *custodes* to describe guardians of stolen treasure is a bitter reminder of the inversion that characterizes so much of Book 2,[13] but it also recalls the earlier description of Pyrrhus' assault on the palace, where no *custodes* could withstand him (*Aen.* 2.491–92): *nec claustra, nec ipsi / custodes sufferre valent*, ("no barriers, not even the guards themselves, can withstand him"). Likewise, the *porticibus vacuis* correspond to the *vacua atria* of the palace through which Pyrrhus hunted Polites (*Aen.* 2.528).[14] Pyrrhus' successful assault thus directly enables Odysseus to assume the role of *custos* over the spoils.

The image of Odysseus in charge of the plunder faintly echoes his Iliadic role in delivering Chryseis back to her father (*Il.* 1.308, 430), but the pairing with Phoenix unmistakably refers us to the embassy scene in *Iliad* 9.[15] There, too, Odysseus and Phoenix are chosen (*lecti*) for the task by Nestor (*Il.* 9.165: ἀλλ' ἄγετε κλητοὺς ὀτρύνομεν, "but come, let us send some chosen men"), and Odysseus' main tactic is to offer Achilles rich spoils from Agamemnon, including the prize that began the feud, Briseis herself. But Virgil's allusion is also marked by the two characters who are absent, Achilles and Ajax. Odysseus' two chief Iliadic rivals are both already dead: Achilles, because of the very destiny he described so vividly in the embassy scene (*Il.* 9.410–16), and Ajax, because Odysseus won Achilles' armor instead of him (*Od.* 11.543–51). As I argued in the Chapter 2, the embassy scene is a key moment in the establishment of Ajax and Achilles as representatives of the Iliadic heroic paradigm against Odysseus and his crafty ways. As I noted earlier, Achilles famously compares his hatred for deceitfulness to his loathing for the gates of death (*Il.* 9.312–13: ἐχθρὸς γάρ μοι κεῖνος ὁμῶς Ἀΐδαο πύλῃσιν / ὅς χ' ἕτερον μὲν κεύθῃ ἐνὶ φρεσίν, ἄλλο δὲ εἴπῃ, "for hateful to me as the gates of

Death is that man who hides one thing in his heart and says another"), but in *Odyssey* 11, we see that both Achilles and Ajax have already passed through those gates, while Odysseus' duplicity has won the war and kept him alive. Here in *Aeneid* 2, he perversely stands guard over stolen treasure in a sanctuary, but it is a powerful reminder that he remains alive and inviolate, just as he tells Achilles that Neoptolemus boarded his ship unscathed (*Od.* 11.535: *askathês*). Once again, Odysseus' excellence is defined in terms of survival. Aeneas, on the other hand, can neither attack Odysseus nor enjoy his own preordained survival, because he has now lost Creusa. Even if she had come to this sanctuary, she would have been captured and included in the *longo ordine* ("long row") of *pueri et pavidae matres* ("children and frightened mothers," *Aen.* 2.766–67) in front of the shrine.

Virgil reinforces the horror of using a sanctuary as a storehouse for stolen *praeda* through an ironic gloss. Servius Auctus (ad *Aen.* 2.761) points out that *asylum* comes from the Greek verb *sulaô*, "carry off as spoil," meaning literally, "a place from which plunder (*praeda*) cannot be removed."[16] An *asylum* is also a place where no person can be harmed, and so it also alludes to the *altaria* where Pyrrhus cut Priam down in violation of the rules of sanctuary (*Aen.* 2.550, cf. 2.515). The substitution of the altar of Jupiter with a sanctuary of Juno is another assertion of Aeneas' precarious status in the aftermath of the war.[17] Not only does it remind us of Juno's hostility toward Aeneas (cf. *Aen.* 1.4, 19–31), but it also recalls Dido's unfinished temple to the goddess and the ambiguous representation of the hero on its walls. As he finishes his own attempted rehabilitation of that image, and perhaps even provides the text for future panels to be added, this glance back to the Carthaginian murals acknowledges the end of the Iliadic world they depict. At the same time, the figure of Odysseus looming large in the portico points forward to the next stage of the story and its more direct engagement with Odysseus' own postwar narrative.

aërias Phaeacum abscondimus arces

Aeneas' narrative of the fall of Troy is, in large part, an attempt to describe the death of the Iliadic world and his own Iliadic character with it. Although he deflects as much of the blame as he can onto the folly of the Trojan populace, the deceitfulness of Odysseus, and the cruelty of Pyrrhus, he nevertheless reveals his own oscillation between inaction and rashness to be a major factor in the demise of the Trojan civilization. In the brief moment when he sees Odysseus guarding the spoils of war in Juno's sanctuary, Aeneas acknowledges that demise and hints at the *Odyssey*'s role as a guide to navigating the post-Iliadic waters. At the same time, he is highlighting the dangers of following that guide too closely. I suggested earlier that Dido might be a reader of Homer, and that one of Aeneas' goals is to preempt any potential reading of the *Odyssey* that might challenge the authority of his own postwar narrative. Thus Virgil's own readers may recognize that Aeneas and Odysseus are about to undertake similar journeys and suffer similar hardships, but to Aeneas' audience in Carthage, their narratives appear to be heading in opposite directions. Odysseus' story seems to be a victor's epic with a definite home in Ithaca to which he can return, while Aeneas is an exile with only vague assurances from two ghosts about a new homeland. Aeneas takes great pains to portray Odysseus as a wholly unsympathetic character who wins the war through trickery and is thus directly responsible for Aeneas' own suffering, but in the process, he also depicts the Greek hero as the ultimate survivor. In Book 3, Virgil uses a very different set of strategies to challenge that status while still using the *Odyssey* as a comprehensive source for the postwar experience. By applying the *Odyssey*'s revisionist techniques to both the Trojan past and to the *Odyssey* itself, Virgil continues to assert the essential differences between the two heroes' trajectories, even as they traverse the same physical time and space.

It is a mark of Virgil's sophisticated intertextuality that while Book 3 appears to be the most Odyssean book in the *Aeneid*, in that it recounts the diverse voyages of the hero across the Mediterranean,[18] only the brief Scylla and Charybdis episode and the encounter with the Cyclops are explicitly Odyssean adventures.[19] Virgil engages other episodes from Odysseus' wanderings, but he does so in oblique ways that acknowledge the source material without slavishly following it. As we will see, even the two expressly Odyssean scenes are part of Virgil's larger scheme to contrast the two heroes' responses to the dangers in their paths. One of the most important functions of even the fleeting references to places or events from the Odyssean wandering tales is to provide independent corroboration for Aeneas' story. A great deal has been written about the reliability of Odysseus as a narrator in general and in *Odyssey* 9–12 in particular,[20] but the "truth" of Aeneas' story in *Aeneid* 3 has not, to my knowledge, ever been questioned.[21] That is to say, Aeneas is not accused of fabricating his adventures precisely because Virgil inserts Odyssean references into his narrative. But this has the curious effect of verifying Odysseus' narrative as well. Either they are both telling the truth or they are both telling the same lies, which would require Aeneas to have already "read" a version of the *Odyssey*. By stressing the synchronicity of their adventures, Virgil cleverly directs us to the first alternative, even though the second one better reflects his own poetic process.

Like Odysseus, Aeneas is describing his own departure from the Iliadic world, but he is also constantly reevaluating it from new angles in order to determine what to preserve and what to discard as he prepares to establish a new Troy. In this regard, an important function of his adventures is to provide him with a better understanding of his real goal, a new home in Italy.[22] This requires a gradual physical and psychological movement away from Troy toward Rome,[23] which is enabled through an alternating series of prophecies and failed attempts to re-found Troy. If Aeneas' very survival in the aftermath of the war is first determined by the prediction of Poseidon in *Iliad* 20, it is not surprising that prophecy figures so prominently in the adventures of *Aeneid* 3.[24] Aeneas' abilities as a reader are once again put to the test as he attempts to decipher these visions of his future and relate them to his Iliadic past. Here again, the *Odyssey*'s central framework of *nostos* serves as guide to the problems of going forward and backward at the same time. Although the *Odyssey* defines Odysseus' departure from the Iliadic world as the very end of that world, it also establishes his journey as an attempt to reassert some of its essential values and institutions. Odysseus wants to return to Ithaca to resume his traditional roles as king, husband, and father, but he must learn to avoid false assumptions about the status of his home. Thus, his explorations of the perversion of hospitality and homecoming are designed to prepare him for the challenges of reintegrating himself into society. Aeneas has similar goals: to re-found Troy, establish a patrimony for his son, and even, as it turns out, to remarry. But he also faces the problem of distinguishing false homes from real ones and false promises from true visions of his destiny. I would like to proceed through Book 3 in a linear fashion, following *la traccia del modello* (to borrow Barchiesi's phrase),[25] in order to elucidate the ways in which Virgil engages his Homeric intertext to define the *Aeneid* as a new kind of *nostos*.[26]

In a resounding statement of posteriority, Book 3 opens with the word *postquam* ("after") followed by a bleak summary of the results of Book 2 (*Aen.* 3.1–3):

> postquam res Asiae Priamique evertere gentem
> immeritam visum superis, ceciditque superbum
> Ilium et omnis humo fumat Neptunia Troia
>
> after the gods saw fit to overturn the power of Asia
> and Priam's blameless race, and proud Ilium had fallen
> and all of Neptune's Troy was smoking from the ground

In that *postquam* there is perhaps more than a hint of the subordinate conjunction *epei* from the second line of the *Odyssey*'s proem (*Od.* 1.2): ἐπεὶ Τροίης ἱερὸν πτολίεθρον ἔπερσε ("after he had sacked the sacred citadel of Troy"). Aeneas is also defining his narrative in relation to the destruction of Troy, but whereas the *Odyssey* makes its hero the active agent of that destruction, Aeneas first attributes it to the gods and then makes *superbum Ilium* the subject of its own fall. The epithetic phrase *superbum Ilium* recalls the Greeks' use of the insult *Trôes huperphialoi* ("arrogant Trojans") in the *Iliad* (*Il.* 13.621, 21.224, 414, 459), and particularly Menelaus' claim that the Trojans defied Zeus as god of hospitality when they stole Helen away, and that the god will one day destroy their city in retribution (*Il.* 13.625: ὕμμι διαφθέρσει πόλιν αἰπήν, "[Zeus] will utterly destroy your steep city").[27]

Aeneas seems to be acknowledging Menelaus' accusation even as he claims that the destruction was *immeritam* ("undeserved"), a contradiction that reflects the dangerous Trojan heritage he carries away from the smoldering ruins.

In the *Iliad*, Hector also recognizes that Paris' wrongful action is to blame for the war (*Il.* 6.328–29, 22.115–16), but this does not prevent him from dying to defend his city. At the same time, the reference to Menelaus' vaunt is also processed through the *Odyssey*, where *huperphialoi mnêstêres* ("arrogant suitors") is one of the standard epithets for the Ithacan suitors (*Od.* 4.790, 13.373, 14.27, 15.315, 16.271, 18.167, 20.12, 291, 23.356).[28] As he embarks on a search for a new homeland that will ultimately involve a conflict over another bride, Aeneas struggles to reconcile the actions of a false suitor with the destruction of a civilization. The tension between *superbum* and *immeritam* also foreshadows Aeneas' own situation with Dido in Book 4. There he will violate the hospitality granted to him by the queen and become a haughty enemy (*Aen.* 4.424: *hostem superbum*) whose actions will lead to an undeserved death for Dido (*Aen.* 4.696: *merita nec morte peribat*).

Like Odysseus, Aeneas frames his journey in terms of the dichotomy between good and bad hospitality. In both cases, this is largely motivated by the desire to secure the right sort of treatment from their respective audiences, but for Aeneas, a central anxiety in Book 3 is not only obtaining good hospitality, but finding it in the right place. Aeneas' first adventure demonstrates that he is still thinking in terms of Iliadic categories, as he arrives in Thrace and founds a city there. In this regard, Virgil is partially echoing Odysseus' first stop (also set in Thrace), the encounter with the Cicones, which is the most "Iliadic" of his adventures.[29] Aeneas describes the land as an *hospitium antiquum Troiae* ("an ancient friend of Troy," *Aen.* 3.15), a status confirmed by the Iliadic catalog of Trojan allies (*Il.* 2.844–45),[30] but adds an ominous temporal qualifier to this claim (*Aen.* 3.16): *dum fortuna fuit* ("while our fortune held"). The destruction of Troy may also signal the dissolution of all sorts of ancient ties: what was once hospitable (*hospitium*) while Troy still stood does not necessarily remain so in the aftermath of the war. In another Iliadic gesture, he names the city he founds *Aeneadae* (*Aen.* 3.18), recalling the two eponymous names of his own land, Troia and Ilium (from Tros and Ilus respectively), which he has just joined in sorrow at the beginning of his narration (*Aen.* 3.3: *Ilium et omnis humo fumat Neptunia Troia*).[31] But this foundation is opposed by the fates (*Aen.* 3.17: *fatis iniquis*), and the naming procedure is marked as a failed attempt to revive old traditions. The city of the future, *Roma*, will not have a name tied to the Trojan past.[32]

The inhospitability of Thrace is revealed by the striking encounter with Polydorus, whose blood and voice pour forth from a plant that Aeneas tries to tear out of the ground in order to build a roof for an altar (*Aen.* 3.24–25). The voice tells Aeneas to leave this cruel land (*Aen.* 3.44: *heu fuge crudelis terras, fuge litus avarum*, "oh, flee these cruel lands, flee this greedy shore") using the same opening words as an earlier mutilated supernatural figure, Hector in the dream vision of Book 2 (*Aen.* 2.289: *heu fuge*). Hector and Polydorus are, of course, brothers, but in the *Iliad* they are especially bound together because they are both killed by Achilles, and more specifically, because Hector's presence at Polydorus' death leads to his first direct challenge to Achilles (*Il.* 20.407–23). Virgil appears to be following a tradition about Polydorus' death first found in Euripides' *Hecuba* (3–10, 767–82, 1132),[33] but by having him speak the same words as Hector, he is also activating the Iliadic story in order to equate the treachery of Thrace with the deceit that led to the destruction of Troy. Aeneas confirms this when he recounts to Dido how Priam had entrusted Polydorus to the Thracian king in order to guarantee the survival of an heir, only to have that king ally himself with Agamemnon, break all oaths (*Aen.* 3.55: *fas omne abrumpit*), and kill Polydorus (*Aen.* 3.55: *obrtruncat*). The verb *obtruncat* is precisely the same word Aeneas used to describe Pyrrhus' killing of Priam in violation of the sanctuary provided by Jupiter's altar (*Aen.* 2.663),[34] which draws attention to the perversion of societal norms demonstrated in both episodes and, in tandem with the earlier Iliadic reference, restates the now familiar chiasmus of Achilles killing a son of Priam, and Achilles' son slaughtering Priam himself.[35] Aeneas acknowledges Polydorus' warnings and decides to leave this *pollutum hospitium* ("this place where hospitality was defiled," *Aen.* 3.61), after building a tomb and performing the proper funeral rites (*Aen.* 3.67–68): *animamque sepulcro / condimus* ("we bury the spirit in its tomb"). The verb *condimus* marks the transformation from city building to burial in the episode.[36]

After the failed foundation in Thrace, the Trojans proceed to Delos to seek advice from Apollo's oracle. They are met by King Anius, who is an old friend of Anchises (*Aen.* 3.82: *veterem . . . amicum*), and he honors the relationship with good hospitality (*Aen.* 3.83: *iungimus hospitio dextras*, "we join right hands in friendship").[37] The contrast with the Thracian king who violates his bonds of friendship is readily apparent,[38] and the episode quickly moves to Aeneas' request that Apollo preserve the *altera Troiae Pergama* ("the second citadel of Troy," *Aen.* 3.86–87), a metonym for the Trojan survivors themselves, and then to his direct questions about his destination (*Aen.* 3.88): *quem sequimur? quove ire iubes? ubi ponere sedes?* ("whom should we follow? where do you command us to go? where should we found our home?").[39] Apollo's famously cryptic reply, *antiquam exquirite matrem* ("seek out your ancient mother," *Aen.* 3.96), is followed by the god's "romanized" version of Poseidon's Iliadic prophecy (*Aen.* 3.97): *hic domus Aeneae cunctis dominabitur oris* ("here Aeneas' house will rule all shores").[40] By telling Aeneas to seek his "ancient mother" and then asserting the boundless dominion of Aeneas' own *domus*, Apollo has reconfigured Aeneas' journey as a *nostos*.[41] The Iliadic prediction of Aeneas' basic narrative has been filtered through the Odyssean ideal of domestic restoration and reintegration, an image further reinforced by the transference of the prophecy away from Poseidon, a god hostile both to the Trojans in the *Iliad* and to Odysseus in his own journey.[42] This is a crucial first step in transforming the *Aeneid* from a loser's to a victor's epic. His homecoming is fraught with all the usual dangers of the Greek *nostoi*, but it also includes the possibility of repeating the Trojan war, and even winning it this time. As Aeneas sees again and again in Book 3, he cannot return to the Troy he knew any more than Odysseus can expect to find the Ithaca of his youth, but he can still approach his journey from the perspective of *nostos* in order to apply the lessons learned in the *Iliad* to the restoration of the Trojan race in the land of their earliest forefather.

Apollo has unmistakably marked that father as Dardanus and the land as Italy by addressing the Trojans as *Dardanidae* at the beginning of his prophecy (*Aen.* 3.94),[43] but Anchises is misled by his Iliadic memory (*Aen.* 3.102: *veterum volvens monimenta virorum*, "thinking of the traditions of ancient men"; 3.107: *si rite . . . recordor*, "if I remember rightly") and announces that the answer to Apollo's riddle is Crete, the homeland of Teucer, who came when *nondum Ilium et arces / Pergameae steterant; habitabant vallibus imis* ("Ilium and the towers of Pergamus did not yet stand, and they lived deep in the valleys," *Aen.* 3.109–10). He has misapplied Aeneas' own description of Dardanus' settlement to Achilles in the *Iliad* (*Il.* 20.216-18): κτίσσε δὲ Δαρδανίην, ἐπεὶ οὔ πω Ἴλιος ἱρὴ . . . ἀλλ' ἔθ' ὑπωρείας ᾤκεον ("he founded Dardania, since there was no sacred Ilium yet . . . but they lived in the foothills").[44] Like Aeneas in Thrace, Anchises' reliance on *monimenta* leads him to select another false homeland for the Trojan people.

As the Trojans prepare to speed away to Crete, Virgil engages the Odyssean narrative in an extremely intricate way. Odysseus does not mention a visit to Crete in the wanderings he describes to the Phaeacians in *Odyssey* 9–12, but it is the central location in three of the lying tales he spins after he returns home to Ithaca.[45] In each case, he represents himself as a Cretan with some close association to Idomeneus, king of Crete: first, he is a fugitive who killed Idomeneus' son (*Od.* 13.259); then, his co-leader in the expedition to Troy (*Od.* 14.237); and finally, the king's brother Aethon (*Od.* 19.181). Odysseus seems to increase the nobility of his own fictional character in order to appear more reliable as the status of his interlocutors grows from Athena in disguise as a herdsman, to Eumaeus his chief swineherd, and finally Penelope herself.[46] The desire to associate himself with Idomeneus may simply reflect the Cretan's high status among the Greek commanders in the *Iliad* (cf., *Il.* 2.645, 13.210–515), but Idomeneus also has a complicated *nostos*.[47] In the *Odyssey*, Nestor tells Telemachus that the Cretan king arrived home safely without losing a single man to the sea (*Od.* 3.191–92): πάντας δ' Ἰδομενεὺς Κρήτην εἰσήγαγ' ἑταίρους, / οἳ φύγον ἐκ πολέμου, πόντος δέ οἱ οὔ τιν' ἀπηύρα ("and Idomeneus brought back to Crete all of his companions who escaped from the war; the sea took none of them"). This seems quite obviously designed to contrast with Odysseus' situation as a captain, already described so prominently in the proem (*Od.* 1.6): ἀλλ' οὐδ' ὧς ἑτάρους ἐρρύσατο ("but he did not save his companions").

In *Aeneid* 3, Aeneas says that a report had reached the Trojans that Idomeneus had been driven out of his homeland (*Aen.* 3.121–22: *pulsum regnis cessisse paternis / Idomenea ducem*, "Idomeneus the chieftain had been driven out and had left his father's kingdom"), and that there was now a home free from the enemy waiting there for them (*Aen.* 3.123: *hoste vacare domum sedesque astare relictas*, "a home empty of enemies and deserted houses await us"). Virgil offers no explanation for these circumstances, but Servius (ad *Aen.* 3.121) tells the story of how Idomeneus was caught in a storm on his way home from Troy and vowed that he would sacrifice the first thing he saw upon arrival if he were saved. This proved to be his son, and when he had sacrificed him, the island was visited by a plague and the people drove him out. This story occurs nowhere else before Servius, but it may be lurking behind Nestor's particular insistence in the *Odyssey* that the sea did not take any of the Cretans on the way home.[48] Even more telling is the first lying tale, where Odysseus claims to be in exile for having killed a son of Idomeneus.[49] Although the details Virgil gives obviously do not correspond to Servius' story, there is nevertheless a strong echo of the king's own disastrous homecoming. For Odysseus, who has just arrived on Ithaca and has not yet seen his son, the Idomeneus scenario is fraught with danger, but we already know that the situation on Ithaca is partially reversed: the suitors have planned to kill the king's son Telemachus as soon as he returns from Sparta (*Od.* 4.658–74).

With this scenario as a guide, Virgil launches Aeneas toward Crete, where he makes his earlier metonymic reference to *Pergama* a reality by founding a city named *Pergamum* (*Aen.* 3.133), once again looking backward to Troy instead of forward to Rome. Even in Book 5, when he is on the very doorstep of Italy, he establishes an *Ilium* and a *Troia* for the veterans who decide to stay in Sicily (*Aen.* 5.756), and in Book 4 he angers Dido by telling her that he gladly would have founded a *recidiva Pergama* ("a restored Pergama," *Aen.* 4.344) on the ruins of Troy if fate had allowed it.[50] After the false interpretation of the prophecy by Anchises, it is not surprising that Aeneas once again builds a false token of the Iliadic past on Crete. But once the settlement has begun, a disastrous plague descends on the Trojans, and Anchises presses Aeneas to return to the oracle at Delos for advice (*Aen.* 3.135–46). Like the horror of Polydorus in Thrace, this pestilence is a sign that Aeneas has chosen the wrong site for his city, but it also refers to the plague that drove Idomeneus from the land in the first place.[51] The point of the allusion is that a hasty *nostos* can be extremely dangerous: Idomeneus' rash promise to sacrifice whatever he sees and Aeneas' rush to re-found Pergamum on Crete both lead to disaster. Against this model is set Odysseus, who uses his three Cretan personae to measure out his return in stages precisely so that he can avoid the kind of mistake that Idomeneus makes. Aeneas does not stop to wonder why Idomeneus has been driven from Crete because he is focused on the idea that a *domus* lies vacant there, but like Thrace, the land has been polluted by the death of an Iliadic king's son. Just as Anchises failed to read the clear signs in Apollo's prophecy, so Aeneas misreads the abandonment of the kingdom.

Aeneas' interpretive failures on his journey up to this point are brought sharply into focus by the corrective prophecy of the Penates. Once again he is visited in a dream (*Aen.* 3.150–51), and as in the vision of Hector, he is ordered to depart Pergamum. But there is a clear rebuke in having to be put on the right path by the very household gods he is supposed to be transporting to Italy (cf. *Aen.* 1.6: *inferretque deos Latio*). This is reinforced by Anchises' realization that Cassandra had predicted the true destination to him long ago, which he follows with a rhetorical question (*Aen.* 3.187): *quem tum vates Cassandra moveret?* ("who would have been moved by Cassandra then?"). After failing to understand Apollo's own words correctly, his belated realization that a prophet who was fated never to be believed actually spoke the truth further confirms that the Trojans are still paying for past mistakes. This pattern is repeated again in the Strophades landing (*Aen.* 3.209–77), where the Trojans slaughter and feast on the cattle of the Harpies without any regard for the lawfulness of their actions. After the Harpies attack twice, Aeneas prepares his men for a full-scale assault, only to be rebuked and then cursed by the chief Harpy, Celaeno. This display of bad guest etiquette is reminiscent of the Thrinacia episode in *Odyssey* 12, where Odysseus' crew slaughter Helios' cattle and are cursed by the sun god (*Od.* 12.353–88).[52] Although Celaeno's curse does not promise the same immediate destruction as Helios' malediction, Aeneas is saddled with another murky prophecy as an obstacle to his *nostos*.

So far, Aeneas has not actually visited any of the places described by Odysseus in his wandering tale.[53] But in a tantalizing reminder of the synchronicity of the two narratives, the Trojans now sail past Ithaca itself, which allows Aeneas to glance back at Book 2 again (*Aen.* 3.272–73): *effugimus scopulos Ithacae, Laertia regna, / et terram altricem saevi exsecramur Ulixi* ("we kept away from the crags of Ithaca, Laertes' kingdom, and we cursed the land that had nourished savage Ulysses"). The scene recalls the Aeolus episode, where Odysseus gets close enough to Ithaca to make out people tending fires, before the crew's curiosity whisks them far away (*Od.* 10.28–30). Although the Trojans' curse here is primarily meant to recall Odysseus' lead role in the destruction of their own *regna*, there is also great deal of irony in the notion that they could easily make landfall in the very place that Odysseus spends ten years trying to reach. The Trojans must flee (*effugimus*) in order to avoid entering the *Odyssey*'s narrative space.[54] We have already seen the attraction that a vacant home on Crete presented to Aeneas, and we are left to wonder what would happen if he chose to preempt Odysseus' homecoming as well. The backhanded compliment of referring to the island as "Laertes' kingdom" (*regna Laertia*) rather than Ulysses',[55] doubly ironizes a political situation that no longer obtains:

in the wake of the Trojan war, neither Laertes nor Odysseus rules the land, leaving it as empty of the Trojans' fiercest enemy (*hoste vacare, Aen.* 3.123) as Crete was.

The contrast between Aeneas' choice to shun Ithaca and Odysseus' involuntary flight away from it is a symbolic representation of Aeneas' superior control over the Odyssean elements of his narrative. After a proleptic Roman interlude at Actium,[56] this commentary is reinforced by an even briefer mention of the Phaeacians (*Aen.* 3.291): *protinus aërias Phaeacum abscondimus arces* ("we soon leave behind the airy heights of the Phaeacians").[57] The striking use of the verb *abscondere*, literally "to hide or bury away," provides a perfect metonym for Virgil's intertextual strategy in Book 3. The fairytales Odysseus tells to the Phaeacians, represented by the *aërias arces*, are "buried away" by Aeneas' own narration. Coming immediately after the historical Actium scene, the implication is similar to that of substituting the Phoenicians for Phaeacians as Aeneas' hosts. The unreliability of the Odyssean narrative is replaced by a more authoritative account. And just as in the earlier Ithaca scene, Virgil toys with the possibility that Aeneas could actually replace Odysseus as the storytelling guest of the Phaeacians.

If this double bypass of Ithaca and the Phaeacians is the closest Aeneas gets to the "real" *Odyssey* as opposed to Odysseus' own narration, then the visit to the Trojans at Buthrotum is his most intimate encounter with the *Iliad*, though as always, the experience is processed through the Odyssean lens. As I pointed out earlier, Book 3 is often said to be the most Odyssean book in the *Aeneid*, but we have already seen very important Iliadic references in Thrace, Delos, and Crete. Here, in the central (and longest) episode in the book (*Aen.* 3.294–505), Aeneas visits a melancholic imitation of Troy, where he finds Helenus and Andromache almost living in a state of suspended animation.[58] The introduction of two more Iliadic characters into the postwar narrative is part of the *Aeneid*'s challenge to the *Odyssey*'s systematic elision of the Trojans. As I have noted before, the *Odyssey* contains the actual appearance of (or significant information about) every major Greek Iliadic figure, but it only makes a handful of oblique references to specific Trojans. By narrating the actual sack of Troy in great detail, Virgil also manages to mention every significant Iliadic Greek except for Telamonian Ajax and Nestor, but in the immediate aftermath of the war, he turns his attention to the scattered remnants of the Trojan people in order to present multiple perspectives on the losers' experience. In Buthrotum he finds yet another son of Priam, Helenus, and more surprisingly, Hector's widow, Andromache.[59] In addition to continuing the pattern of Priam's sons offering predictions to Aeneas, the long middle section of the scene, which contains Helenus' detailed instructions on the remaining stages of the journey (*Aen.* 3.374–462), corresponds in several ways to Tiresias' prophecies to Odysseus in *Odyssey* 11.[60] In particular, Helenus offers Aeneas the vision of the white sow as a definitive token by which

Virgilian Reflection 105

to determine when he has reached the end of his wanderings (*Aen.* 3.388: *signa tibi dicam*, "I will tell you signs"), which corresponds to Tiresias' sign of the man who mistakes an oar for a winnowing fan (*Od.* 11.126: σῆμα δέ τοι ἐρέω, "I will tell you a sign").[61]

The rest of the prophecy contains a great deal of practical information for Aeneas, but like its Tiresian model, its greatest virtue lies in the contrast it provides with the scenes surrounding it. In the *Odyssey*, once the business of consultation for the future has been disposed of, Odysseus turns his attention to the extended exploration of the past. Similarly, Aeneas' two encounters with Andromache, as well as Helenus' non-prophetic activities, provide an opportunity to investigate the devastating effects of the Iliadic world's demise.[62] When Aeneas first approaches the city, he finds Andromache making offerings to Hector's empty tomb (*Aen.* 3.304: *Hectoreum ... tumulum ... inanem*) beside a brook that he calls a "false Simois" (*Aen.* 3.302: *falsi Simoentis*). Aeneas has entered a world of make-believe, a life-sized dollhouse of Troy where Andromache can endlessly revisit her former life.[63] Again, there is a strong echo of Odysseus' visit to the underworld as Andromache attempts to summon the *manes* (*Aen.* 3.303) to the tomb of Hector on twin altars (*Aen.* 3.305: *geminas aras*).[64] But in an inversion of that model, she sees Aeneas and momentarily believes that she has conjured up his ghost (*Aen.* 3.310–12): *verane te facies, verus mihi nuntius adfers, / nate dea? vivisne? aut, si lux alma recessit, / Hector ubi est?* ("are you a real form, a real messenger who comes to me, son of a goddess? Are you alive? Or if the kind light has withdrawn, where is Hector?")[65] In fact, it is Andromache who turns out to be the figurative *manes* in this pseudo-underworld scene, but the reversal reinforces the delusional nature of her postwar existence. She begins to play the more traditional role of the Odyssean shade when she asks Aeneas about his journey and then about Ascanius (*Aen.* 3.339), recalling Agamemnon's inquiry about Orestes (*Od.* 11.458) and Achilles' eager questions about Neoptolemus (*Od.* 11.492–93),[66] but the moment is marked by another inversion since she asks about the visitor's child rather than her own. Just as the false Simois and the cenotaph of Hector are replicas of sites from Troy, so Andromache thinks of Ascanius as a double of her own dead son Astyanax.[67] She wonders whether the thought of *avunculus Hector* ("uncle Hector") stirs the boy to *antiquam virtutem* ("ancient courage," *Aen.* 3.342–43), and in the departure scene later, she gives the boy a mantle as *manuum monimenta* ("memorials of [her own] handiwork," *Aen.* 3.486), because he is her last *imago* of Astyanax (*Aen.* 3.489–90): *o mihi sola mei super Astyanactis imago* ("o you, the only image left of my Astyanax").[68]

Throughout this last scene of the episode, as in the whole of Book 3, Ascanius is notably absent from text, even though Andromache addresses him directly. His absence underscores the sterility of this false Troy. When Aeneas approaches the actual city after the initial encounter with Andromache, he sees a *parvam Troiam simulataque magnis / Pergama et arentem*

Xanthi cognomine rivum ("a little Troy, a Pergama that imitates the great one, and a dry stream named after the Xanthus," *Aen.* 3.349–50). The contrast between *parva* and *magnis* is both physical and symbolic: the attempt to re-create Troy is doomed to be a *parva* endeavor, as Aeneas' own failed attempt to found a *Pergama* has already shown him.[69] Even more revealing is the reference to the second great river of Troy, the Xanthus, which is replicated here by a dry (*arentem*) brook in sharp contrast to its Iliadic description (*Il.* 20.73: *megas potamos bathudinês*, "a great, deep-eddying river"). This is not only a striking image of the sterility of the land,[70] but it is also a metonym for Astyanax's absence from the scene, since both the Xanthus and Astyanax share the alternate name *Scamander* (cf. *Il.* 6.402; 20.74). The omission of any description of Ascanius' physical presence in the final scene thus brings us full circle to Andromache's first appearance: the *dona extrema* ("last gifts") (*Aen.* 3.488) she gives the shadow of Ascanius complete the offering of the *tristia dona* ("sad gifts") (*Aen.* 3.301) to the *manes* at the twin altars.[71]

Like Odysseus' visit to the underworld, Aeneas' encounter with the shades of Troy allows him to redefine his own relationship to the Iliadic world. Helenus' prophecy alludes to the wars to come in Italy (*Aen.* 3.458: *ventura bella*), and he sends the hero forth with a mandate to make Troy great again (*Aen.* 3.462): *vade age et ingentem factis fer ad aethera Troiam* ("now go, and through your deeds raise great Troy to the heavens"). The repeated emphasis on the sterility of Helenus' city, and the loss of Hector and Astyanax in particular, allows Aeneas to assert that the future of the Trojan race lies with himself and his own son Ascanius. Just as Odysseus assumes control of Achilles' incomplete role as the destroyer of Troy and father-figure to Neoptolemus, so Aeneas uses his meeting with Andromache to claim Hector's role as the defender of Troy. This reinforces the dream vision in Book 2, where Aeneas depicts Hector giving him a specific mandate to survive. Andromache's literal placing of the mantle on Ascanius (*Aen.* 3.484: *chlamydem*) in the final scene thus seals the transfer of power to the line of Aeneas.

The departure from Epirus marks a clear passage into the Italian space of Aeneas' future, but even as he moves closer to his destiny, Virgil draws him into the world of Odysseus' wanderings in order to challenge the Greek hero's highly effective presentation of himself as the ultimate survivor of the Trojan war. The Buthrotum episode uses the Odyssean model to redefine a key Iliadic paradigm by contrasting Aeneas' survival of the Trojan war with Hector's bitter death, but in the last scenes of Book 3, Virgil moves to differentiate the two heroes' species of survival. After the brief stop at Acroceraunia and the landing at Castrum Minervae in Italy (*Aen.* 3.506–47), the Trojans sail across the Gulf of Tarentum and approach the twin dangers of Scylla and Charybdis. Many of the details in the scene are modeled on Odysseus' own encounter (*Od.* 12.201–59),[72] but the major difference is that Aeneas escapes with no loss of crew, while Odysseus loses six men. Aeneas thus shows himself to be the better leader, a more responsible captain who can preserve the people in his care. The *Odyssey* itself constantly draws attention to Odysseus' failure to bring his men home,[73] but in Odysseus' embedded narrative, he either assigns the blame to the crew themselves (as in the Aeolus and Thrinacia episodes) or he redirects our attention to his own miraculous survival in each case. By entering one of these Odyssean situations and demonstrating that it is possible to make different choices that can ensure the survival not only of the hero but also of the passengers and crew, Aeneas draws attention to Odysseus' own narrative misdirections and the essential selfishness of his survival instinct.

This strong challenge to the *Odyssey*'s views on survival becomes even more pronounced in the encounter with Achaemenides and the Cyclopes (*Aen.* 3.588–691).[74] The episode is full of intricate allusive gestures to its Odyssean model, but the central element of the story, the encounter with a man left behind by Odysseus in his hasty departure, is another clear assertion of Aeneas' ability to ensure the survival of other people. But even before the Trojans encounter this Odyssean castaway, Virgil makes another subtle allusion by relocating the Cyclopes from their unnamed land to Sicily. In the *Aeneid*, Sicily is always called *Trinacria* (here, at *Aen.* 3.582), which is a variation on the Homeric form *Thrinakiê*, "Thrinacia."[75] As the Trojans land on the island, this reference to the last stop on Odysseus' journey creates an expectation that they will encounter a similar definitive disaster. This is reinforced by the vivid description of the destructive power of Mount Etna, which belches smoke and shakes the land as they try to sleep (*Aen.* 3.569–87). Virgil has already used the story of Helios' cattle in the encounter with the Harpies, but here the point is to remind us that, by the end of his journey, Odysseus manages to lose every last crew member.

While we are still absorbing this central fact of the first half of the *Odyssey*, Virgil announces a bold revision to that text: there is at least one survivor, but of which disaster is not immediately clear.[76] The very first words used to describe him, *macie confecta suprema* ("exhausted by final hunger," *Aen.* 3.590), suggest that he might have survived precisely because he refrained from joining in the feast. He has maintained the state of hunger that led the crew to slaughter Helios' cattle, and has now reached the very limits of that condition.[77] Although he is filthy and dressed in rags, the Trojans recognize him as a Greek (*Aen.* 3.594: *at cetera Graius*, "but otherwise a Greek"),[78] and after a momentary fright at the sight of his former enemies, he rushes forward to supplicate them. This is Aeneas' first encounter with a Greek since Book 2, and the circumstances show how far he has come from that humiliation: here, a Greek is groveling on his knees before the Trojans, marking Aeneas' growing control over his destiny.[79] There is even the slight suggestion that this strange Greek might be Odysseus himself, forced to beg his former enemies for mercy. The Trojans ask him the same sorts of questions Arete puts to the suppliant Odysseus (*Od.* 7.238–39), which are later amplified by Alcinous (*Od.* 8.550–55, 574–77), and his very first words maintain the suspense about his identity (*Aen.* 3.613–14): *sum patria ex Ithaca, comes infelicis Ulixi, / nomine Achaemenides* ("I am from the land of Ithaca, a comrade of unfortunate Ulysses; my name is Achaemenides"). The first clause, positioned so that it falls entirely before the pause at the caesura, is similar to Odysseus' statement to Alcinous (*Od.* 9.21: ναιετάω δ' Ἰθάκην, "I live on Ithaca"), and the name of *Ulixes* is delayed until the very end of the line.

Even once he makes clear that he is not Odysseus, the unlikely epithet *infelix* also causes some surprise, since we have come to expect adjectives like *dirus* and *saevus*.[80] It recalls Odysseus' description of himself to Arete as *dustênos* ("unfortunate," *Od.* 7.248), and it appears to soften the harsh view of the hero reflected in *Aeneid* 2. Achaemenides' speech is being quoted, so the sentiment is at least presented as his rather than Aeneas', but it seems strange that Achaemenides would transfer an especially apt epithet for himself to the man who abandoned him. He soon reveals that he is not a survivor of the Thrinacia disaster, but one of the men who was trapped in the Cyclops' cave. Odysseus, of course, does not describe any sailor left behind in that episode, but Virgil makes his intervention into the Homeric narrative credible by making Achaemenides' account of the events follow the *Odyssey* very closely.[81] Thus, when Polyphemus inevitably appears, Aeneas corrects Odysseus' mistake and brings Achaemenides along with him.

The implications are even stronger here than in the Scylla and Charybdis episode: not only does Aeneas preserve his own people, he even saves Odysseus' men. Aeneas has trumped Odysseus within the Greek hero's own narrative. In a clever intertextual cap to the episode, the Trojans sail along the coast as Achaemenides retraces his wanderings (*Aen.* 3.690–91): *talia monstrabat relegens errata retrorsus / litora Achaemenides, comes infelicis Ulixi* ("such were the shores that Achaemenides, comrade of unfortunate Ulysses, showed us as he retraced his wanderings in reverse").[82] These, of course, would be the *errata* of Odysseus, but just as he inserted Achaemenides into the story of the Cyclops, Virgil now makes his creation assume the role of Odyssean narrator as well. Finally, in an ironic repetition of Achaemenides own self-identification, Aeneas refers to him as *comes infelicis Ulixi*.[83] This time, the epithet is appropriate: Achaemenides has now assumed the roles of survivor and narrator, while Odysseus is somewhere in the Mediterranean awaiting his next misfortune.[84]

The final port of call on Aeneas' Sicilian cruise is Drepanum, which he describes as an *inlaetabilis ora* ("joyless shore," *Aen.* 3.707).[85] Here, Anchises' death marks the final passing of the old Troy, and more importantly, of Aeneas' Trojan identity. As Aeneas brings his story to an end, Virgil confirms the transition by referring to Aeneas as *pater* (*Aen.* 3.716).[86] The last son of Troy is now ready to become the father of Rome, though he will still require Anchises' help to do so. Aeneas the reader has still not mastered all the signs, as he demonstrates when he optimistically describes this death as his own *labor extremus* ("final struggle," *Aen.* 3.714).[87] He adds to this a second description that more aptly describes his situation (*Aen.* 3.714): *longarum haec meta viarum* ("this was the limit of my long journey"). Aeneas' greatest *labores* still lie ahead of him in Italy, and he is about to learn that Carthage is by no means the end of his voyaging, but his work as a storyteller has already reached its limit (*meta*) in the Achaemenides episode, where he proves himself to be the definitive meta-Odyssean narrator.

videmus nunc per speculum in aenigmate

In this chapter, I have mainly been concerned with the detailed ways in which Aeneas himself reads the Iliadic world through the application of Odyssean and meta-Odyssean narrative techniques. In this last section, I would like to examine briefly one of the broader implications of that reading process for the later books of the poem, where Aeneas is forced to adapt his experiences to the challenges of establishing a new homeland. This argument is meant to demonstrate the possibilities of applying my views on Virgil's sophisticated Odyssean intertextuality to large-scale questions of structure and theme in the *Aeneid*, but it is not intended to be a comprehensive analysis of the scenes in question.

As Aeneas' experiences in Book 1–3 have repeatedly demonstrated, it is not so easy to break free from one's past. Aeneas' own failed foundations in Thrace and Crete, as well as his visit to Helenus and Andromache at *parva Troia*, reflect the dangers of trying to replicate one's memories. If, as Virgil tells us in the proem, Aeneas must undergo many years of wandering and war *dum conderet urbem* ("until he founded the city," *Aen.* 1.5), then we must acknowledge that *condere* means both "to found" and "to bury." To found Rome, he must bury Troy, but from the moment Aeneas arrives in Italy, several signs point to a repetition of the *Iliad*. In Book 6, the Cumaean Sibyl announces that "another Achilles has been born in Latium" (*Aen.* 6.89: *alius Latio iam partus Achilles*) and that the *causa mali* will "again be a bride and a foreign marriage" (*Aen.* 6.93–94: *coniunx iterum ... externique iterum thalami*). Likewise, Virgil ominously restarts his poem in Book 7 with a second proem, in which he declares, *primae revocabo exordia pugnae* ("I will recall the beginnings of the first battle," *Aen.* 7.40). This echoes the starting point of the *Iliad* as defined by its proem (*Il.* 1.6: ἐξ οὗ δὴ τὰ πρῶτα διαστήτην ἐρίσαντε, "from the time when they first stood divided in strife"), and the verb *revocabo* stresses the repetition of the past.[88]

Moreover, Aeneas faces the prospect of playing three different disastrous Trojan roles in this re-enactment of the *Iliad*. In response to his planned marriage to Lavinia, Juno calls him *Paris alter, / funestaeque iterum recidiva in Pergama taedae* ("a second Paris, and there are deadly

110 *Virgil's Homeric Lens*

torches again for a restored Pergama," *Aen.* 7.321–22), a charge echoed by Amata a few lines later (*Aen.* 7.362: *perfidus . . . abducta virgine praedo*, "faithless . . . with the stolen girl as his prize"), and later by Turnus (*Aen.* 9.136–39), Numanus (*Aen.* 9.600), and Juno again (*Aen.* 10.97).[89] At the same time, the existence of an *alius Achilles* in Latium suggests that Aeneas will play the role of Hector as well, and as I pointed out earlier, Aeneas positions himself as Hector's heir early in the poem through both the dream vision in Book 2 and the visit to Andromache in Book 3. Finally, the most dangerous possibility is that Aeneas will play his former Iliadic role, the impotent challenger of Diomedes and Achilles who has to be rescued by the gods on two occasions. This seems especially likely early in the war, when the Latin envoy Venulus is sent to ask Diomedes, who has settled in the new city of Arpi, to fight the Trojans a second time (*Aen.* 8.9–17).[90] If Aeneas does revert to this third model, there is the further danger of repeating the cycle of survival and destruction. In Book 5, Neptune remembers the crucial Iliadic scene where he saves Aeneas from Achilles (*Il.* 20.318–29), and promises Venus that, despite his hostility to the Trojans, he is still willing to protect her son (*Aen.* 5.812: *nunc quoque mens eadem perstat mihi*, "now also my mind remains the same"), and one can almost imagine Aeneas being whisked away from an endless series of *alii Achilles*, fleeing from Troy after Troy, and trying to found cities *ad infinitum*.

In order to break free from the Iliadic cycle and transform his narrative from a loser's to a victor's epic, Aeneas must find a way to activate what I referred to in Chapter 3 as a cycloidal motion: the wheel must move forward even as it turns back on itself. If the repetition of the *Iliad* is in some sense inevitable, the obvious solution is to trade in the Trojan roles for Greek ones. The great advantage of having witnessed the events of the *Iliad* firsthand, and then processing its consequences in the narrative of *Aeneid* 2–3, is that Aeneas now has an intimate knowledge of what to emulate and what to avoid. An *Iliad* requires an Achilles figure, and even though Turnus immediately attempts to claim the title promised him by the Sibyl's prophecy (*Aen.* 9.148, 742),[91] Aeneas can wrest that role away from him. Nor is he limited to Achilles alone: Neoptolemus, whose brutally effective tactics he witnessed firsthand in the palace of Priam, offers a clear model for transforming old heroes into "new warriors." But above all, Odysseus points the way for the definitive revision of the Iliadic experience. As we have seen, the *Odyssey* establishes a heroic paradigm with two main goals: to avoid Achilles' fate by both winning and surviving the war, and to avoid Agamemnon's (or Idomeneus' or Little Ajax's) fate by winning and surviving the *nostos*.[92] Aeneas has already demonstrated that he knows how to survive the war and win the homecoming, but now surviving his *nostos* means winning a replica of the very war he lost the first time. Virgil thus establishes an intricate pattern of multiple correspondence and role reversal for the second half of the poem, but the solution to Aeneas' specific dilemma lies in an Odyssean reading of Iliadic material. By understanding the war in Italy as a repetition of the *Iliad* fought from the perspective of Odysseus' violent homecoming, we can describe a coherent model that explains the various inversions of the Iliadic intertext.

If the initial accusations of Juno and the various Italians suggest that the Trojans will play their familiar Iliadic role of failed defenders, the progress of the war brings about significant role reversals. Thus when Turnus claims that he is an Achilles who does not need Vulcan's armor (*Aen.* 9.148: *non armis mihi Volcani*), his words betray him, since we have just seen Aeneas take possession of that armor at the end of Book 8.[93] There is no need to multiply examples; the notion of Aeneas as Achilles and Turnus as Hector is a standard feature of Virgilian interpretation.[94] But as I briefly suggested in earlier chapters, there is another kind of inversion that has not been explored in any systematic way. If Aeneas is modeled on Achilles once he arrives in Italy, then he appears to be moving backward through the *Iliad* in respect to the central theme of Achilles' anger.[95] From the opening word of the poem, *mênin* ("wrath"), through the killing and desecration of Hector, the action of the *Iliad* is defined in relation to Achilles' various states of anger. As the poem progresses, his anger toward Agamemnon gives way to a combination of anger and grief over the death of Patroclus, and finally to grief alone after he avenges that death. But in the last three books of the poem, Achilles achieves a threefold resolution to his anger: first the revenge killing of Hector in Book 22, then Patroclus' funeral in Book 23, and finally, the return of Hector's corpse to the suppliant Priam, which is punctuated by another funeral and burial in Book 24.

In Aeneas' case, this pattern is partially inverted. Book 7 begins with the burial of Caieta (*Aen.* 7.1–4), followed immediately by a reference to *pius Aeneas* (7.5) to mark his respect and self-possession, but at the end of the poem, Aeneas kills Turnus in full rage (*Aen.* 12.946–47: *furiis accensus et ira / terribilis*, "burning with fury and terrible in his anger").[96] The inversion is further marked by the opposition between the burial of a Trojan mother in the beginning of the second half of *Aeneid* and a Trojan son at the end of the *Iliad*,[97] as well the similarities between the two sources of anger. Not only does Aeneas' anger over Pallas' death correspond to Achilles' feeling about Patroclus, but the reason for Achilles' first *mênis* toward Agamemnon, the unlawful seizure of Briseis, is recalled in the commencement of hostilities due to Turnus' claim to Lavinia.[98] Finally, Aeneas' hesitation before killing Turnus (*Aen.* 12.940: *cunctantem*) also recalls Achilles' hesitation over whether to kill Agamemnon at the beginning of the poem (*Il.* 1.189: διάνδιχα μερμήριξεν, "he was debated in two ways").

The key to this large-scale pattern lies in Virgil's refraction of the war in Italy through the lens of Odyssean *nostos*. Unlike Agamemnon or Menelaus, the Iliadic Odysseus has no personal stake in the Trojan war beyond the standard desires of a Homeric hero, nor does he suffer any significant psychological wound, like Achilles, that might motivate him further. But as he returns to Ithaca, he faces a conflict that is extremely personal, or perhaps more aptly, domestic. Now he is very much a Menelaus figure who sets a war in motion to get his wife back, but he is also like Achilles in his desire to exact vengeance on those who have wronged his loved ones (cf. *Od.* 22.35–41).[99] However, he does not undertake what we might call a proportional response. Achilles kills Hector, who is directly responsible for Patroclus' death, and then abuses the body, but this is in the context of a full-scale war, and he eventually relents and makes an appropriate gesture of conciliation for his excesses. In sharp contrast, Odysseus slaughters all the suitors in his house, none of whom have physically harmed either Telemachus or Penelope, and then is prepared to fight all their kinsmen to death until Zeus and Athena forcibly intervene. This is a bold revision of the Achillean mode of vengeance, a statement to the effect that Achilles' actions were not harsh enough. Having spent the first half of the poem, and especially his visit to the underworld in Book 11, hearing about Agamemnon's murder upon his arrival and Achilles' regrets that he did not return home, Odysseus makes a choice to use maximum force in order to achieve a successful reintegration into his society.

In Chapter 3, I discussed how this Odyssean paradigm of ruthlessness is reflected in Neoptolemus' actions in *Aeneid* 2. The transferred snake simile (*Aen.* 2.540–43; *Il.* 22.93–95) defines Neoptolemus in terms of both Achilles and Hector simultaneously, and his subsequent murder of Polites and Priam engages the image of Odysseus as a "defender" of the home wreaking havoc inside that home itself. In describing the killing of Priam, perhaps the climactic moment in the fall of Troy, as a kind of Achillean vengeance filtered through the ethical lens of the *Odyssey*, Virgil both uses the *Odyssey*'s revision of the *Iliad* and, at the same time, questions the reliability of Odysseus' own presentation of that revision. By defining Neoptolemus in terms that clearly depend on the ending of the *Odyssey*, but inserting that description into the internal Homeric timeline at a point earlier than the *Odyssey*'s own narrative, Virgil, or more properly, Aeneas as narrator, preempts Odysseus' calculated praise of Neoptolemus and announces his own claim as the definitive interpreter of both the Iliadic aftermath and its Odyssean revision. But given that Aeneas personally witnesses this ostentatious violation of *pietas* and the sanctity of the altar in the palace courtyard but does not intervene at all, it becomes clear throughout the rest of the *Aeneid* that he too is transformed into a "new warrior" by the experience, and that the foundation of the new Troy is shaped by the vivid memory of this Odyssean Neoptolemus and the impotence of his former Iliadic self to challenge him.

This transformation is explicitly marked in Aeneas' visit to Buthrotum, where Helenus actually gives the hero Neoptolemus' armor as a parting gift (*Aen.* 3.469: *arma Neoptolemi*).[100] But while Aeneas and Turnus both play the part of Achilles at different times during the war, they also both reflect Neoptolemus' revision of that role. Thus, when Turnus addresses Pandarus before killing him in Book 9, he says (*Aen.* 9.742): *hic etiam inventum*

Priamo narrabis Achillem ("you will tell Priam that, here too, you found an Achilles"). This makes his claim as an *alius Achilles* explicit, but it does so through the same technique of sending a message to the dead that Pyrrhus uses in Book 2 (*Aen.* 2.548–49): *illi mea tristia facta / degeneremque Neoptolemum narrare memento* ("remember to tell him of my sorrowful deeds and how degenerate Neoptolemus was").[101] Turnus makes Pyrrhus' messenger, Priam, the recipient of this new message, and Pyrrhus' recipient, Achilles, the new topic. This inversion confirms the killing of Priam as a new rendition of Hector's death at the hands of Achilles. By sending this message to Priam, Turnus is asserting his own ability to repeat the same pattern successfully.

But just as Turnus eventually yields the dominant Achillean role to Aeneas, he also watches as his enemy filters that role through his own first-hand experience with Neoptolemus in Book 2. When Aeneas returns to battle in Book 10, his first victim is Magus, who begs for his life only to be killed in the middle of his supplication (*Aen.* 10.535–36): *sic fatus galeam laeva tenet atque reflexa / cervice orantis capulo tenus applicat ensem* ("thus speaking, he held the helmet with his left hand and, bending back the suppliant's neck, drove in the sword up to the hilt"). The episode is modeled in large part on Achilles' killing of Lycaon, which is both the first individual encounter after the hero resumes fighting and a prominent example of a suppliant being killed.[102] But the specific description of the killing also strongly recalls Pyrrhus' slaughter of Priam (*Aen.* 2.552–53): *implicuitque comam laeva, dextraque coruscum / extulit ac lateri capulo tenus abdidit ensem* ("and he held [Priam's] hair with his left hand, and with his right he drew the glistening blade and buried it into his side up to the hilt"). Both the posture of the victims and the use of the unusual phrase *capulo tenus* ("up to the hilt") signal the close connection between these two scenes.[103] Aeneas is re-enacting the first steps of Achilles' vengeance, but he processes that vengeance through his own memory of Pyrrhus' actions. Similarly, in Book 12, when Juturna attempts to rescue Turnus from the fighting as Aeneas approaches, she is compared to a mother swallow who flies through the halls of a mansion (*Aen.* 12.474: *alta atria lustrat*) and is heard gathering food for her children in the empty colonnades (*Aen.* 12.476: *porticibus vacuis*), which recalls the description of Polites as he flees from Pyrrhus through the long porticoes and empty halls of Priam's palace (*Aen.* 2.528: *porticibus longis fugit et vacua atria lustrat*, "he flees through the long colonnades and roams the empty halls").[104] And later on in Book 12, Aeneas, *ipse inter primos* ("he himself among the leaders," *Aen.* 12.579), threatens the walls of Latinus' city, just as Pyrrhus breaks down the doors of Priam's palace *ipse inter primos* (*Aen.* 2.479).[105]

Turnus' reaction when he finally realizes the magnitude of the destruction around him confirms Aeneas' mastery of Neoptolemus' violent methods (*Aen.* 12.665–66): *obstipuit varia confusus imagine rerum / Turnus et obtutu tacito stetit* ("confused by the various images of ruin, Turnus was dumbstruck and stood silently staring"). Not only is *obstipuit* the same verb Aeneas uses to describe his own reaction to Priam's death (*Aen.* 2.560), but Turnus' utter helplessness in the face of the *varia imago rerum* reflects the inversion that has taken place as Aeneas and his Trojan survivors have assumed the roles of the Greek destroyers of Troy described in Book 2.[106] As Troy fell, Aeneas' "confused mind was seized by fear" (*Aen.* 2.735: *trepido ... confusam eripuit mentem*), causing him to lose Creusa; here, Turnus is *confusus* by the chaos around him, and he is also about to lose a bride (*Aen.* 12.937: *tua est Lavinia coniunx*, "Lavinia is your bride"). In this regard, Turnus not only plays the role of Hector to Aeneas' Achilles, but he also reflects the impotent earlier version of Aeneas himself.[107]

While Aeneas appears to be transformed into the Greek destroyer of his former home, he is nevertheless fighting this war in Italy in order to secure his claim to a new home. In conflating the roles of Hector and Achilles as keeper of the home and private avenger respectively, Aeneas is following the Odyssean example that underlies the representation of Neoptolemus in Book 2. The inversion of Achilles' anger, or more specifically, the lack of any Achillean gesture of reconciliation at the end of Book 12, reflects Aeneas' assimilation of Neoptolemus' degeneracy, his literal falling away from the *genus* of Achilles. Virgil locates the ultimate source for that transformation in the portrait of Odysseus as simultaneous defender and avenger in his own palace, but he uses the figure of Neoptolemus in Book 2 to embody the application of Odyssean ruthlessness to Achillean vengeance. At the same time, he uses other elements of the *Odyssey* to refract the Iliadic correspondences in the second half of the poem. Thus, early on in Book 7, Virgil tells us that Lavinia has many suitors, but that Turnus is the most handsome by far (*Aen.* 7.54–56): *multi illam magno e Latio totaque petebant / Ausonia; petit ante alios pulcherrimus omnis / Turnus* ("many men sought her from great Latium and all of Ausonia; Turnus, most handsome of all the others, sought her, too").[108] This equates him with Antinous, Penelope's chief suitor, whose good looks are contrasted with his intelligence on two occasions (*Od.* 17.381, 454).[109] Even before Juno and Amata declare Aeneas to be a false suitor like Paris, Virgil is already preparing us for the inevitable Odyssean reclamation of home and wife by Aeneas.

In killing Turnus, Aeneas essentially enacts an Achillean vengeance through the ethical lens of the *Odyssey*. His unbridled rage and unrepentant attitude is, like Odysseus' own response, not just specific retribution against his victim, but also an attempt to ensure his own survival in the aftermath of that retribution through a display of maximum force. After his own conspicuous failures to act in the *Iliad* and during the fall of Troy depicted in *Aeneid* 2, Aeneas adopts the Odyssean paradigm in order to guarantee his future survival. As we saw in Book 3, asserting his ability to survive is a key part of Aeneas' own narration, but there it is clearly distinguished from Odysseus' selfish type of survival. Aeneas depicts himself as both an ideal survivor and one who can ensure the safety of his own people. If Odysseus cannot bring even a single crewman home, it is not surprising that he also cannot restrain himself and keep a single suitor or maid alive. His personal survival instinct overrides all consideration for the welfare of his household or kingdom. Aeneas does manage to ensure the survival of most of his Trojans on the way "home" to Italy, but as the predictions of Jupiter and Anchises show, he must also preserve them for the Roman future, which means integrating them into the Latin population. The lessons he learns at sea are supposed to prepare him for this unifying task, but Aeneas raises doubts about his abilities by choosing a dangerous model for his vengeance. In the end, the legend of Aeneas founding Rome *met' Odusseô* proves to be a disturbing commentary on Aeneas' lack of self-restraint, and by extension on the destiny of the Roman people. At the same time, Virgil demonstrates that his own complex dialogue with the Homeric poems can lead to troubling interpretations. But then, we do not always like what we see in the mirror.

Notes

NOTES TO CHAPTER 1

1. See *OLD* s.v. deff. 1, 4, 5.
2. For detailed discussions on this issue, see Conte 1986; Thomas 1986; Hinds 1998, 17–21, 46–51; Edmunds 2001, 19–38.
3. On types of *imitatio* in Latin literature generally, see Reiff 1959; West and Woodman 1979.
4. See Conte (1999, 27–28), who actually interprets the priority of the two goals in reverse: "his first aim was *Augustum laudare a parentibus* . . ." On the similarly axiomatic nature of this second goal in the history of Virgilian scholarship, see Thomas 2001, 25–54.
5. On the privileging of Greek literature in general and Homer in particular over the Latin classics in the English and German traditions, see Habinek 1992; Pfeiffer 1976; Wilamowitz 1982; Conte 1999, 17–18; Selden 2006; Simonsuuri 1979.
6. In a letter to Thomas Moore, dated April 11th, 1817 (Marchand 1976, 211). Cf. Coleridge's famous statement: "If you take from Virgil his diction and metre, what do you leave him?" (Wooding 1990, 240).
7. See Knauer 1981, 871–74.
8. The terminology was first introduced by C.S. Lewis in his *Preface to Paradise Lost* (Lewis 1942). Cf. also W.H. Auden's famous attack on Virgil in the poem "Secondary Epic" (Auden 1991, 598).
9. Newton 1672, 5095.
10. See Fowler 1997, 26–27; Edmunds 2001, 159–63.
11. All citations from Homer are from Allen and Monro 1920. Cf. also the similar prophecy in *Homeric Hymn to Aphrodite* 196–97.
12. All citations of Virgil are from Mynors 1969 unless otherwise noted. The similarity between these two pairs of lines was recognized as early as Macrobius (*Saturnalia* 5.3.8).
13. On the question of Poseidon's words as a *post eventum* prophecy in the *Iliad*, see Smith 1981; Casali 2010, 40–41.
14. Cf. Williams 1962, 76. For the opposing view that Virgil based his line on the preexisting variant reading, see Horsfall 2006, 108; 1979, 373; Smith 1981, 44n49.
15. But note that Scholia A and T do record a very similar variant: μεταγράφουσί τινες „Αἰνείω γενεὴ πάντεσσιν ἀνάξει", ὡς προθεσπίζοντος τοῦ ποιητοῦ τὴν Ῥωμαίων ἀρχήν. There is no precise way to date these scholia, but there is a general consensus that they reflect the critical tradition of the first century BCE and the first and second centuries CE. See Richardson 1980, 265; Lausberg 1983, 210n28; Wlosok 1986, 83n19–22; Erbse 1960, 171–73. On the

influence of the Homeric scholia on Virgil's work, see the seminal study by Schlunk (1974), and cf. Schmit-Neuerberg 1999; Hexter 2010; Farrell 1997, 222–28; Wlosok 1986; Lausberg 1983, 210.
16. On the textual transmission of Homer and the range of variants see, e.g., West 2001; Haslam 1997; Nagy 1996, 107–52; West 1967; and the still useful Pasquali 1952, 201–47.
17. On the question of Virgil's reading habits, cf. Nelis 2010.
18. Cf. the massive intertextual tradition inspired by the two fluid Sanskrit epics, the *Mahâbhârata* and *Râmâyana* (Ghosh 1963). For the provocative idea that the *Aeneid* may have been influenced by the *Mahâbhârata*, see Lallemand 1959.
19. For the valuable results of these other inquiries, see, among others, Panoussi 2009; Nelis 2001; Clausen 1987; Kopf 1981; George 1974; Wigodsky 1972; Fraenkel 1932; Norden 1915.
20. On "proems in the middle," see Conte 1992; on the framing function of this second proem, see Kyriakidis 1998; on the dual influence of Homer and Apollonius here, see Mariotti 1981.
21. For other early views of the *Aeneid* in a Homeric context, cf. Quint. *Inst.* 10.1.85, 12.11.26; Juvenal 6.436. Cf. Schmit-Neuerberg 1999, 2n6.
22. Even if we count by line number instead of books, the halfway mark in the poem would be 7.193, not 7.36.
23. Cf. Peerlkamp 1843 *ad* 7.37; Gastinel 1926, 90.
24. Cf. Fraenkel 1945, 1.
25. Cf. Harrison 1980, 375–76; Fowler 1989, 95; Hinds 1998, 109.
26. Thomas (1985, 63) notes that similarly delayed invocation to Maecenas in *Georgics* 2.35–46, and argues that the practice is "essentially Alexandrian in nature." Cf. Thomas 2004, 139.
27. But note for now that in this last stage of the journey, Aeneas and his fleet sail past "Odyssean" Circe's island.
28. Cf. Duckworth 1957.
29. Cf. Anderson 1969.
30. Cf. Conway 1928; Stadler 1942.
31. Cf. Knauer 1981, 871–74; 1964, 41–53.
32. On the problem of studies of local contact displacing the study of systematic contact in Latin studies, see Hinds 1998, 101–4.
33. See *OLD* s.v.
34. For *error* as the cause of a mistake, i.e., "deception," cf. *Aen.* 2.412, Livy 22.1.3.
35. The adjective *Iliacus* occurs twenty-four times in the *Aeneid*, of which sixteen are directly connected to things or events at Ilium. Of the remainder, four (4.64, 4.537, 4.658, 5.607) refer to the fleet that has sailed from Ilium, three refer to the Trojan army in Italy (10.635, 11.393, 12.861), and only one applies the term to the actual race of the Trojans (6.875). Compare *Troianus*, which specifically refers only to the homeland in seven out of forty occurrences, and *Teucri*, which refers only to race of people (cf. 10.662 where *Iliacos* and *Teucris* are specifically contrasted). *Iliacus* thus seems to mark the Trojans' relationship to their homeland and especially to the events surrounding the war itself.
36. See *OLD* s.v. def. 2.
37. See *OLD* s.v. deff. 2 and 1.
38. Cf. Virgil's unique use of the word without a genitive, *quantum instar in ipso*, referring to young Marcellus (*Aen.* 6.865). Here it seems to mean something like "presence," which points both to his inherent qualities and to their effect on others.

97. Cf. Fowler 1997, 27.

NOTES TO CHAPTER 2

1. Cf. Rutherford 1993, 37–38; Cairns 1989, 179–82.
2. Plato has a brief discussion on the differences between Achilles and Odysseus as characters (*Hipp. Min.* 363c–65c, 369a–71e), but he does not distinguish between the two poems and all his quoted examples are from the *Iliad*.
3. Cf. Lockwood 1929.
4. Cf. Cic. *Orator* 128, Quint. 6.2.8–24 for ancient formulations of this definition; also on the general contrast cf. Auerbach 1957, 25–27.
5. For the idiom, see Russell 1964 ad loc.
6. The word occurs in extant Greek texts only here and again later in the same passage in the accusative singular.
7. See the passages cited earlier in Chapter 1 n. 65.
8. Cf. Cairns 1989, 180; Bühler 1964, 55; and Russell 1964 ad loc. citing Schol. BT on *Il.* 24.804a, which gives the view of Aristarchus' disciple Menecrates of Nysa that Homer retains the τὰ λοιπὰ...τῶν διηγημάτων [ζητημάτων MS] "the rest of the stories" for the *Odyssey* and that the latter contains τὰ λείψανα of the *Iliad*. For more parallels, cf. also Schol. HQ ad *Od.* 1.284; Schol. E ad *Od.* 4.69; Schol. Q ad *Od.* 4.187; Schol. E ad *Od.* 3.248; also Eustathius *Comm.* ad *Od. proem.* and *Od.* 3.108; and more generally *Certamen* 275f. For more details, see esp. Bühler 1964, 46–55.
9. Cf. *Schol. in Arist. Ran.* 1500:Ἔκθεσις τοῦ δράματος, ὃ καὶ ἐπίλογος καλεῖται. Cf. also *Schol. in Soph. Oed. Tyr.* 1515.
10. Arist. *Rhet.* 1414b1–18, 1419b10–1420a8.
11. On the differences between the *Iliad* and *Odyssey* on the one hand and the Cycle on the other, cf. Griffin 1977; Rutherford 1993, 39–40; and on the Cycle in general, Davies 1987.
12. On the *Odyssey* as a poem of the aftermath, cf. Rutherford 1993, 49–53.
13. In his 1673 treatise *The Rehearsal Transpros'd* (Grosart 1874, 251).
14. Cf. Bassett 1923, 346.
15. On the general relationship between these two episodes, cf. Macleod 1982, 32–34.
16. For *aithe opheles* expressing a regret or wish that cannot be fulfilled, see Chantraine 1963, 228.
17. On the phrase *aisa miunutha*, cf. Slatkin 1991, 37–38.
18. Cf. Slatkin 1986, 7–8 (= Slatkin 1991, 44–45).
19. See *LSJ* s.v.
20. The word is an *hapax legomenon*, but Schol. B defines it as ἐπὶ κακῷ τὸν ἄριστον τεκοῦσα, ἄριστον καὶ δύστηνον. Cf. Schol. A ad loc.; *Etym. Magnum*, *Suda*, Hesychius' *Lexicon* s.v.
21. Cf. *Il.* 9.410–16.
22. Note that Aristophanes, Aristarchus, and Didymus all athetize this line on various grounds (cf. scholion A on *Il.* 19.327).
23. See Schol. T on *Il.* 2.260, ABT on *Il.* 4.354. On the question of Iliadic anticipation of later events in the Trojan cycle including the *Odyssey*, cf. Richardson 1980, 269.
24. There is only a small body of secondary literature on this phrase: Geddes 1878, 46–51; Leaf 1902, i.67–68; Rank 1951, 69; Higbie 1995, 159. On potential wordplay with the name Telemachus here, cf. Martin 1989, 70; Louden 1995, 39.

25. Cf. Higbie 1995; Meyer 1907. On their less frequent use in the *Odyssey*, cf. Scott 1912.
26. But cf. Geddes (1878, 84n5) and Leaf (1902, i.68) who cite the two-word Ibycus fragment *Althaia Meleagris* (PMG 9) as another example.
27. This theory was first proposed by Tylor 1889 who also coined the term *teknonymy*. For other views on the origins of the practice, cf. Steinmetz 1894, 236; Parsons 1914; Lowie 1925, 107–9, 262; Geertz 1964. Note that Leaf (1902, i.67) coins the term *paedonymic* instead, but this term is never used outside of the few secondary references mentioned earlier, which all trace back to his usage.
28. Cf. Finkelberg 1991; Miller 1953, 49–52.
29. On the succession problem in the *Odyssey*, cf. Finkelberg 1991, 306–7; Halverson 1986; Finley 1977, 84–95; Clarke 1963, 129–33.
30. Cf. Heubeck, West, and Hainsworth 1988, 101 citing parallels in Euripides for this sort of abdication.
31. On the inconsistencies of Homeric marriage customs, see Snodgrass 1974.
32. On the naming of Odysseus, see Russo, Fernández-Galiano, and Heubeck 1992, 97; Rank 1951, 52–60; Stanford 1952; Dimock 1956; Austin 1972; Clay 1983, 54–68; Peradotto 1990, 120–42.
33. Diomedes 3.180; Idomeneus 3.191; Big Ajax 3.109; Achilles 3.109; Little Ajax 4.499–511; Agamemnon 1.29, 298–301, 3.193–98, 306–10, 4.512–37.
34. As opposed to *anchemachos* (*Il.* 13.5, 16.248, 272, 17.165). Luc. *Lex.* 12.15 offers the only example of a common noun *têlemachos* in reference to Artemis. On the children of Homeric heroes bearing names related to their fathers' lives, cf. Kamptz 1981, 31–32; Heubeck, West, and Hainsworth 1988, 91–92.
35. Cf. Louden 1995, 37–38; Rank 1951, 68–69; Dimock 1956, 60–62.
36. On this idiom, see de Jong 2001, 419, 248; Combellack 1981; Leaf 1902, i.368.
37. On *êmar*, cf. Fränkel 1960, 5–6; Santiago 1962. For *têlou* = "long ago", see LSJ s.v.
38. See de Jong 2001, 387–89. Also cf. Podlecki 1971, 89; Moulton 1977, 132–33; Foley 1978, 7.
39. For a valuable analysis of Telemachus' "recognition" of Odysseus in this scene, see Pucci 1987, 94–97.
40. None of these meanings suits every occurrence of the word and comparative evidence offers no further help, but the ancient sources at least suggest that the word was understood to be derived from *têle/-ou* and *gignomai*. See further Ciani 1964–65; Stanford 1937.
41. This patronymic only occurs once in any historical period of extant Greek literature: Eustathius *Comm.* ad *Hom. Od.* 1.119.12.
42. Cf. de Jong 2001, 27.
43. Cf. de Jong 2001, 3–4; Olson 1995, 77.
44. Athena as Mentor *Od.* 2.270–78; Nestor 3.122–25; Helen 4.141–46; Menelaus 4.149–50, 611; Odysseus 16.300–10.
45. On Pisistratus' role as a facilitator, see Race 1993, 89–90.
46. On the similarities between Telemachus and Nausicaa, see Belmont 1967; Besslich 1981.
47. These lines are repeated in Thetis' speech to Hephaestus (*Il.* 18.339–441).
48. On the syntax of these lines, see Heubeck and Hoekstra 1989, 89 against which Ahl and Roisman 1996, 131; on the defective verb *apêura*, see Strunk 1958.
49. De Jong 2001, 281 also draws attention to the anaphora, but without further comment.

50. For a similar point with different conclusions, cf. Ahl and Roisman 1996, 304n13. There may be an even stronger accusation lurking in a play on the homonym *mêdea* "genitals," suggesting that his belated return is not just due to his wartime schemes, but also to his amorous adventures of which we have just heard an account regarding Circe, and which will recur with Calypso. In this regard, *pothos* may also refer to his sexual desire, despite the suggestion (Weiss 1998, 32–33) that the word never bears this familiar later meaning in Homer.
51. The only other occurrence of the word is in *Il.* 24.772, where Helen praises Hector for possessing the quality.
52. For the opposing view that Odysseus is not connected with gentleness elsewhere, see Ahl and Roisman 1996, 132, 305n17. But note that they do not cite the Iliadic passages at all.
53. On the poetics of *achos* in the *Iliad* specifically, see Gregory Nagy's valuable chapter "The Name of Achilles" (Nagy 1999, 69–93).
54. See Louden 1995, 33–34. For the proposed etymology of Achilles' name from *achos* and *laos*, see Palmer (1963, 79) and the subsequent discussions in Nagy 1976, Palmer 1979, Palmer 1980, 37–38, Nagy 1994, Nagy 1999, 69–70. For a revised etymology, see Holland 1993.
55. There does not appear to be any difference in meaning between the masculine *pothos* and the feminine *pothê* (cf. Weiss 1998, 32n2 against Gagnepain 1959, 69–70), but the masculine word never occurs in the *Iliad*.
56. Eumaeus' later description of Anticleia's death suggests that her *pothos* was understood by others to be a kind of *achos* (*Od.* 15.358): ἡ δ' ἄχεϊ οὗ παιδὸς ἀπέφθιτο κυδαλίμοιο ("she died in grief over her glorious son").
57. Cf. *OED* s.v.: "The current spelling *ache* is erroneous; the vb. being historically *ake*... Dr. Johnson is mainly responsible: ignorant of the history of the words, and erroneously deriving them from the Gr. ἄχος (with which they have no connexion) he declared them 'more grammatically written *ache*.'"
58. Cf. *Od.* 20.53, where Athena reassures an impatient Odysseus: κακῶν δ' ὑποδύσεαι ἤδη ("you will soon emerge from your troubles").
59. The lengthened form *theîon* also occurs once at *Od.* 22.493, when Eurycleia actually brings the sulphur. On the etymology of *theeion* and related forms, see Russo, Fernández-Galiano, and Heubeck 1992, 306–7.
60. Even in the "Cretan" tale that he recounts to Eumaeus, the ship's destruction is attributed to Zeus' wrathful thunderbolt (*Od.* 14.305–6). On the description of thunderbolts in Homer, cf. Hainsworth 1958, 55.
61. For other expressions of Achilles' overwhelming *achos*, cf. *Il.* 19.8, 57, 307, 367, 23.137, 167.
62. Cf. also *Il.* 18.330–35.
63. On the arrival of Achilles, cf. de Jong 2001, 289; Edwards 1985, 47–48; Heubeck and Hoekstra 1989, 105.
64. Note that Nestor arranges the order so that he can end his description with his own son Antilochus. Cf. de Jong 2001, 76.
65. Cf. *Od.* 24.78–79: χωρὶς δ' Ἀντιλόχοιο, τὸν ἔξοχα τῖες ἁπάντων / τῶν ἄλλων ἑτάρων μετὰ Πάτροκλόν γε θανόντα ("and apart from those of Antilochus, whom you valued above all your other companions after Patroclus died").
66. As well as his cousin in some traditions (cf. Pindar *Isthm.* 6.19–27; Apollod. 3.12.6; Plut. *Thes.* 10.3; Schol. ad Eur. *Andr.* 687; Schol. ad Pind. *Nem.* 5.12.). For an explicit alternate tradition attributed to Pherecydes, also cf. Apollod. 3.12.6. The Homeric poems themselves take no stand on the issue.
67. This exact Iliadic phrase is used by Odysseus in his encounter with Ajax a few lines later at *Od.* 11.550–51, while the alternate form reappears at *Od.* 24.18.

124 Notes

68. See Dowden 1996, 58; cf. also Willcock 1987, 191; Kullman 1960, 316; Bethe 1914, 100.
69. Various other details of this story are described in Pind. *Pyth.* 6.28–39; Quint. Smyrn. 2.244–548; Apollod. epit. 5.1–6; Philostr. *Imag.* 2.7.
70. The prevalent view has been that the *Iliad* is familiar with some form of the *Aethiopis* material, with the main dispute being whether that material took the form of the *Aethiopis* poem attributed to Arctinus and summarized by Proclus. The most useful extensive studies of the relationship are Schoeck 1961 and Kullman 1960, but see also Dowden 1996; Erbse 1993; Willcock 1987; Willcock 1983; Kullman 1981; Willcock 1973; Schadewaldt 1951, 155–202; Kakridis 1949, 93–95; Pestalozzi 1945.
71. The content of these lines resemble, but do not necessarily contradict, *Il.* 24.574–75, where Achilles is said to honor Automedon and Alcimus beyond all others after the death of Patroclus. However, Pestalozzi 1945, 24 condemns them as inauthentic; cf. also Dowden 1996, 57n50.
72. Cf. Edwards 1985, 48; on Achilles' withdrawal in the *Aethiopis*, see Schoeck 1961, 1–3.
73. Whether *katestuge* means "hated intensely" or "was horrified at" as the context seems to demand in the only other occurrence of the verb when Odysseus' crew encounter the queen of the Laestrygonians (*Od.* 10.112–13: τὴν δὲ γυναῖκα / εὗρον ὅσην τ' ὄρεος κορυφήν, κατὰ δ' ἔστυγον αὐτήν, "and they found a woman as big as a mountain top, and they were horrified at her"), the entire phrase seems to be an inversion of Hector's happy response to Paris' willingness to enter single combat in Book 3 (*Il.* 3.76) and then to Helenus' suggestion that he himself participate in such combat in Book 7 (*Il.* 7.54):Ὣς ἔφαθ', Ἕκτωρ δ' αὖτ' ἐχάρη μέγα μῦθον ἀκούσας ("thus he spoke, and Hector heard his word and rejoiced").
74. Cf. *Il.* 23.222–23, where Achilles' mourning for Patroclus is compared to a father mourning his son.
75. Note that the last line and two feet also describe Eurycleia's tearful recognition of Odysseus' scar (*Od.* 19.471–72), which further supports the notion that this kind of emotional reaction is associated with figures who feel a sense of responsibility for the other person.
76. Although Antilochus' killing of the Trojan Atymnius earlier in Book 16 appears to be inspired by Patroclus' leadership in the battle (cf. Willcock 1983, 479).
77. This is not incompatible with the suggestion of Schol. A ad loc.: πολλῷ περιπαθέστερον ἄνοπλον ὄντα καὶ τρέχοντα παραστῆναι τῷ Ἀχιλλεῖ ("he inspires much more *pathos* because he runs off unarmed to stand by Achilles").
78. Cf. Whitehead 1984, 122.
79. Again Proclus' summary of the *Aethiopis* (*Chr.* 193–95) adds further details about the recovery of the body (cf. Willcock 1987, 192). For the view that the details of the battle described in the *Aethiopis* would have been quite similar to the Patroclus episode, see Fenik 1968, 232–33.
80. The Odyssean version of the description (with the necessary shift to the third person) is also used to describe the death of Cebriones, Hector's charioteer (*Il.* 16.775–76). For the view that all three passages containing "this most impressive epitaph in the *Iliad*" (Willcock 1976, 189) echo a pre-Homeric passage referring to Achilles, cf. Pestalozzi 1945, 18; Schadewaldt 1951, 168n65; Kullman 1960, 38. For the opposing view that the phrase originally described Cebriones and was then extended to Achilles, cf. Russo, Fernández-Galiano, and Heubeck 1992, 364.
81. Cf. Whitehead 1984, 121; Whitman 1958, 202; Kakridis 1949, 65–95.
82. The scholia offer two alternative intepretations of this emotional moment in order to avoid the notion that Achilles is actually contemplating suicide:

Schol. A *ad* 18.34, that Antilochus feared that Achilles might cut his (Antilochus') throat; Schol. bT *ad* 18.34, that Achilles feared that Hector might cut the head off Patroclus' corpse. Even if we do not believe that the reference to Ajax's death at *Od.* 11.548–51 refers to his suicide, Menelaus wishes he were dead when he learns about Agamemnon's murder (*Od.* 4.539–40) and Odysseus also considers suicide after the disastrous Aeolus episode (*Od.* 10.50–52), so it is not so far-fetched that a Homeric hero might try to kill himself. On *autothanasia* in general, see van Hooff 1990.
83. The identical phrases occur as follows: *Pêleiadeô Achilêos*: *Il.* 1.1, 322, 9.166, 16.269, 653, 24.406; *amumona Pêleiôna*: *Il.* 2.674, 770, 9.181, 9.698, 10.323, 17.280, 22.278; *podôkeos Aiakidao*: *Il.* 2.860, 874, 16.134, 165, 865, 17.388, 486, 23.28. Examples of two different names for the hero appearing in close succession include: *Il.* 2.769–70, 874–75, 16.165–66, 22.277–78.
84. Cf. Whitehead 1984, 121 on the appearance of Achilles in the second underworld scene (*Od.* 24.15–18), where lines 15b–18 are identical to 11.467b–70 here. Note, however, that the line that completes the patronymic triplet (11.471) does not occur in the later passage.
85. For a different reading of this passage in support of the same point about the enmity between Ajax and Odysseus, see Ahl and Roisman 1996, 145.
86. I cite only the parts of the passage that are directly relevant to my argument. My brief analysis of this scene mainly follows Pucci (1987, 145–47), who offers fuller details about the mechanics of the simile itself.
87. On Homeric lion similes in general, cf. Lonsdale 1990a; Friedrich 1981; Scott 1974, 58–62; Fränkel 1921.
88. For details on the disputes concerning the meanings of these two epithets, see Pucci 1987, 59n14–15.
89. *Polymêtis* is only used to describe Odysseus, and among the Achaeans, *megas* belongs exclusively to Ajax. The distribution of these epithets in the poems is so wide as to render any judgment about their function here tenuous at best, but they do nicely underscore the contrast between the two heroic modes.
90. The meanings of *kerdos* and its derivatives fall into two semantic categories: "profit" and "skill." In the Homeric poems, the plural form *kerdea* almost always means skill, with the specific nature of the skill provided by the context. Thus when there is some artifice or trickery involved, *kerdea* means something like "cunning or craftiness" as in *Od.* 2.88, 13.297, 299, 20.257, 23.217 and possibly also *Il.* 23.322, 515. On the semantics of *kerdea* and related words, see Roisman 1990 (esp. 23–24); Wheeler 1988, 245–49; Cozzo 1988; Roisman 1987, 66–67; Bamberger 1976 (esp. 1–10); Seiler 1973.
91. Cf. Gardiner 1905, 24 and Leaf 1902 ad loc., who both cite Pausanias' (8.40) description of a similar situation in a boxing match: Creuges and Damoxenus agree to strike one another in turn without defending themselves.
92. Cf. Helen's description at *Il.* 3.202 and Agamemnon's insult at *Il.* 4.339.
93. Cf. Pucci 1987, 147.
94. For an analysis of the narrative structure of the Ajax encounter, see de Jong 2001, 292–93.
95. For the legalistic imagery, cf. the description of the murder arbitration on the shield of Achilles (*Il.* 18.497–508).
96. For the view that the story of the contest is pre-Homeric, see Kullman 1960, 79–84; on the Cyclic version, cf. Bethe 1922, 168–73.
97. Cf. Ahl and Roisman 1996, 146.
98. These lines have often been criticized as an interpolation: see Schwartz 1924, 319; Wilamowitz 1884, 141–42. For the view that Odysseus' curiosity about the other shades compels him to move on, see Heubeck and Hoekstra 1989,

111; Focke 1943, 222–24. For the view that these lines are an attempt to save face after being rebuffed, see de Jong 1992, 5; Eisenberger 1973, 184.
99. See Austin 1975, 53. For the important qualification that this only applies universally to the *Odyssey* and a brief discussion of the Iliadic contexts, see Pucci 1987, 33–34.
100. On *schetlios* as a compliment, cf. Ahl and Roisman 1996, 143; as an insult, cf. Edwards 1985, 49–50; Stanford 1965 ad loc.
101. *Od.* 10.526 where Circe tells Odysseus to make offerings to the *nekroi* when he arrives in Hades; *Od.* 11.34 where he carries out those instructions; *Od.* 11.632 where the hordes of ghosts gathering around Odysseus cause him to flee; also *Il.* 23.51 is an ambiguous case. Cf. the use of *nekus*, which is distributed more widely between the meanings of "corpse" and "dead person."
102. *Kamontôn* is also used to refer to the dead at *Il.* 3.278. For more on this phrase, see Bergold 1977, 86–87.
103. This is true even of the other living veterans in the *Odyssey*: Nestor is relegated even more than in the *Iliad* to a life of perpetual reminiscence, while Menelaus coasts through middle age with the help of Helen's analgesic *nepenthe*.
104. According to Circe, only Tiresias still possesses his *phrenes* in Hades (*Od.* 10.493).
105. Cf. Odysseus' description of Heracles in the underworld (*Od.* 11.601–3), though this passage is usually thought to be an interpolation. Cf. Hexter 1993, 156–57; Heubeck and Hoekstra 1989, 110–11, 114.
106. The only other occurrence of the line also involves such an attempt, when Patroclus pleads with Achilles to aid the Achaeans (*Il.* 16.21).
107. For a different, but compatible analysis of this scene, cf. Pucci 1987, 166–69.
108. On the word *phertatos* in Homer, cf. Nagy 1999, 26n2; Palmer 1955, 11–12.
109. "Throw down": *Il.* 1.458, 2.421, 23.255, *Od.* 3.447; "hurl together": *Il.* 11.529, *Od.* 5.331.
110. Cf. Pucci 1979, 122.
111. Cf. Rutherford 1986, 149.
112. On the irreverence of *gaster* in this somber context, see Pucci 1987, 168 and cf. Leaf 1902 ad loc.
113. The phrase *nêlei thumôi* is also used of the Cyclops at *Od.* 9.272, 287, 938.
114. On the Hesiodic qualities of Odysseus' advice in *Iliad* 19, see Codino 1965, 112.
115. Cf. Heubeck and Hoekstra 1989, 106.
116. For the provocative suggestion that he may actually be dead, or even lord of the dead, in *Il.* 24 in light of the katabasis-like journey of Priam, see Dowden (1996, 58), who cites Hommel 1980.
117. Cf. Louden 1995, 34n20; Rank 1951, 42.
118. *Il.* 18.61–62, 442–43; 23.46–47. See my earlier discussion of these passages.
119. Cf. Pucci 1987, 167.
120. LSJ suggest "speak lightly of" for this passage; Merry 1887, 129 offers "console"; likewise, Ameis, Hentze, and Cauer (1928 ad loc.) paraphrase it as ". . . jemandem durch Zuspruch etwas annehmbar zu machen suchen . . ."; Heubeck and Hoekstra 1989, 106 give "Do not try to reconcile me to death!"
121. Cf. Edwards 1985, 50–52; Rüter 1969, 252–53; Hölscher 1967, 7–8; Reinhardt 1960, 108–9.
122. This word is *hapax legomenon*, but it should literally mean "someone living on the earth," and may echo Achilles' description of himself as *etôsion achthos arourês* ("a useless weight on the earth," *Il.* 18.104), see Heubeck and

Hoekstra 1989, 106; Stanford 1965 ad loc., but also cf. the suitors' similar comment about Odysseus disguised as a beggar (*Od.* 20.379).
123. On the contrary-to-fact condition here, see Schmiel (1987, 36–37), who cites the only three other occurrences of this type of *bouloimên* formulation as evidence (*Il.* 23.592–95, *Od.* 3.232–35, 16.106–7).
124. Cf. Edwards 1985, 59; for details on Achilles as the *promos* of all the Achaeans, cf. Edwards 1984, 61–65.
125. Cf. Ahl and Roisman 1996, 144; Edwards 1985, 65.

NOTES TO CHAPTER 3

1. To repeat my earlier data from Chapter 1, the only Trojans mentioned in the *Odyssey* are: Deiphobus (4.276, 8.518), Cassandra (11.422), Priam (3.107, 130, 5.106, 11.533, 13.316, 14.241, 22.230 all in periphrastic phrases for the city Troy, and 11.421 as a parental genitive with the one occurrence of Cassandra).
2. On this repetition, see the classic account by Lord 1960, 186.
3. On symmetrical composition in Odysseus' wandering tales, see Most 1989; Scully 1987; Redfield 1983; Niles 1978; cf. also the earlier Whitman 1958; Germain 1954, 332–33.
4. To this point and the following comment on the Laertes episode it can certainly be objected, following the famous scholiast's comment on *Od.* 23.296, that Book 24 is not an original part of the poem. On this long controversy, see the excellent overview and bibliography in Russo, Fernández-Galiano, and Heubeck (1992, 342–45 and 354–55), and cf. also West 1989; Oswald 1993. For my purposes in this chapter, the solution to this problem is not crucial since Virgil surely had Book 24 in his text, but his reading of that book could certainly have been influenced by the Alexandrian opinions. On Virgil and the scholia, see Schlunk 1974; Schmit-Neuerburg 1999. It is worth noting, however, that there are several lines in *Odyssey* 24 that have been posited over the centuries as "sources" for passages in the *Aeneid* (cf. Knauer 1964, 526–27).
5. E.g., Wilamowitz 1927, 82; Scheliha 1943, 19–20; Kirk 1962, 250; Ahl and Roisman 1996, 275, 314n1. In defense of Odysseus, cf. Focke 1943, 378; Kakridis 1971, 160–61; Stanford 1965, 216–18.
6. See de Jong 2001, 576 for the compatible view that this deception serves to lend greater dramatic weight to the reunion scene.
7. On the legends concerning Odysseus' death, see Hartmann 1917.
8. On Odysseus' potential unreliability as a narrator, cf. Most 1989 and 1985. On the veracity of Odysseus' tales in particular, cf. Richardson 1996; Parry 1994; Alden 1992, 9–14; Peradotto 1990, 92–93; Murnaghan 1987, 172–73; Griffin 1980, 48–49.
9. Quint 1993.
10. Ibid. 9.
11. Ibid. 376n1 citing the first Renaissance theorists of Romance, Giovambattista Pigna (1554, 23–24) and Giovambattista Giraldi Cinzi (1564, 65). See further Weinberg 1961, 445, 970.
12. See especially his second chapter, "Repetition and Ideology in the *Aeneid*" (Quint 1993, 50–96).
13. Ibid. 51.
14. Ibid. 45.
15. Cf. *Il.* 15.68–71 for a potential allusion. For the Cyclical accounts of the horse in the *Ilias Parva* and the *Ilioupersis*, see Proclus' summaries (*Chr.* 205–75). On the story in the *Odyssey*, see Andersen 1977.

128   Notes

16. This is true of other Latin poets as well: cf. Hor. *Carm.* 1.6.6; Prop. 2.22.34; Ov. *Met.* 12.605; Stat. *Silv.* 2.7.97; Juv. 3.280.
17. On these forms in Homer, cf. Higbie 1995, 6–7, 51–52. Note that while most of the occurrences of *Aiakidês* refer to Achilles, the name is also applied to Peleus three times (*Il.* 16.15, 18.433, 21.189). Cf. Shive 1987, 42.
18. Fifty-two instances and twelve more of the longer forms beginning in *Pêlêiad-*.
19. Cf. my discussion in Chapter 2 of *têlemachos* as an appropriate epithet for Odysseus. Kenney (1979, 224n6) makes the different, but perhaps compatible, point that Neoptolemus "usurps" his father's patronymic. Horsfall (2008, 232) argues against Kenney, citing Vinchesi (1984–91) for the "remarkable flexibility" of the patronymic in Virgil.
20. Cf. Knauer 1964, 380; Austin 1964 ad loc.; Horsfall 2008, 362.
21. See Bowie 1990, 471. On Achillean light imagery and in its associations with future victory, cf. Whitman 1958, 128–53.
22. The name does not appear in Greek poetry until Theocritus (15.40), but according to Pausanias (10.26.4), it was used in the Cyclical *Cypria*. For the history of the name and its use in the *Aeneid*, see O'Hara 1996, 133; Kenney 1979, 105–12; Austin 1964 ad loc.; Mørland 1960, 24; Rank 1951, 92–93; Knox 1950, 394; Wijdeveld 1942.
23. Knox 1950, 393–95. The point about *novus* should be weighed against the fact that this line is identical to Verg. *G.* 3.437 (cf. Thomas 1986, 183). For other accounts of the rebirth imagery, cf. Mills 1978.162–63, Bowie 1990, 471; Hornsby 1970, 62; West 1969, 42. On this simile more generally, cf. Putnam 1965, 33–35; Kenney 1979, 106–9; Williams 1983, 256–57; Scafoglio 2001, 200; Schwarz 1983, 448; Briggs 1980, 63, 66–67.
24. Cf. Knox 1950, 394; Mills 1978, 162.
25. In his four appearances in the *Iliad*, he is a swift watchman (*Il.* 2.791–94), he pulls his wounded brother Deiphobus to safety (*Il.* 13.533–35), kills the Greek Echius with no particular distinction (*Il.* 15.339), and is included in Priam's angry rant against his surviving sons after Hector's death (*Il.* 24.250).
26. On Neoptolemus completing his father's work, cf. Smith 1999, 248; Putnam 1965, 33–37.
27. Cf. Carnes 2001, 103.
28. On the differences between Priam's depiction of Achilles here and the portrait on the temple walls, cf. Smith 1999, 248–50.
29. See Carnes 2001, 101–2.
30. On the significance of the name in general, see Mühlestein 1971, 46–47. Eupeithes' rhetorical ability is evident in his speech to mobilize the Ithacans against Odysseus, which ends with this clever wordplay: ἀλλ' Εὐπείθει / πείθοντ' (*Od.* 24.465–66). Cf. Janko 1988, 219.
31. For a different account of the contrast with the Iliadic ending, cf. Cairns 1989, 200.
32. Stanford (1965 ad *Od.* 24.439f.) points out that Eupeithes deserves to die at the end of the poem because he fails to return the favor Odysseus once did for him.
33. Bowie 1990, 471n13 raises the point that this transference of the simile from "victim to victor" has not been explained by commentators.
34. For an early account of this etymology, see Schol. T ad *Il.* 24.730. On wordplay in the *Iliad* involving the etymology, see Louden 1995, 29.
35. The word *polites* occurs as a common noun at *Il.* 15.558, 22.429; *Od.* 7.131, 17.206. Cf. Paschalis 1997, 89; Mørland 1968, 65–66; and for a more different interpretation of the name's significance in this passage, cf. Bowie 1990, 476n52.

36. See especially the various periphrastic phrases for Troy as "city of Priam" in Homer: *Priamoio poli-s/n* (*Il.* 1.19, 12.15, 13.14, 18.288, 22.165, *Od.* 3.130, 11.533, 13.316); *Priamou polin* (*Il.* 2.37); *poli-s/n Priamoio* (*Il.* 2.373, 4.18, 4.290); *polin Priamou* (*Od.* 14.241); (*Priamoio...polis*: *Il.* 12.11); *astu mega Priamoio* (*Il.* 2.332, 2.803, 7.296, 9.278, 16.448, 17.160, 21.309, 22.251, *Od.* 3.107); *astu...Priamoio* (*Il.* 22.173, 230, *Od.* 5.106). For Priam as a symbol for Troy in the *Aeneid*, cf. the following phrases: *Priami regna* (*Aen.* 2.22, 12.545); *Priami arx alta* (2.56); *Priami imperio Phrygibusque* (2.191); *patriae Priamoque* (2.291); *res Asiae Priamique...gentem* (3.1); *Priami tecta* (4.343); and see Bowie 1990, 472n21; Pomathios 1987, 25.
37. Cf. Putnam 1965, 172–75.
38. On scenes of taunting in the *Aeneid*, see Highet 1972, 116–17. Horsfall (2008, 413–14) argues against reading any sarcasm in this reply.
39. The *figura etymologica* of *genitori . . . degenerem* reinforces this notion.
40. Cf. Knauer 1964, 381; Bowie 1990, 472; Horsfall 2008, 415.
41. Cf. Carnes 2001, 102.
42. Virgil elsewhere uses the phrase *sine nomine* to mean "nameless" (*Aen.* 6.776), "inglorious, unrenowned" (*Aen.* 11.846), and, as in the case of Priam's corpse, a combination of the two (*Aen.* 9.343). Cf. Serv. ad *Aen.* 2.557: "SINE NOMINE: sine agnitione, aut sine dignitate. aut simpliciter 'sine nomine'; a capite enim quis nomen ducit?" ("SINE NOMINE: without acknowledgment or without honor; or simply, 'without a name.' For who can derive a name from a head?")
43. Carnes (2001) argues that Neoptolemus' brief speech borrows from, and subverts, the conventions of the epinician genre, especially as reflected in the odes of Pindar. In that context, "[s]ending a message to the dead is *tour de force*, an illustration of the poet's power to grant his patrons immortal glory. Typically the victor's dead father is the intended recipient of the message" (Carnes 2001, 102).
44. He is described in the *Aeneid* as *durus* (2.7), *pellax* (2.90), *scelerum inventor* (2.164), *dirus* (2.261, 762), *saevus* (3.273), and *fandi fictor* (9.602). Cf. Cairns 1989, 193–94.
45. See Austin 1964, 198, who draws attention to the similarity between the line that introduces the scene (*Aen.* 2.506: *forsitan et Priami fuerint quae fata requiras*, ("and perhaps you ask what was Priam's fate"), and the typical first question put to a messenger in Greek tragedy, e.g., Eur. *El.* 772–73; Soph. *El.* 679; Eur. *Med.* 1134. Cf. Austin 1959, 16, 20.
46. On Aeneas' "evanescent, or diluted, viewpoint" in his narration of this scene, see Reed 2007, 179–80.
47. On the long debate regarding the authenticity of this passage, see Goold 1970; Austin 1964, 217–19; Austin 1961. Heinze (1915, 49–51) proposes that it replaces an original episode by Virgil in which Aeneas debates about whether to kill himself by his own hand or by attempting to avenge Priam's death. While he can offer no actual evidence that this episode existed, his theory does reflect the strong uneasiness that Aeneas' inaction generates.
48. Cf. Carnes (2001, 103): "the *Aeneid* speech occurs at an earlier point in the fictive narrative history of the Trojan war, and thus ostentatiously preempts the apparently truthful and unironic praise of Odysseus." While I believe that Odysseus' praise is quite ironic, in that he claims to be extolling Neoptolemus as the son of great Achilles but actually uses his account to praise his own role as a surrogate father and victor in the war, Virgil's preemptive strategy certainly calls into question the truthfulness of Odysseus' account.
49. Note that even Aeneas' story at Carthage takes place at an earlier point in Homeric history than Odysseus' tale to the Phaeacians, since only seven

years have passed since the end of the war (cf. *Aen.* 1.755), while Odysseus is in his tenth year of wandering.
50. E.g., *Aen.* 2.298–308; 604–7; 735–36. Cf. Carnes 2001, 101, 111.
51. Cf. Aristotle's explanation of the length of Odysseus' narration (*Rhet.* 1417a12–15): ἔτι πεπραγμένα δεῖ λέγειν ὅσα μὴ πραττόμενα ἢ οἶκτον ἢ δείνωσιν φέρει· παράδειγμα ὁ Ἀλκίνου ἀπόλογος, ὃς πρὸς τὴν Πηνελόπην ἐν ἑξήκοντα ἔπεσιν πεποίηται ("further, we must only speak of past events that cause pity or indignation by being described in the present. The story of Alcinous is an example [of a brief retelling], when it is told again to Penelope in sixty verses.") On the purpose of Odysseus' storytelling to the Phaeacians, see Most 1989.
52. Cf. Williams 1972, 251; Austin 1964, 559.
53. *Aen.* 2.787 alludes to her as Priam's daughter. For explicit statements of the lineage, cf. Dion. Hal. *Ant. Rom.* 3.31.4; schol. Lycophr. 1263; Apollod. *Bibl.* 3.12.5; Hygin. *fab.* 90.
54. Cf. Knauer 1964, 381; Austin 1964, 218; Horsfall 2008, 425.
55. This trope will be activated again when Aeneas recalls his father's image in similar terms (*Aen.* 10.824: *mentem patriae subiit pietatis imago*, "the image of my father rose to my mind") after he kills Lausus, the son of Mezentius, and declines the privilege of stripping his armor.
56. Cf. Mills 1978, 166.
57. Cf. Smith 1999, 251–52; Williams 1983, 249–50; and more generally on the reprisal, Horsfall 2006, 263; Quint 1993, 59–60; Cartault 1926, 246n3.
58. On the Oresteia story in the *Odyssey*, see D'Arms and Hulley 1946; Hommel 1955; Hölscher 1967 and 1989, 297–310; Lesky 1967, 5–21; Clarke 1967, 10–12; Friedrich 1975, 86–87; Felson-Rubin 1994, 95–107; Katz 1991, 29–53; Olson 1990 and 1995, 25–42.
59. Cf. Carnes 2001, 101; Fowler 1990, 51.
60. Cf. her similar assertion at *Od.* 6.277–79.
61. For various theories concerning this reticence, see Ahl and Roisman 1996, 71–72; Goldhill 1991, 24–37; Murnaghan 1987, 8; Friedrich 1975, 42–43; Fenik 1974, 7–55; Dolin 1973, 274; Kilb 1973, 78; Austin 1972, 5; Rose 1969, 391; Besslich 1966, 60–69; Reinhardt 1960, 116–17; Schadewaldt 1959, 13–20; Mattes 1958, 151–63; Hölscher 1939, 67–68.
62. Cf. de Jong 2001, 181; Ahl and Roisman 1996, 72; Besslich 1966, 42–47. On indirect dialogue in the *Odyssey*, cf. Hölscher 1989, 128–30; Hohendahl-Zoetelief 1980, 170–73; Fenik 1974, 68–71.
63. Cf. Ahl and Roisman 1996, 75.
64. This is sometimes called a "mirror story." Cf. de Jong 2001, 184; de Jong 1985, 6; Létoublon 1983, 24–27. Note the numerous verbatim (or near-verbatim) repetitions of the earlier narrative: 7.249–51 = 5.131–33; 7.256–57 = 5.135–36; 7.266 = 5.268; 7.267–68 = 5.278–79; 7.281–82 = 5.442–43.
65. I am not making any particular claims here about separate authorship of the Homeric poems. The *Odyssey* uses Demodocus as a way to distinguish between an Iliadic and an Odyssean representation of Odysseus, regardless of who composed these descriptions.
66. On this passage, see Edwards 1985, 11–13; Maehler 1963, 16–17. Cf. also the descriptions of competition in Hesiod's *Works and Days* 23–26, 654–59, *Homeric Hymn to Apollo* 146–52, 160–61, 169–76, and Peabody 1975, 268–72, who proposes that the entire *Works and Days* was a contest song.
67. On the character doublets, cf. Fenik 1974, 172–207. On singers in Homer in general, cf. Segal 1992; Ford 1992, 90–130; Goldhill 1991, 49–68; Ritook 1989; de Jong 1987, 44–53; Poetscher 1986; Thalmann 1984, 157–84; Murray 1981 and 1983; Svenbro 1976, 16–45; Harriott 1969, 24–46; Maehler 1963, 21–34; Fränkel 1962, 6–27; Schadewaldt 1959, 66–86; Lanata 1954–56.

68. For various interpretations of the first song, cf. Finkelberg 1987; Nagy 1999, 42–58; Olson 1995, 56; Goldhill 1991, 50; Taplin 1990; Clay 1983, 97–106, 241–46; Rüter 1969, 247–54; Marg 1956.
69. Cf. Nagy 1999, 57–58; Macleod 1983, 4–9; Rüter 1969, 247–54; Marg 1956, 16–29.
70. Cf. Ahl and Roisman 1996, 84.
71. Note that in his discussion of the third type of recognition, the kind due to memory, Aristotle cites the tale of Alcinous as one of his examples (Arist. *Poet*. 1455a): καὶ ἡ ἐν Ἀλκίνου ἀπολόγῳ, ἀκούων γὰρ τοῦ κιθαριστοῦ καὶ μνησθεὶς ἐδάκρυσεν, ὅθεν ἀνεγνωρίσθησαν ("and in the story of Alcinous, where Odysseus hears the bard on the cithara, remembers, and weeps, whence they recognize him"). Either there was an alternate version of the story in which Alcinous instantly recognizes Odysseus from his tears, precisely as Menelaus recognizes Telemachus earlier in the poem (*Od*. 4.116–19), or Aristotle may be suggesting that Alcinous' ignorance was feigned.
72. *Od*. 7.61–63, 146, 205–6 show that Odysseus is aware of Alcinous' relationship to the Cyclopes and Poseidon. Furthermore, Polyphemus would be half-brother to Alcinous' father, Nausithous (Ahl 1989, 14).
73. The motif of a guest remembering his host occurs elsewhere in the *Odyssey* as well: 4.591–92, 8.461–62, 467–68, 15.54–55, 125–28, 181, 19.332–34. Cf. de Jong 2001, 198–99.
74. Cf. the references to Phoenicians and Thesprotians in his longest lying tale to Eumaeus (*Od*. 14.192–359, repeated by Eumaeus at 16.61–67 and 17.522–27). On the lying tales and their relationship to the narrated adventures of Odysseus, see Olson 1995, 129–31; Reece 1993; Pratt 1993, 85–94; Goldhill 1991, 36–48; Hölscher 1989, 210–34; Emlyn-Jones 1986; Haft 1984; Maronitis 1981; Walcot 1977; Fenik 1974, 159, 167–71; Gaisser 1969, 26–31; Trahman 1952; Woolsey 1941, 173–75.
75. Cf. Ahl (1989, 16) and de Jong (2001, 327), who refers to them quite usefully as "allomorphs."
76. He adds that some authorities believe it is a description of the harbor at New Carthage in Spain, for which see Polyb. 10.10.2. For a summary and criticism of modern attempts to locate a specific geographic source for the description, see Austin 1971, 71–72.
77. Cf. Macrob. *Sat*. 5.3.18: "Videte . . . portum ad civitatem Didonis ex Ithaca migrantem" ("you see the gate to the city of Dido transported from Ithaca").
78. On the combination of sources, see Clay 1988, 197–98; Krischer 1979, 144–47; Williams 1968, 637–43; Knauer 1964, 152–73. For a discussion of the Goat island, see Clay 1980.
79. See, e.g., Austin 1971, 51; Williams 1972, 66–67.
80. See Knauer 1964, 158–59. Cf. also the girl who shows Odysseus' men the way to the palace of the Laestrygonian king (*Od*. 10.103–11), a model that reinforces the potential dangers ahead.
81. Macrobius (*Sat*. 5.2.13) already recognized the influence of Nausicaa on Dido, while the appropriateness of this particular simile was famously criticized in antiquity by Probus (ap. Gell. *NA* 9.9.12–17). For the simile itself, see Polk 1996; Lonsdale 1990b; Glei 1990; Thornton 1985; Pöschl 1977, 85–90; West 1969, 43–44; Timpanaro 1986, 29n18. On Nausicaa as a model for Dido in general, see Cairns 1989, 129–35.
82. Williams 1963, 271.
83. Cf. Feeney 1998; Harrison 1982; Knauer 1964, 209–14.
84. Cf. Clay 1988, 198.
85. There is more than a hint of impatience (*nec plura querentem passa*) in Venus' interruption, as if she is trying to keep Aeneas on track. For the relationship

132   Notes

of this scene to Polyphemus' interrogation of Odysseus (*Od*. 9.252–55), see Clay 1988, 199–200.
86. Austin 1971, 138. The active meaning is reinforced by the echo of Odysseus' words to Nausicaa (*Od*. 6.175–77): σὲ γὰρ κακὰ πολλὰ μογήσας / ἐς πρώτην ἱκόμην, τῶν δ' ἄλλων οὔ τινα οἶδα / ἀνθρώπων, οἳ τήνδε πόλιν καὶ γαῖαν ἔχουσιν ("for you are the first person I have come to after suffering much, and I know no one else of the people who possess this city and land").
87. See Ahl 1989, 25.
88. Although, as Austin 1971, 157 points out, the *aliquam* demonstrates that he is careful not to hope for too much.
89. For discussions of the ecphrasis, see Putnam 1998a (revised as Putnam 1998b, 23–54); Barchiesi 1994a ; Hexter 1992, 353–57; Heffernan 1993, 22–36; Lowenstam 1993; Clay 1988; Thomas 1983; Johnson 1976, 99–105; Williams 1960.
90. Clay 1988, 202. Cf. Putnam 1998a, 247–48.
91. Cf. Lowenstam 1993, 41, who connects this to the description of Aeneas in Book 12.
92. Cf. the excellent discussion of this relationship in Putnam 1998a, 268–71.
93. Cf. also the suggestion in Servius (mss. *WN* ad *Aen*. 1.488) that Aeneas' name was written over the scene.
94. See Hexter 1992, 353–54, 381; Ahl 1989, 27.
95. Cf. Smith 1997, 34–37; Hexter 1992, 353; Clay 1988, 204n28.
96. On the verb *condere* in the *Aeneid*, see Hexter 1992, 359.
97. See Putnam 1998a, 265–67; Lowenstam 1993; Clay 1988, 203–5; Johnson 1976, 103–4; Stanley 1965, 274–77; Knauer 1964, 305–9, 328–29, 349–50.
98. Cf. Putnam 1998a, 269–70 on the distinction between public and private in the two scenes.
99. And perhaps an apt messenger, if he is at all associated with the Ilioneus killed at *Il*. 14.489–505, about whose father is said τόν ῥα μάλιστα / Ἑρμείας Τρώων ἐφίλει ("whom Hermes loved most of all the Trojans," *Il*. 14.490–91).
100. On the post-Iliadic story of Teucer, see Austin 1971, 1919. In the *Iliad*, Teucer and Aeneas are involved in three battles together (*Il*. 14.425, 515; 15.302, 332; 16.511, 536), but they never meet each other face to face.
101. Cf. Clay 1988, 200, who cites Dante's imitation of her language in *Inferno* 1.79 to describe his reaction to Virgil: *or se' tu quel Virgilio...?* ("are you that Virgil then?").
102. Cf. Quint. *Inst*. 11.3.176, who cites this line as one example of his views on the effects of changing the delivery of a single word: "Quid quod eadem verba mutata pronuntiatione indicant adfirmant exprobrant negant mirantur indignantur interrogant inrident elevant?" ("do not the same words, by a change in their pronunciation, indicate, affirm, reproach, deny, marvel, show indignation, interrogate, deride, and mock?")
103. Cf. Serv. ad *Aen*. 1. 488, 647; Dion. Hal. *Ant Rom*.1.48.3–4; Dares Phrygius 37; Dictys 4.18, 22. Dares and Dictys are obviously much later than Virgil, but Dionysus attributes the accusation to the fourth-century Lycian historian Menecrates. On this tradition, see Galinsky 1969, 40–46; Ussani 1947; Gabba 1976; Bracessi 1984; and on the possible implications for Aeneas' narration of *Aeneid* 2, see Ahl 1989, 24–29; Casali 1999, 206–11.
104. Although, as Putnam 1998a 271–74 demonstrates, the content of Iopas' song has more to do with the surrounding stories than it seems to at first glance.
105. Serv. ad loc. (and cf. Austin 1971, 226) claims that Dido means the horses Diomedes stole from Rhesus, which she would certainly know about from the panel in the temple, but this does not explain why she would assume that Aeneas knew anything specific about the quality of these horses. For the

Notes   133

view that Dido means the horses of Diomedes the Thracian king instead, see Nethercut 1976.
106. On Aeneas as *hospes*, see Gibson 1999.
107. Later, Dido doubts that the Trojans will remember her at all (*Aen.* 4.538–39). Cf. Gibson 1999, 193. A Virgilian reader familiar with the *Odyssey* will already suspect that Dido will be elided by the hero much as Alcinous is.
108. Cf. the references to the Greek *dolus* at 2.34, 44, 62, 152, 196, 252, 264, 390.
109. Cf. my discussion of *error* in Chapter 1.
110. Or more properly, that the sorrowful story is itself "unspeakable." *Infandum* often describes something monstrous or accursed. See *OLD* s.v. and cf. *Aen.* 1.251, 525, 597, 2.84, 132, 3.644, 4.85, 613, 7.583, 8.483, 489, 578, 10.673, 11.257, 267, 12.804.
111. For the Latin form *Ulixes*, see Stanford 1954, 8. For the epithets used to describe his cruelty in the *Aeneid*, see note 44.
112. Cf. his ranking of Neoptolemus as the third best speaker among the Achaeans after himself and Nestor (*Od.* 11.511–12).
113. Virgil does not explicitly say whether the images on the temple of Juno are carved or painted. For a summary of opinions, see Lowenstam 1993, 37n3.
114. Cf. *Verg. G.* 4.345, *E.* 6.78, and Austin 1964, 210. Cf. Horsfall 2008, 414–15.
115. On this verse and the unusual verb *renarrabat*, see Fernandelli 1999 and the literature cited there; Gasti 2010.
116. On the erotic effects of Aeneas' account and the question of narrative control, see Biow 1994.

NOTES TO CHAPTER 4

1. See Gruen 1992, 9–12, 16–21, 30–31; Solmsen 1986; Horsfall 1979, 377–83; Prinz 1979, 155; Galinsky 1969, 100–5; Perret 1942, 370–73. The words *met' Odusseôs* are usually construed with what follows, though Galinsky (1969, 103n1) argues that they should be taken with the preceding participle only.
2. MS Urbinas 105. Most scholars have preferred the genitive reading. See Solmsen 1986, 94; Horsfall 1979, 379; Cornell 1975, 18; Pearson 1939, 191.
3. On the importance of Odysseus as sacker of Troy, cf. Eustath. 1382.57–58; Schol. AT ad *Il.* 2.278.
4. Though it is possible that Virgil has in mind the tradition that Odysseus was the father of Latinus by Circe (Hes. *Theog.* 1013) when he uses Laertes as a model for the king.
5. *OLD* s.v. and cf. my discussion in Chapter 1.
6. Coroebus seems to have earned a reputation for stupidity in antiquity because of this *error*. See Ael. *VH* 13.15 and cf. Ahl 1989, 29.
7. Though it was not necessarily Virgil's only source. The story of the horse was told in the *Ilias Parva* and the *Iliupersis* (Procl. *Chr.* 222–56), and Livius Andronicus and Naevius both wrote plays on the subject (Nonius 475.10; Macrob. *Sat.* 6.1.38). For other accounts of the horse in antiquity, see Andersen 1977; Austin 1964, 34. The description of the Greek soldiers emerging (*Aen.* 2.260: *cavo se robore promunt*, "they emerge from the hollow wood") corresponds to Demodocus' account (*Od.* 8.515: κοῖλον λόχον ἐκπρολιπόντες, "leaving their hollow hiding place"); cf. *Od.* 8.507.
8. When Aeneas tells his story to Dido, only seven years have passed since the end of the war (cf. *Aen.* 1.755), while Odysseus arrives at Scheria in his tenth year of wandering.

134 Notes

9. Cf. Knauer 1964, 380; Austin 1964, 128.
10. On Aeneas' confusion here, cf. Williams 1983, 107–8.
11. In Homer, *atê* usually means "folly" or "blindness," but here it has often been understood to have its common post-Homeric meaning of "ruin" or "destruction." See Finkelberg 1995, 19 and cf. Doyle 1984, 18; Verdenius 1985, 215; Dodds 1951, 19n17. Cf. Odysseus' similar claim after the Aeolus episode (*Od.* 10.67).
12. Cf. Fernandelli 1999, 104–5; Horsfall 2008, 523.
13. Cf. Austin 1964, 275.
14. Cf. Horsfall 2008, 527. On the layout of the palace, see Wistrand 1960.
15. Austin 1964, 275 notes the allusion but offers no explanation for it.
16. O'Hara 1996, 135. Cf. Bartelink 1965, 86; Hanssen 1948, 122; and on the problematic text of Serv. Auct. in this comment, Fraenkel 1948, 142–43; Mühmelt 1965, 61–62.
17. Virgil does not explicitly identify the altar where Priam is killed as belonging to Jupiter, but its position in the middle of the courtyard (*Aen.* 2.512: *aedibus in mediis nudoque sub aetheris axe*, "in the middle of the halls, under the naked vault of heaven") corresponds to the altar of Zeus in *Iliad* 24 (*Il.* 24.306: μέσῳ ἕρκεϊ, "in the middle of the enclosure"). Cf. Austin 1964, 199–200; Williams 1972, 248–49.
18. Hexter 1999, 67; Putnam 1980, 1.
19. Cf. Williams 1962, 13.
20. See Richardson 1996; Parry 1994; Alden 1992, 9–14; Peradotto 1990, 92–93; Most 1989 and 1985; Murnaghan 1987, 172–73; Griffin 1980, 48–49.
21. This should be distinguished from the thorny question of how well his account represents the pre-Virgilian Aeneas legend (cf. Williams 1962, 7–12), as well as the issue of narrative point of view, which has been discussed by Sanderlin 1975–76. Note, however, the doubts raised about the truthfulness of Aeneas' account in Book 2 by Casali (1999, 206–11).
22. Hexter 1999, 66, 70.
23. On the transformation of Aeneas from Trojan to Roman, see Semple 1955.
24. On prophecy in the *Aeneid*, see O'Hara 1990.
25. This is the title of his illuminating study of Virgilian intertextuality (Barchiesi 1984). Cf. my discussion of this phrase in Chapter 1.
26. For other readings of *Aeneid* 3, see Hexter 1999; Quint 1993, 53–65; Hershkowitz 1991; Putnam 1980; di Cesare 1974, 61–76; Klinger 1967, 420–36; Otis 1964, 251–64; Lloyd 1957a and 1957b; Allen 1951–52; and the introduction and longer notes throughout Horsfall 2006.
27. Fowler 1990, 49–50. Cf. Traiana 1984–91, 1072–76, who notes the allusion but denies that that *superbum* has any negative force in this context, and similarly, Horsfall 2006, 41.
28. The adjective is also used several times without the noun to describe the suitors: 1.134, 2.310, 3.315, 11.116, 15.12, 376, 21.289.
29. Cf. Knauer 1964, 184. On the Iliadic qualities of the episode, see de Jong 2001, 229; Heubeck and Hoekstra 1989, 15–16; Reinhardt 1960, 60–62; Focke 1943, 161–62.
30. The Cicones are also allies of Trojans (*Il.* 2.846, 17.73).
31. This recalls, albeit in inverted order, Odysseus' own juxtaposition of the two names as he begins his story (*Od.* 9.38–39: Τροίηθεν . . . Ἰλιόθεν). See Knauer 1964, 185n1, 382. On *omnis* as an intensifier of the sorrow, see Horsfall 2006, 41. On the existence of an actual town called Aenus in Thrace, see Williams 1962, 56; Horsfall 2006, 50–51.
32. Hexter 1999, 78. In this context, contrast Dionysius' story of the foundation quoted at the beginning of this chapter (Dion. Hal. *Ant. Rom.* 1.72.2) with its eponymous Trojan woman named *R(h)ome*.

33. On the Polydorus legend, see Casali 2005; Caviglia 1984–91; Horsfall 2006, 50–53; Williams 1962, 57–58.
34. On the apparent inconsistency with the description of Polydorus' death by a crop of spears a few lines earlier (*Aen.* 3.45–46), see Casali 2007, 186–88; Williams 1962, 65; Paschalis 1997, 113.
35. Note also that the word Aeneas uses to describe his reaction to Polydorus' voice is *obstipui* (*Aen.* 3.48), which is the same word he used earlier in response to Priam's death.
36. Quint 1993, 58.
37. Hexter 1999, 72.
38. On the connection between the Thracian and Delian episodes, see Jens 1948.
39. On the apparent inconsistency between Aeneas' total ignorance here and Creusa's earlier mention of Hesperia and the Tiber, see Williams 1962, 20.
40. See my discussion in Chapter 1, and cf. Heyworth 1993, 256; Barchiesi 1994b, 441.
41. This is further emphasized by the *figura etymologica* of *domus/dominabitur*, which Horsfall (2006, 108) notes without discussing its emphatic function.
42. On the transfer of the prophecy from "anti-Trojan Poseidon . . . to pro-Trojan Apollo," see Heyworth 1993, 256n2.
43. Cf. Servius' comment (ad *Aen.* 3.94): "dicendo 'Dardanidae' ostendit Italiam, unde Dardanus fuit. quod si Cretam significaret, Teucriadae diceret" ("by saying *Dardanidae* he designates Italy, whence Dardanus came. For if he had meant Crete, he would have said *Teucriadae*"). Cf. also Casali 2007, 192–93; Horsfall 2006, 105–6.
44. Cf. Horsfall 2006, 115; for the version of the Trojan legend in which Teucer already ruled Troy when Dardanus arrived from Italy, see Apollod. *Bibl.* 3.12.1.
45. The lie to Athena (*Od.* 13.253–86); to Eumaeus (*Od.* 14.192–359; and to Penelope (*Od.* 19.165–202, 221–48, 268–99. Cf. also the lying tale told by the anonymous Aetolian (*Od.* 14.379–85). Cf. my discussion of the lying tales in Chapter 3 and the references there.
46. Cf. Hexter 1993, 240–41.
47. On Odysseus and Idomeneus, see Haft 1984.
48. For a different explanation of Idomeneus' absence in a fragment of Lycophron, see West 2003, 305–8.
49. He thus adopts the familiar position of many characters in the Homeric poems: cf. *Il.* 2.661–67, 13.694–97 = 15.335–36, 15.430–32, 16.570–76, 23.85–90, 24.480–83, *Od.* 14.380, 15.224, 23.118–20. Cf. Schlunk 1976.
50. Quint 1993, 58. Cf. Horsfall's (2006, 133) criticism of this view.
51. Cf. Quint 1993, 378n12. Given the scant evidence for earlier versions of Idomeneus' homecoming story, we must admit the possibility that Servius constructed his account based on what happens to Aeneas on Crete. However, I believe that the subtle echoes of the story in the *Odyssey* weigh against this view. For other views on the plague, see Horsfall (2006, 133–34) and the literature cited there.
52. Cf. Knauer 1964, 198, 383; Williams 1962, 98; Nelis 2001, 37; Horsfall 2006, 207.
53. I am excluding Thrace, since Aeneas did not actually encounter the Cicones there.
54. I mean here the actual Homeric framing narrative, not Odysseus' own story in Books 9–12, which Aeneas will enter later. On the notion that the two heroes are crossing each other's paths across the Mediterranean without ever meeting, cf. Hexter 1999, 67.
55. Cf. Servius' point (ad *Aen.* 3.272) about the ironic juxtaposition of *regna* to *scopuli*, and Horsfall (2006, 217).

136 Notes

56. See Horsfall 2006, 223; Hexter 1999, 74; Putnam 1980, 6.
57. On Virgil "passing by" a Homeric episode, see Horsfall 2006, 231; Nelis 2001, 61. Horsfall, however, pursues different implications of the metaphoric use of *abscondimus*.
58. On this episode, see esp. Hexter 1999, 74–77; Bettini 1997; Quint 1993, 58–61; Cova 1992, 87–139; Bright 1981; Putnam 1980, 8–9; Grimm 1967; Van Ooteghem 1937. For further bibliography, see Horsfall 2006, 236.
59. For Helenus in the *Iliad*, see *Il.* 6.76, 7.44, 13.576, 758.
60. On the "two-tiered" allusion to Homer's Tiresias and Apollonius' Phineus, see Nelis 2001, 38–44.
61. Quint 1993, 58–59. Cf. Klinger 1967, 426–27. There are also strong echoes of Circe's advice throughout the scene, for which see Horsfall 2006, 294–95.
62. On the encounter with Andromache, cf. Smith 2005, 71–77.
63. Hexter 1999, 75–76. Cf. Bettini 1997, 12–13. On Buthrotum as a world of the living dead, see Bright 1981; Nelson 1961; Starry West 1983, 258–59.
64. On the echoes of the underworld, see Bright 1981. Hexter (1999, 315n19) suggests quite persuasively that the twin altars reflect the double loss of Hector and her son Astyanax (cf. Serv. ad *Aen.* 3.305), rather than simply marking some special emphasis on the ceremony as Warde-Fowler (1917) argues (cf. Bettini 1997, 12n19; Grimm 1967, 154; Williams 1962, 305). I would add that the ambiguity in the noun *manes*, which can be either singular or plural, supports Hexter's position. Andromache seems to be summoning both husband and son in one gesture.
65. Cf. Serv. Auct. ad *Aen.* 3.307.
66. Quint 1993, 59.
67. On the relationship between Ascanius and Astyanax in the poem, see Feldman 1957–58 and cf. Smith 2005, 76–77. The two boys are already doubles in themselves, since they both carry two names: Ascanius-Iulus and Astyanax-Scamandrius.
68. Quint 1993, 60.
69. Cf. Bettini 1997, 16–21.
70. See Hexter (1999, 76, 316n31), who makes the valuable point that the whole episode suggests that the marriage between Andromache and Helenus will produce no offspring.
71. Cf. Horsfall 2006, 351.
72. Knauer 1964, 187–90.
73. Cf. my foregoing discussion of the contrast with Idomeneus.
74. On this episode in general, see esp. Hexter 1999, 77–79; Ramminger 1991; Moskalew 1988; Harrison 1986; Putnam 1980, 11–13; Kinsey 1979; Römisch 1976; McKay 1966. For further bibliography, see Horsfall 2006, 409.
75. On the identification with Sicily, see Serv. Auct. ad *Aen.* 3.687 and cf. Thuc. 6.2.2; Strab. 6.2.1; Dion. Hal. *Ant. Rom.* 1.22.2; Plin. *HN* 3.86.
76. Cf. Hexter 1999, 79 for the notion that Virgil is "correcting" Homer in this episode.
77. Williams (1962, 183) and Horsfall (2006, 410) note the frequent association of the word *suprema* with death. Cf. *Aen.* 3.68, 482, 6.213, 735, 11.25, 61.
78. On the importance of this recognition to the "complex play of sympathies," see Horsfall 2006, 413.
79. Putnam 1980, 12.
80. On *infelix* here, cf. Putnam 1980, 11–13; Ramminger 1991, 60–61; Rengakos 1993, 118; Kinsey 1979, 114; Klinger 1967, 433; Cartault 1926, 257; Horsfall 2006, 421–22.
81. Cf. Knauer 1964, 385; Williams 1962, 190; 1963, 268–69.

82. On Achaemenides rereading (*relegens*) the text of Homer in reverse, see Papanghelis 1999, 284. On these lines more generally, cf. Horsfall 2006, 459; Nelis 2001, 53; Moskalew 1988, 120; Cartault 1926, 261.
83. Cf. Geymonat 1993, 325.
84. Cf. the different, but compatible, interpretation in Williams 1983, 263–64.
85. Heyne 1832 *ad* 3.707 suggests Tiresias' description of the underworld (*Od.* 11.94: ἀτερπέα χῶρον, "a place without pleasure") as a possible model for this phrase. See further Horsfall 2006, 470.
86. Quint 1993, 60; cf. Roti 1983.301n4.
87. On *labor* here as "a metaphor for the toil involved in poetic activity," see Geymonat 1993, 323.
88. Cf. Horsfall 2000, 73.
89. Earlier in Carthage, Iarbas levels a similar accusation at Aeneas (*Aen.* 4.138). On Aeneas as Paris, see Cairns 1989, 120–21, 158; Lyne 1987, 109; Anderson 1957, 21.
90. Cf. Quint 1993, 70.
91. Cf. Quint 1993, 67; Anderson 1957, 24–25; Hardie 1994, 231–32.
92. On the significance of the Oresteia story as a warning in the *Odyssey*, see Felson-Rubin 1994, 95–107; Katz 1991, 29–53; Olson 1990 and 1995, 25–42; Friedrich 1975, 86–87; Hölscher 1967, 1989, 297–310; Lesky 1967, 5–21; Clarke 1967, 10–12; Hommel 1955; D'Arms and Hulley 1946.
93. Quint 1993, 67. Note, however, that Turnus does have a sword made by Vulcan (*Aen.* 12.90–91). On the slight inconsistency, see Serv. ad *Aen.* 9.146; Hardie 1994, 101.
94. Particularly those interpretations that press the bipartite model. See, e.g., Gransden 1984; Van Nortwick 1980; West 1974; Anderson 1957; MacKay 1957.
95. On Achilles' anger, see Muellener 1996; Nagy 1999, 69–93.
96. The bibliography on Aeneas' anger in the final scene is vast. Among the most useful recent accounts, see Putnam 1995, 201–45; Putnam 1990; Galinsky 1994 and 1988; Quint 1993, 65–83; Thomas 1991; Cairns 1989, 78–79; West 1974; Little 1970.
97. On the nurse Caieta as a substitute for Aeneas' immortal mother, see Segal 1966, 57. For other views, cf. Dyer 1995, 290–91; Wiltshire 1989, 110.
98. The latter point is made by Cairns (1989, 87) with reference to Schenk 1984.
99. On the crimes of the suitors, see Yamagata 1994, 28–31; Fisher 1992, 162–75; Saïd 1978, 305–17.
100. Horsfall (2006, 340–42) notes that such transfers of armor are regularly ill omens in the *Aeneid* (e.g., Camilla and Chloreus, Turnus and Pallas, Androgeos and Coroebus, etc.), but he argues that Aeneas benefits here from the Homeric attitude toward the re-use of armor. See further Horsfall (1995, 176, 205) and the literature cited there. However, he may be too quick in his assertion that Virgil "makes nothing of" the issue of ill fortune in the transferred armor, especially in light of the moral ambiguities at the end of the poem.
101. Cf. Hardie 1994, 231–32.
102. Cf. Harrison 1991, 204. Some of the details in this episode are also drawn from the scenes of unsuccessful supplication by Adrestus (*Il.* 6.37–65) and Dolon (*Il.* 10.376–457). On the killing of suppliants in the *Iliad*, see Fenik 1968, 83; Macleod 1982, 15–16.
103. Cf. Nethercut 1968, 86. The word *capulus*, "hilt," only occurs in one other passage in the *Aeneid* (12.734) and is fairly rare before Virgil. Cf. Harrison 1991, 207.

104. Putnam 1965, 172; cf. Nethercut 1968, 86.
105. Putnam 1965, 175.
106. On the Trojans as invaders, see Nethercut 1968.
107. On the ways in which Turnus is assimilated to the Iliadic Aeneas, see Quint 1993, 65–75.
108. For other descriptions of Turnus' beauty, see *Aen.* 7.473, 649, 783.
109. Cairns 1989, 211.

Bibliography

Ahl, F. 1989. "Homer, Vergil, and Complex Narrative Structures in Latin Epic: An Essay." *ICS* 14: 1–31.
Ahl, F., and H. M. Roisman. 1996. *The Odyssey Re-formed*. Ithaca, NY.
Alden, M. J. 1992. "Ψεύδεα πολλὰ ἐτύμοισιν ὁμοῖα." *Liverpool Classical Papers* 2: 9–14.
Allen, A. W. 1951–2. "The Dullest Book of the *Aeneid*." *CJ* 47: 119–23.
Allen, T. W., and D. B. Monro, eds. 1920. *Homeri Opera I–V.*³ Oxford.
Ameis, F., C. Hentze, and P. Cauer. 1928. *Homers Odyssee*. Leipzig-Berlin.
Andersen, O. 1977. "Odysseus and the Wooden Horse." *SO* 52: 5–18.
Anderson, W. S. 1957. "Vergil's Second *Iliad*." *TAPA* 88: 17–30.
Anderson, W. S. 1969. *The Art of the Aeneid*. Englewood Cliffs, NJ.
Auden, W. H. 1991. *Collected Poems*. Ed. E. Mendelson. New York.
Auerbach, E. 1957. *Mimesis*. New York.
Austin, J. N. H. 1972. "Name Magic in the *Odyssey*." *ClAnt* 5: 1–19.
Austin, N. A. 1975. *Archery at the Dark of the Moon: Poetic Problems in Homer's Odyssey*. Berkeley.
Austin, R. G. 1959. "Virgil and the Wooden Horse." *JRS* 49: 16–25.
Austin, R. G. 1961. "Virgil, *Aeneid* 2.567–88." *CQ* 11: 185–98.
Austin, R. G. 1964. *P. Vergili Maronis Aeneidos Liber Secundus*. Oxford.
Austin, R. G. 1971. *P. Vergili Maronis Aeneidos Liber Primus*. Oxford.
Bamberger, F. 1976. "Κέρδος et sa famille (emplois homérique), Contribution aux recherches sur le vocabulaire de la 'richesse' en grec." *Centre de Recherches Comparatives sur les Langues de la Méditeranée Ancienee* 3: 1–37.
Barchiesi, A. 1984. *La Traccia Del Modello: Effetti Omerici Nella Narrazione Virgiliana*. Pisa.
Barchiesi, A. 1994a. "Rappresentazioni del dolore e interpretazione nell'Eneide." *A&A* 40: 109–24.
Barchiesi, A. 1994b. "Immovable Delos: Aeneid 3.73–98 and the Hymns of Callimachus." *CQ* 44: 438–43.
Barta, P. I., P. A. Miller, C. Platter, and D. Shepherd. 2001. *Carnivalizing Difference: Bakhtin and the Other*. London.
Bartelink, G. J. M. 1965. *Etymologisering bij Vergilius*. Mededelingen der Kon. Neder. Akad. van Wetenschappen 28.3. Amsterdam.
Bassett, S. E. 1923. "The Proems of the *Iliad* and the *Odyssey*." *AJPh* 44: 339–48.
Belmont, D. E. 1967. "Telemachus and Nausicaa: A Study of Youth." *CJ* 63: 1–9.
Bergold, W. 1977. *Der Zweikampf des Paris und Menelaos*. Bonn.
Berres, T. 1993. "Vergil und Homer: ein Beitrag zur Entmythologisierung des Verhältnisses." *Gymnasium* 100: 342–69.
Besslich, S. 1966. *Schweigen, Verschweigen, Übergehen. Die Darstellung des Unausgesprochenen in der Odyssee*. Heidelberg.

Besslich, S. 1981. "Nausikaa und Telemach. Dichterische Funktion und Eigenwert der Person bei der Darstellung des jungen Menschen in der *Odyssee.*" In Kurtz, Müller, and Nicolai 1981, 103–16.
Bethe, E. 1914. *Homer: Dichtung und Sage, vol. 1. 'Ilias.'* Leipzig-Berlin.
Bethe, E. 1922. *Homer: Dichtung und Sage, vol. 2. 'Odysee, Kyklos, Zeitbestimmung.'* Leipzig-Berlin.
Bettini, M. 1997. "Ghosts of Exile: Doubles and Nostalgia in Vergil's *parva Troia (Aeneid* 3.294ff.)." *ClAnt* 16: 8–33.
Biow, D. 1994. "Epic Performance on Trial: Virgil's Aeneid and the Power of Eros in Song." *Arethusa* 27: 223–46.
Bowie, A. M. 1990. "The Death of Priam: Allegory and History in the Aeneid." *CQ* 40: 470–81.
Bracessi, L. 1984. *La leggenda di Antenore da Troia a Padova.* Padua.
Bradley, R. 1954. "Backgrounds of the Title *Speculum* in Mediaeval Literature." *Speculum* 29: 100–115.
Bremer, J. M., I. J. F. de Jong, and J. Kalff. 1987. *Homer: Beyond Oral Poetry: Recent Trends in Homeric Interpretation.* Amsterdam.
Briggs, W. W., Jr. 1980. *Narrative and Simile from the Georgics in the Aeneid.* Mnemosyne Suppl. 58. Leiden.
Bright, D. F. 1981. "Aeneas's Other Nekyia." *Vergilius* 27: 40–47.
Bühler, W. 1964. *Beiträge zur Erklärung der Schrift vom Erhabenen.* Göttingen.
Burden, M., ed. 1998. *A Woman Scorn'd. Responses to the Dido Myth.* London.
Cairns, F. 1979. *Tibullus: A Hellenistic Poet at Rome.* Cambridge.
Cairns, F. 1989. *Virgil's Augustan Epic.* New York.
Carnes, J. S. 2001. "Praise Poetry and the Novelization of the *Aeneid.*" In Barta, Miller, Platter, and Shepherd 2001, 99–118.
Cartault, A. 1926. *L'Art de Virgile dans l'Enéide.* Paris.
Casali, S. 1999. "*Facta Impia* (Virgil, Aeneid 4.596–99)." *CQ* 49: 203–11.
Casali, S. 2005. "La vite dietro il mirto: Lycurgus, Polydorus e la violazione delle piante in Eneide 3." *SIFC* 4th ser. 3: 233–50.
Casali, S. 2007. "Correcting Aeneas's Voyage: Ovid's Commentary on *Aeneid* 3." *TAPA* 137: 181–210.
Casali, S. 2010. "The Development of the Aeneas Legend." In Farrell and Putnam 2010, 38–51.
Caviglia, F. 1984–91. "Polidoro." In Della Corte 1984–91, 4: 162–64.
Cesare, M. di 1974. *The Altar and the City.* New York.
Chantraine, P. 1958. *Grammaire homérique, I.* 3rd ed. Paris.
Chantraine, P. 1963. *Grammaire homérique, II.* 2nd ed. Paris.
Ciani, M. G. 1964–65. "La parola omerica τηλύγετος." *AIV* 123: 157–66.
Cinzi, G. G. 1564. *Discorsi.* Venice.
Clarke, H. W. 1963. "Telemachos and the *Telemacheia.*" *AJPh* 84: 129–45.
Clarke, H. W. 1967. *The Art of the Odyssey.* Englewood Cliffs, NJ.
Clausen, W. 1987. *Virgil's Aeneid and the Tradition of Hellenistic Poetry.* Sather Classical Lectures 51. Berkeley.
Clay, D. 1988. "The Archaeology of the Temple to Juno in Carthage (*Aen.* 1.446–93)." *CPh* 83: 195–205.
Clay, J. S. 1980. "Goat Island: *Od.* 9.116–41." *CQ* 30: 261–64.
Clay, J. S. 1983. *The Wrath of Athena. Gods and Men in the Odyssey.* Princeton.
Codino, F. 1965. *Introduzione a Omero.* Turin.
Combellack, F. M. 1981. "The Wish without Desire." *AJPh* 102: 115–19.
Conte, G. B. 1981. "A proposito dei modelli in letteratura." *MD* 6: 147–60.
Conte, G. B. 1985. *Memoria dei poeti e sistema letterario.* 2nd ed. Turin.
Conte, G. B. 1986. *The Rhetoric of Imitation: Genre and Poetic Memory in Virgil and Other Latin Poets.* Ed. C. Segal. Cornell Studies in Classical Philology 44. Ithaca, NY.

Conte, G. B. 1992. "Proems in the Middle." *YCS* 29: 147–59.
Conte, G. B. 1999. "The Virgilian Paradox." *PCPhS* 45: 17–42.
Conte, G. B., and A. Barchiesi. 1989. "Imitazione e arte allusiva. Modi e funzioni dell' intertestualità." *Lo spazio letterario di Roma antica* 1: 81–114.
Contini, G. 1970. *Varianti e altra linguistica: una raccolta di saggi (1938–1968)*. Turin.
Conway, R. S. 1928. *Harvard Lectures on the Vergilian Age*. Cambridge, MA.
Cornell, T. J. 1975. "Aeneas and the Twins." *PCPhS* 21: 1–32.
Cova, P. V. 1992. *Letteratura latina dell' Italia settentrionale*. Milan.
Cozzo, A. 1988. *Kerdos, Semantica, Ideologie e Società nella Grecia antika*. Rome.
Craik, E. M., ed. 1990. *Owls to Athens. Essays on Classical Subjects Presented to Sir Kenneth Dover*. Oxford.
D'Arms, E. F., and K. K. Hulley. 1946. "The Oresteia-Story in the *Odyssey*." *TAPA* 77: 207–13.
Davies, A. M., and W. Meid, eds. 1976. *Studies in Greek, Italic, and Indo-European Linguistics Offered to Leonard R. Palmer on the Occasion of His Seventieth Birthday, June 5, 1976*. Innsbrucker Beiträge zur Sprachwissenschaft 16. Innsbruck.
Davies, M. 1987. *The Epic Cycle*. Bristol.
Della Corte, F., ed. 1984–91. *Enciclopedia Virgiliana*. Rome.
Dimock, G. E. 1956. "The Name of Odysseus." *The Hudson Review* 9: 52–70.
Dodds, E. R. 1951. *The Greeks and the Irrational*. Berkeley.
Dolin, E. 1973. "Odysseus in Phaeacia." *GB* 1: 273–82.
Dowden, K. 1996. "Homer's Sense of Text." *JHS* 116: 47–61.
Doyle, R. E. 1984. *ATH. Its Use and Meaning*. New York.
Duckworth, G. E. 1957. "The Aeneid as Trilogy." *TAPA* 88: 17–30.
DuQuesnay, I. M. Le M. 1977. "Vergil's Fourth *Eclogue*." *PLLS* 1: 25–99.
Dyer, R. R. 1995. "Cicero at Caieta in Vergil's *Aeneid*." *Latomus* 54: 290–97.
Edmunds, L. 2001. *Intertextuality and the Reading of Roman Poetry*. Baltimore.
Edwards, A. T. 1984. "*Aristos Achaion*: Heroic Death and Dramatic Structure in the *Iliad*." *QUCC* 46: 61–80.
Edwards, A. T. 1985. *Achilles in the Odyssey*. Beiträge zur klassischen Philologie 171. Königstein.
Eisenberger, H. 1973. *Studien zur Odyssee*. Wiesbaden.
Emlyn-Jones, C. 1986. "True and Lying Tales in the *Odyssey*." *G&R* 33: 1–10.
Erbse, H. 1960. *Beiträge zur Überlieferung der Iliasscholien*. Munich.
Erbse, H. 1993. "Nestor und Antilochos bei Homer und Arktinos." *Hermes* 121: 385–403.
Farrell, J. 1997. "The Virgilian Intertext." In Martindale 1997, 222–38.
Farrell, J., and M. C. J. Putnam, eds. 2010. *A Companion to Vergil's Aeneid and Its Tradition*. Malden, MA.
Feeney, D. C. 1998. "Leaving Dido: The Appearance(s) of Mercury and the Motivations of Aeneas." In Burden 1998, 105–27.
Feldman, L. H. 1957–8. "Ascanius and Astyanax." *CJ* 53: 361–67.
Felson-Rubin, N. 1994. *Regarding Penelope: From Courtship to Poetics*. Princeton.
Fenik, B. C. 1968. *Typical Battle Scenes in the Iliad. Studies in the Narrative Techniques of Homeric Battle Description*. Wiesbaden.
Fenik, B. 1974. *Studies in the Odyssey*. Wiesbaden.
Fernandelli, M. 1999. "Sic pater Aeneas... fata renarrabat divom: esperienza del racconto e esperienza nel racconto in Eneide II e III." *MD* 42: 95–112.
Finkelberg, M. 1987. "The First Song of Demodocus." *Mnemosyne* 40: 128–32.
Finkelberg, M. 1991. "Royal Succession in Heroic Greece." *CQ* 41: 303–16.
Finkelberg, M. 1995. "Patterns of Human Error in Homer." *JHS* 115: 15–28.

Finley, M. I. 1977. *The World of Odysseus*. 2nd ed. London.
Fisher, N. R. E. 1992. *Hybris*. London.
Focke, F. 1943. *Die Odyssee*. Berlin.
Foley, H. P. 1978. "Reverse Similes and Sex Roles in the *Odyssey*." *Arethusa* 11: 7–26.
Ford, A. 1992. *Homer. The Poetry of the Past*. Ithaca.
Fowler, D. P. 1989. "First Thoughts on Closure: Problems and Prospects." *MD* 22: 75–122.
Fowler, D. P. 1990. "Deviant Focalization in Virgil's *Aeneid*." *PCPhS* 36: 42–63.
Fowler, D. P. 1991. "Subject Review of Roman Literature." *G&R* 38: 85–97.
Fowler, D. P. 1997. "On the Shoulders of Giants: Intertextuality and Classical Studies." *MD* 39: 13–34.
Fraenkel, E. 1932. "Vergil und die Aithiopis." *Philologus* 87: 242–48.
Fraenkel, E. 1945. "Some Aspects of the Structure of *Aeneid* VII." *JRS* 35: 1–14.
Fraenkel, E. 1948. "Rev. of E. K. Rand et al. *Serviani in Vergili Carmina Commentarii*. Part 1." *JRS* 39: 131–43.
Fränkel, H. 1921. *Die homerischen Gleichnisse*. Göttingen.
Fränkel, H. 1960. *Wege und Formen frühgriechischen Denkens*. 2nd ed. Munich.
Fränkel, H. 1962. *Dichtung und Philosophie des frühen Griechentums*. Munich.
Friedrich, R. 1975. *Stilwandel im homerischen Epos. Studien zur Poetik und Theorie der epischen Gattung*. Wiesbaden.
Friedrich, R. 1981. "On the Compositional Use of Similes in the Odyssey." *AJP* 102: 120–37.
Gabba, E. 1976. "Sulla valorizzazione politica della leggenda delle origini troiane di Roma fra III e II secolo a.C." In Sordi 1976, 84–101.
Gagnepain, J. 1959. *Les noms grec en -os et en -a*. Paris.
Gaisser, J. H. 1969. "A Structural Analysis of the Digressions in the *Iliad* and the *Odyssey*." *HSCP* 73: 1–43.
Galinsky, G. K. 1969. *Aeneas, Sicily, and Rome*. Princeton.
Galinsky, G. K. 1988. "The Anger of Aeneas." *AJPh* 109: 321–48.
Galinsky, G. K. 1992. *The Interpretation of Roman Poetry: Empiricism or Hermeneutics?* Studien zur klassischen Philologie Bd. 67. Frankfurt am Main.
Galinsky, G. K. 1994. "How to Be Philosophical about the End of the Aeneid." *ICS* 19: 191–201.
Gardiner, E. N. 1905. "Wrestling." *JHS* 25: 14–31.
Gasti, H. 2010. "Narrative Self-Consciousness in Virgil's *Aeneid* 3." *Dictynna* 10: 59–68.
Gastinel, G. 1926. "Carthage et l'Énéide." *RA* 23: 75–100.
Geddes, W. 1878. *The Problem of the Homeric Poems*. London.
Geertz, H. and C. Geertz. 1964. "Teknonymy in Bali: Parenthood, Age-Grading and Genealogical Amnesia." *Journal of the Anthropological Institute of Great Britain and Ireland* 94: 94–108.
George, E. V. 1974. *Aeneid VIII and the Aitia of Callimachus*. Leiden.
Germain, G. 1954. *Genèse de l'Odyssée. Le fantastique et le sacré*. Paris.
Geymonat, M. 1970. *P. Vergili Maronis Opera*. Turin.
Geymonat, M. 1993. "Callimachus at the End of Aeneas' Narration." *HSCP* 95: 323–31.
Ghosh, J. 1963. *Epic Sources of Sanskrit Literature*. Calcutta.
Gibson, R. K. 1999. "Aeneas as *Hospes* in Vergil, *Aeneid* 1 and 4." *CQ* 49: 184–202.
Glei, R. 1990. "Von Probus zu Pöschl: Vergilinterpretation im Wandel." *Gymnasium* 97: 321–40.
Goldhill, S. 1991. *The Poet's Voice. Essays on Poetics and Greek Literature*. Cambridge.

Goold, G. P. 1970. "Servius and the Helen Episode." *HSCP* 74: 101–68.
Görgemanns, H., and E. A. Schmidt, eds. 1976. *Studien zum antiken Epos*. Beiträge zur Klassischen Philologie 72. Meisenheim am Glan.
Grabes, H. 1973. *Speculum, Mirror und Looking-Glass: Kontinuität und Originalität der Spiegelmetapher in den Buchtiteln des Mittelalters und der englischen Literatur des 13. bis 17. Jahrhunderts*. Tübingen.
Gransden, K. W. 1984. *Virgil's Iliad: An Essay on Epic Narrative*. New York.
Gransden, K. W., P. Murray, and T. Winnifrith, eds. 1983. *Aspects of Epic*. London.
Griffin, J. 1977. "The Epic Cycle and the Uniqueness of Homer." *JHS* 97: 39–53.
Griffin, J. 1980. *Homer*. Oxford.
Grimm, R. E. 1967. "Aeneas and Andromache in *Aeneid* III." *AJPh* 88: 151–62.
Grosart, A. B. 1874. *Complete Works in Verse and Prose of Andrew Marvell*. London.
Gruen, E. S. 1992. *Culture and National Identity in Republican Rome*. Ithaca, NY.
Habinek, T. N. 1992. "Grecian Wonders and Roman Woe: the Romantic Rejection of Rome and Its Consequences for the Study of Roman Literature." In Galinsky 1992, 227–42.
Haft, A. 1984. "Odysseus, Idomeneus, and Meriones; the Cretan Lies of *Odyssey* 13–19." *CJ* 79: 286–306.
Hainsworth, J. B. 1958. "No Flames in the Odyssey." *JHS* 78: 49–56.
Halverson, J. 1986. "The Succession Issue in the *Odyssey*." *G&R* 33: 119–28.
Händel, P., and W. Meid, ed. 1983. *Festschrift für Robert Muth zum 65. Geburtstag am 1. Januar 1981 dargebracht von Freunden und Kollegen*. Innsbruck.
Hanssen, J. S. T. 1948. "Vergilius ἐπιθέτως λέγων: Vergilian Notes 2." *SO* 26: 113–25.
Hardie, P. 1994. *Virgil. Aeneid Book IX*. Cambridge.
Harriott, R. 1969. *Poetry and Criticism before Plato*. London.
Harrison, E. L. 1980. "The Structure of the Aeneid: Observations on the Links between the Books." *ANRW* 31.1: 359–93.
Harrison, E. L. 1982. "Vergil's Mercury." In McKay 1982, 1–47.
Harrison, E. L. 1986. "Achaemenides' Unfinished Account: Vergil *Aen*. 3.588–69." *CP* 81: 146–47.
Harrison, S. J. 1991. *Vergil: Aeneid 10*. Oxford.
Hartmann, A. 1917. *Untersuchungen über die Sagen vom Tod des Odysseus*. Munich.
Haslam, M. 1997. "Homeric Papyri and Transmission of the Text." In Morris and Powell 1997, 55–97.
Heffernan, J. A. W. 1993. *Museum of Words*. Chicago.
Heinze, R. 1915. *Virgils epische Technik*. 3rd ed. Leipzig.
Hershkowitz, D. 1991. "The *Aeneid* in *Aeneid* 3." *Vergilius* 37: 69–76.
Heubeck, A., and A. Hoekstra. 1989. *A Commentary on Homer's Odyssey, Vol. II*. Oxford.
Heubeck, A., S. West, and J. B. Hainsworth. 1988. *A Commentary on Homer's Odyssey, Vol. I*. Oxford.
Hexter, R. J. 1992. "Sidonian Dido." In Hexter and Selden 1992, 332–84.
Hexter, R. J. 1993. *A Guide to the Odyssey: A Commentary on the English Translation of Robert Fitzgerald*. New York.
Hexter, R. J. 1999. "Imitating Troy: A Reading of *Aeneid* 3." In Perkell 1999, 64–79.
Hexter, R. J. 2010. "On First Looking into Vergil's Homer." In Farrell and Putnam 2010, 26–36.
Hexter, R. J., and D. Selden, eds. 1992. *Innovations of Antiquity*. New York.

Heyne, C. G. 1832. *P. Vergilius Maro varietate lectionis et perpetua adnotatione illustratus*. 4th ed. Ed. G. P. Wagner. Vol. 2. Leipzig and London.
Heyworth, S. J. 1993. "Deceitful Crete: Aeneid 3.84. and the Hymns of Callimachus." *CQ* 43: 255–57.
Higbie, C. 1995. *Heroes' Names, Homeric Identities*. Alfred Bates Lord Studies in Oral Tradition vol. 10. New York.
Highet, G. 1972. *The Speeches in Vergil's Aeneid*. Princeton.
Hinds, S. 1987. *The Metamorphosis of Persephone*. Cambridge.
Hinds, S. 1998. *Allusion and Intertext: Dynamics of Appropriation in Roman Poetry*. New York.
Hohendahl-Zoetelief, I. M. 1980. *Manners in the Homeric Epic*. Leiden.
Holland, G. 1993. "The Name of Achilles: A Revised Etymology." *Glotta* 71: 17–27.
Hölscher, U. 1939. *Untersuchungen zur Form der Odyssee*. Berlin.
Hölscher, U. 1967. "Die Atridensage in der Odyssee." In Singer and von Weise 1967, 1–16.
Hölscher, U. 1989. *Die Odyssee. Epos zwischen Märchen und Roman*. 2nd ed. Munich.
Hommel, H. 1955. "Aigisthos und die Freier." *Studium Generale* 8: 237–45.
Hommel, H. 1980. *Der Gott Achilleus*. Heidelberg.
Hoof, A. J. L. van. 1990. *From Autothanasia to Suicide: Self-Killing in Classical Antiquity*. London.
Hornsby, R. A. 1970. *Patterns of Action in the Aeneid: An Interpretation of Vergil's Epic Similes*. Iowa City.
Horsfall, N. 1979. "Some Problems in the Aeneas Legend." *CQ* 29: 372–90.
Horsfall, N. 1995. *A Companion to the Study of Virgil*. Leiden.
Horsfall, N. 2000. *Virgil, Aeneid 7: A Commentary*. Leiden.
Horsfall, N. 2006. *Virgil, Aeneid 3: A Commentary*. Leiden.
Horsfall, N. 2008. *Virgil, Aeneid 2: A Commentary*. Leiden.
Hügi, M. 1952. *Vergils Aeneis und die hellenistische Dichtung*. Bern.
Janko, R. 1988. Review of *Odissea. 6. (Libri xxi–xxiv)*. Ed. M. Fernandez-Galiano and A. Heubeck. Trans. G. A. Privitera. *JHS* 108: 218–19.
Jens, W. 1948. "Der Eingang des dritten Buches der *Aeneis*." *Philologus* 97: 194–97.
Johnson, W. R. 1976. *Darkness Visible: A Study of Vergil's Aeneid*. Berkeley.
Jong, I. J. F. de. 1985. "*Iliad* 1.366–92: A Mirror Story." *Arethusa* 18: 1–22.
Jong, I. J. F. de. 1987. *Narrators and Focalizers. The Presentation of the Story in the Iliad*. Amsterdam.
Jong, I. J. F. de. 1992. "The Subjective Style in Odysseus' Wanderings." *CQ* 42: 1–11.
Jong, I. J. F. de. 2001. *A Narratological Commentary on the Odyssey*. Cambridge.
Kakridis, J. T. 1949. *Homeric Researches*. Lund.
Kakridis, J. T. 1971. *Homer Revisited*. Lund.
Kamptz, H. von. 1981. *Homerische Personennamen. Sprachwissenschaftliche und historische Klassifikationenen*. Göttingen.
Katz, M. A. 1991. *Penelope's Renown. Meaning and Indeterminacy in the Odyssey*. Princeton.
Kazazis, J. N., and A. Rengakos, eds. 1999. *Euphrosyne. Studies in Ancient Epic and Its Legacy in Honor of Dimitris N. Maronitis*. Stuttgart.
Keany, J. J., and R. Lamberton, eds. 1992. *Homer's Ancient Readers*. Princeton.
Kenney, E. J. 1979. "*Iudicium transferendi*: Virgil, Aeneid 2.469–505 and Its Antecedents." In West and Woodman 1979, 103–20 and 224–29.
Kilb, M. 1973. *Strukturen epischen Gestaltens im 7. und 23. Gesang der Odysse*. Munich.

Kinsey, T. E. 1979. "The Achaemenides Episode in Virgil's Aeneid III." *Latomus* 38: 110–24.
Kirk, G. S. 1962. *The Songs of Homer*. Cambridge.
Klinger, F. 1967. *Virgil*. Zurich.
Knauer, G. N. 1964. *Die Aeneis und Homer: Studien zur poetischen Technik Vergils mit Listen der Homerzitate in der Aeneis*. Hypomenmata 7. Göttingen.
Knauer, G. N. 1981. "Vergil and Homer." *ANRW* 2.31.2: 870–918.
Knox, B. M. W. 1950. "The Serpent and the Flame: The Imagery of the Second Book of the Aeneid." *AJPh* 71: 379–400.
Kohl, J. W. 1917. *De Chorizontibus*. Darmstadt.
Kopf, E. C. 1981. "Virgil and the Cyclic Epics." *ANRW* 2.31.2: 919–47.
Krapp, G. P. 1932. *The Paris Psalter and the Meters of Boethius*. Anglo-Saxon Poetic Records 5. New York.
Krischer, T. 1979. "UnHomeric Scene-Patterns in Vergil." *PLLS* 2: 143–54.
Kullman, W. 1960. *Die Quellen der Ilias (troischer Sagenkries)*. Hermes Einzelschriften 14. Wiesbaden.
Kullman, W. 1981. "Zur Methode der Neoanalyse in der Homerforschung." *WS* 15: 5–42.
Kurtz, G., D. Müller, and W. Nicolai, eds. 1981. *Gnomosyne. Menschliches Denken und Handeln in der frühgriechischen Literatur*. Munich.
Kyriakidis, S. 1998. *Narrative Structure and Poetics in the Aeneid. The Frame of Book 6*. Bari.
Kyriakidis, S., ed. 2004. *Middles in Latin Poetry*. Bari.
Laffitte, J. 1983. *Mélanges Édouard Delebecque*. Aix-en-Provence.
Lallemand, M. 1959. "Une source de l'Énéide: le Mahâbhârata." *Latomus* 18: 262–87.
Lanata, G. 1954–56. "Il problema della tecnica poetica in Omero." *Antiquitas* 9–11: 27–36.
Lausberg, M. 1983. "Iliadisches im ersten Buch der Aeneis." *Gymnasium* 90: 203–39.
Leaf, W. 1902. *The Iliad*. 2nd ed. 2 vols. London.
Lesky, A. 1967. "Die Schuld der Klytaimestra." *WS* 80: 5–21.
Létoublon, F. 1983. "Le miroir et la boucle." *Poétique* 53: 19–35.
Lewis, C. S. 1942. *Preface to Paradise Lost*. New York.
Little, D. A. 1970. "The Death of Turnus and the Pessimism of the Aeneid." *AUMLA* 33: 67–76.
Lloyd, R. B. 1957a. "*Aeneid* III: A New Approach." *AJPh* 78: 133–51.
Lloyd, R. B. 1957b. "*Aeneid* III and the Aeneas Legend." *AJPh* 78: 383–400.
Lockwood, J. F. 1929. "ΗΘΙΚΗ ΛΕΞΙΣ and Dinarchus." *CQ* 23: 180–85.
Lonsdale, S. H. 1990a. *Creatures of Speech: Lion, Herding and Hunting Similes in the Iliad*. Stuttgart.
Lonsdale, S. H. 1990b. "Simile and Ecphrasis in Homer and Virgil; the Poet as Craftsman and Choreographer." *Vergilius* 36: 7–30.
Lord, A. B. 1960. *The Singer of Tales*. Cambridge, MA.
Louden, B. 1995. "Categories of Homeric Wordplay." *TAPA* 125: 27–46.
Lowenstam, S. 1993. "The Pictures on Juno's Temple in the *Aeneid*." *CW* 87: 37–49.
Lowie, R. H. 1925. *Primitive Society*. New York.
Lyne, R. O. A. M. 1987. *Further Voices in Vergil's* Aeneid. Oxford.
MacKay, L. A. 1957. "Achilles as Model for Aeneas." *TAPA* 88: 11–16.
Macleod, C. W. 1982. *Homer: Iliad Book XXIV*. Cambridge.
Macleod, C. W. 1983. *Collected Essays*. Cambridge.
Maehler, H. 1963. *Die Auffassung des Dichterberufs im frühen Griechentum bis zur Zeit Pindars*. Göttingen.

Marchand, L. 1976. *Byron's Letters and Journals Vol. 5*. Cambridge, MA.
Marg, W. 1956. "Das erste Lied des Demodokos." In *Navicula Chiloniensis. Studia Philologa Felici Jacoby Professori Chiloniensi emerito octogenario oblata*, 16–29. Leiden.
Mariotti, I. 1981. "Il secondo proemio dell' Eneide." In *Letterature comparate, problemi e metodo : studi in onore di Ettore Paratore* 1: 459–64. Bologna.
Maronitis, D. N. 1981. "Die erste Trugrede des Odysseus in der *Odyssee*. Vorbild und Variationen." In Kurz, Müller, and Nicolai 1981, 117–34.
Martin, R. P. 1989. *The Language of Heroes: Speech and Performance in the Iliad*. Ithaca.
Martindale, C., ed. 1997. *The Cambridge Companion to Virgil*. Cambridge.
Mattes, W. 1958. *Odysseus bei den Phäaken*. Würzburg.
McCarty, W. 1989. "The Shape of the Mirror: Metaphorical Catoptrics in Classical Literature." *Arethusa* 22: 161–95.
McKay, A. G. 1966. "The Achaemenides Episode: Vergil, 'Aeneid' III, 588–591." *Vergilius* 12: 31–38.
McKay, A. G., ed. 1982. *Vergilian Bimillenary Lectures 1982*. Vergilius Suppl. 2. College Park, Maryland.
Merry, W. W. 1887. *Homer: "Odyssey."* Oxford.
Meyer, W. 1907. *De Homeri patronymicis*. Göttingen.
Miller, M. 1953. "Greek Kinship Terminology." *JHS* 63: 46–52.
Mills, D. H. 1978. "Vergil's Tragic Vision: The Death of Priam." *CW* 72: 159–66.
Monro, D. B. 1901. *Odyssey 13–20*. Oxford.
Mørland, H. 1960. "Zu den Namen in der Aeneis." *SO* 36: 21–29.
Mørland, H. 1968. "'Horaz', 'Vergil' und andere Gestalten in der Aeneis." *SO* 43: 57–67.
Morris, I., and B. Powell, eds. 1997. *A New Companion to Homer*. Suppl. Mnemosyne 163. Leiden.
Moskalew, W. 1988. "The Cyclops, Achaemenides, and the Permutations of the Guest-Host Relationship in *Aeneid* 1–4." *Vergilius* 32: 25–34.
Most, G. W. 1985. "The Stranger's Stratagem: Self-Disclosure and Self-Sufficiency in Greek Culture." *JHS* 109: 119–43.
Most, G. W. 1989. "The Structure and Function of Odysseus' Apologoi." *TAPA* 119: 115–30.
Moulton, C. 1977. *Similes in Homeric Poems*. Göttingen.
Muellener, L. C. 1996. *The Anger of Achilles: Mênis in Greek Epic*. Ithaca, NY.
Mühlestein, H. 1971. "Sieben Personennamen aus der Odyssee." *Ziva Antika* 21: 45–48.
Mühmelt, M. 1965. *Griechische Grammatik in der Vergilerklärung*. Zetemeta 37. Munich.
Murnaghan, S. 1987. *Disguise and Recognition in the Odyssey*. Princeton.
Murray, P. 1981. "Poetic Inspiration in Early Greece." *JHS* 101: 87–100.
Murray, P. 1983. "Homer and the Bard." In Grandsen, Murray, and Winnifrith 1983, 1–15.
Muth, R., and G. Pfohl, eds. 1979. *Serta Philologica Aenipontana*. Innsbrucker Beiträge zur Kulturwissenschaft 20. Innsbruck.
Mynors, R. A. B. 1969. *P. Vergilii Maronis opera*. Oxford.
Nagy, G. 1976. "The Name of Achilles: Etymology and Epic." In Davies and Meid 1976, 209–37.
Nagy, G. 1994. "The Name of Achilles: Questions of Etymology and 'Folk Etymology.'" *ICS* 19: 3–9.
Nagy, G. 1996. *Poetry as Performance: Homer and Beyond*. Cambridge.
Nagy, G. 1999. *Best of the Achaeans*. 2nd ed. Baltimore.

Nelis, D. 2001. *Vergil's Aeneid and the Argonautica of Apollonius Rhodius.* ARCA: Classical and Medieval Texts, Papers and Monographs 39. Leeds.
Nelis, D. 2010. "Vergil's Library." In Farrell and Putnam 2010, 13–25.
Nelson, L., Jr. 1961. "Baudelaire and Virgil: A Reading of *Le Cygne.*" *Comparative Literature* 13: 332–45.
Nethercut, W. R. 1968. "Invasion in the *Aeneid.*" *G&R* 15: 82–95.
Nethercut, W. R. 1976. "Foreshadowing in *Aeneid* 1.751-52." *Vergilius* 22: 30–33.
Newton, I. 1672. "Mr. Isaac Newton's Answer to Some Considerations upon His Doctrine of Light and Colors; Which Doctrine Was Printed in Numb. 80. of These Tracts." *Philosophical Proceedings* 7: 5084–103.
Niles, J. D. 1978. "Patterning in the Wanderings of Odysseus." *Ramus* 7: 46–60.
Norden, E. 1915. *Ennius und Vergilius; Kriegsbilder aus Roms grosser Zeit.* Leipzig.
O'Hara, J. J. 1990. *Death and the Optimistic Prophecy in Vergil's Aeneid.* Princeton.
O'Hara, J. J. 1996. *True Names: Vergil and the Alexandrian Tradition of Etymological Wordplay.* Ann Arbor, MI.
Olson, S. D. 1990. "The Stories of Agamemnon in Homer's *Odyssey.*" *TAPA* 120: 57–71.
Olson, S. D. 1995. *Blood and Iron. Stories and Storytelling in Homer's Odyssey.* Leiden.
Oswald, R. 1993. *Das Ende der Odyssee. Studien zu Strukturen epischen Gestaltens.* Graz.
Otis, B. 1964. *Virgil: A Studied in Civilized Poetry.* Oxford.
Page, D. L. 1955. *The Homeric Odyssey.* Oxford.
Palmer, L. R. 1955. *Achaeans and Indo-Europeans: An Inaugural Lecture Delivered Before the University of Oxford on 4 November 1954.* Oxford.
Palmer, L. R. 1963. *The Interpretation of Mycenaean Greek Texts.* Oxford.
Palmer, L. R. 1979. "A Mycenaean 'Akhilleid'?" In Muth and Pfohl 1979, 3: 255–61.
Palmer, L. R. 1980. *The Greek Language.* London.
Panoussi, V. 2009. *Greek Tragedy in Vergil's Aeneid: Ritual, Empire, and Intertext.* Cambridge.
Papanghelis, T. D. 1999. "*Relegens errata litora*: Virgil's Reflexive 'Odyssey.'" In Kazazis and Rengakos, 275–90.
Parry, H. 1994. "The *Apologos* of Odysseus: Lies, All Lies?" *Phoenix* 48: 1–20.
Parsons, E. C. 1914. "Teknonymy." *American Journal of Sociology* 19: 649–50.
Paschalis, M. 1997. *Vergil's Aeneid: Semantic Relations and Proper Names.* Oxford.
Pasquali, G. 1952. *Storia della tradizione e critica del testo.* 2nd ed. Florence.
Peabody, B. 1975. *The Winged Word.* Albany, NY.
Pearson, L. 1939. *The Early Ionic Historians.* Oxford.
Peerlkamp, P. 1943. *P. Virgilii Maronis Aeneidos libri VII–XII.* Leiden.
Peradotto, J. 1990. *Man in the Middle Voice, Name and Narration in the Odyssey.* Princeton.
Perkell, C., ed. 1999. *Reading Vergil's* Aeneid: *An Interpretive Guide.* Norman, OK.
Perret, J. 1942. *Les Origines de la Légende troyenne de Rome.* Paris.
Pestalozzi, H. 1945. *Die Achilleis als Quelle der Ilias.* Erlenbach.
Pfeiffer, R. 1976. *History of Classical Scholarship from 1300 to 1850.* Oxford.
Pigna, G. 1554. *I romanzi.* Venice.
Podlecki, A. J. 1971. "Some Odyssean Similes." *G&R* 18: 81–90.
Poetscher, W. 1986. "Das Selbstverständnis des Dichters in der homerischen Poesie." *Literaturwissenschaftliches Jahrbuch* 27: 4–22.

Polk, G. C. 1996. "Vergil's Penelope: The Diana Simile in *Aeneid* 1.498–502." *Vergilius* 42: 38–49.

Pomathios, J. L. 1987. *Le pouvoir politique et sa représentation dans l'Énéide de Virgile*. Brussels.

Pöschl, V. 1977. *Die Dichtkunst Virgils: Bild und Symbol in der Aeneis*. 3rd ed. Berlin.

Pratt, L. H. 1993. *Lying and Poetry from Homer to Pindar. Falsehood and Deception in Archaic Greek Poetics*. Ann Arbor, MI.

Prinz, F. 1979. *Gründungsmythen und Sagenchronologie*. Zetemeta 72. Munich.

Pucci, J. 1998. *The Full-Knowing Reader: Allusion and the Power of the Reader in the Western Literary Tradition*. New Haven.

Pucci, P. 1979. "The Song of the Sirens." *Arethusa* 12: 121–32.

Pucci, P. 1987. *Odysseus Polutropos: Intertextual Readings in the* Odyssey *and* Iliad. Ithaca.

Putnam, M. C. J. 1965. *The Poetry of the Aeneid*. Cambridge, MA.

Putnam, M. C. J. 1980. "The Third Book of the *Aeneid*: From Homer to Rome." *Ramus* 9: 1–21.

Putnam, M. C. J. 1990. "Anger, Blindness, and Insight in Virgil's Aeneid." *Apeiron* 23: 7–40.

Putnam, M. C. J. 1995. *Vergil's Aeneid: Interpretation and Influence*. Chapel Hill, NC.

Putnam, M. C. J. 1998a. "Dido's Murals and Virgilian Ekphrasis." *HSCP* 98: 243–75.

Putnam, M. C. J. 1998b. *Virgil's Epic Designs: Ekphrasis in the Aeneid*. New Haven.

Quint, D. 1993. *Epic and Empire: Politics and Generic Form from Virgil to Milton*. Princeton.

Race, W. H. 1993. "First Appearances in the *Odyssey*." *TAPA* 123: 79–107.

Ramminger, J. 1991. "Imitation and Allusion in the Achaemenides Scene (Vergil, *Aeneid* 3.588–691)." *AJPh* 112: 53–71.

Rank, L. P. 1951. *Etymologiseering en Verwante Verschijnselen bij Homerus*. Assen.

Redfield, J. M. 1983. "The Economic Man." In Rubino and Shelmerdine 1983, 218–47.

Reece, S. 1993. *The Stranger's Welcome. Oral Theory and the Aesthetics of the Homeric Hospitality Scene*. Ann Arbor, MI.

Reed, J. D. 2007. *Virgil's Gaze: Nation and Poetry in the Aeneid*. Princeton.

Reiff, A. 1959. *Interpretatio, imitatio, aemulatio, interpretatio: Begriff und Vorstellung literarischer Abhängigkeit bei den Römern*. Cologne.

Reinhardt, K. 1960. "Die Abenteuer des Odysseus." In *Tradition und Geist*, 47–124. Göttingen.

Rengakos, A. 1993. "Zum Griechenbild im Vergils Aeneis." *Antike und Abenland* 1993: 112–24.

Richardson, N. J. 1980. "Literary Criticism in the Exegetical Scholia to the *Iliad*: A Sketch." *CQ* 30: 265–87.

Richardson, S. 1996. "Truth in the Tales of the *Odyssey*." *Mnem.* 49: 393–402.

Ritook, Z. 1989. "The Views of Early Greek Epic on Poetry and Art." *Mnem.* 42: 331–48.

Roisman, H. 1987. "Penelope's Indignation." *TAPA* 117: 59–68.

Roisman, H. 1990. "*Kerdion* in the *Iliad*: Profit and Trickiness." *TAPA* 120: 23–35.

Römisch, E. 1976. "Die Achaemenides-Episode in Vergils Aeneis." In Görgemanns and Schmidt 1976, 208–27.

Rose, G. P. 1969. "The Unfriendly Phaeacians." *TAPA* 98: 391–98.

Roti, G. C. 1983. "'Omnibus Unus' (*Aeneid* 3.716)." *CQ* 33: 300–301.
Rubino, C. A., and C. W. Shelmerdine. 1983. *Approaches to Homer*. Austin, TX.
Russell, D. A. 1964. *'Longinus': On the Sublime*. Oxford.
Russo, J., M. Fernández-Galiano, and A. Heubeck. 1992. *A Commentary on Homer's Odyssey, Vol. III*. Oxford.
Rüter, K. 1969. *Odysseeinterpretationen. Untersuchungen zum ersten Buch und zur Phaiakis*. Göttingen.
Rutherford, R. B. 1986. "The Philosophy of the Odyssey." *JHS* 106: 145–62.
Rutherford, R. B. 1993. "From the Iliad to the Odyssey." *BICS* 38: 37–54.
Saïd, S. 1978. *La Faute tragique*. Paris.
Sanderlin, G. 1975–6. "Aeneas as Apprentice–Point of View in the Third *Aeneid*." *CJ* 71: 53–56.
Santiago, R. A. 1962. "Observaciones sobre algunos usos formularios de ἦμαρ en Homero." *Emerita* 30: 139–50.
Scafoglio, G. 2001. "La tragedia di Euripide e la mediazione romana arcaica nel libro II dell' *Eneide*." *Vichiana* 4a: 187–212.
Schadewaldt, W. 1951. *Von Homers Welt und Werk*. 2nd ed. Stuttgart.
Schadewaldt, W. 1959. "Kleiderdinge: Zur Analyse der Odyssee." *Hermes* 87: 13–26.
Scheliha, R. von. 1943. *Patroklos: gedanken über Homers Dichtung und Gestalten*. Basel.
Schenk, P. 1984. *Die Gestalt des Turnus in Vergils Aeneis*. Beiträge zur klassischen Philologie 164. Könignstein.
Schlunk, R. R. 1974. *The Homeric Scholia and the Aeneid: A Study of the Influence of Ancient Homeric Literary Criticism on Vergil*. Ann Arbor, MI.
Schlunk, R. R. 1976. "The Theme of the Suppliant-Exile in the *Iliad*." *AJPh* 97: 199–209.
Schmidt, E. G. 1983. "Achilles-Odysseus-Aeneas: zur Typologie des vergilischen Helden." *Listy Filologické* 106: 24–28.
Schmiel, R. 1987. "Achilles in Hades." *CPh* 82: 35–37.
Schmit-Neuerburg, T. 1999. *Vergils Aeneis und die antike Homerexegese, Untersuchungen zum Einfluss ethischer und kritischer Homerrezeption auf imitatio und aemulatio Vergils*. Untersuchungen zur antiken Literatur und Geschichte 56. Berlin.
Schoeck, G. 1961. *Ilias und Aithiopis: Kyklische Motive in homerische Brechung*. Zurich.
Schwartz, E. 1924. *Die Odyssee*. Munich.
Schwarz, F. F. 1983. "Fumat Neptunia Troia. Feuerzeichensprache im zweiten Buch der *Aeneis*." In Händel and Meid 1983, 443–61.
Scott, J. A. 1912. "Patronymics as a Test of the Relative Age of the Homeric Books." *CPh* 7: 293–301.
Scott, W. C. 1974. *The Oral Nature of the Homeric Simile*. Suppl. Mnem. 28. Leiden.
Scully, S. 1987. "Doubling in the Tale of Odysseus." *CW* 80: 401–17.
Segal, C. P. 1966. "*Aeternum per saecula nomen*. The Golden Bough and the Tragedy of History." Part 2. *Arion* 5: 34–72.
Segal, C. P. 1992. "Bard and Audience." In Keany and Lamberton 1992, 3–29.
Seiler, H. 1973. "Methodologisches zu κέρδιον, κέρδιστος." *Glotta* 51: 96–98.
Selden, D. L. 2006. "Vergil and the Satanic *Cogito*." *Literary Imagination* 8: 345–85.
Semple, W. H. 1955. "A Short Study of Aeneid, Book III." *Bulletin of the Rylands Library* 38: 225–40.
Shive, D. 1987. *Naming Achilles*. New York.
Simonsuuri, K. 1979. *Homer's Original Genius: Eighteenth-Century Notions of Early Greek Epic*. Cambridge.

Singer, H., and B. von Weise, eds. 1967. *Festschrift für Richard Alewyn.* Cologne.
Slatkin, L. M. 1986. "The Wrath of Thetis." *TAPA* 116: 1–24.
Slatkin, L. M. 1991. *The Power of Thetis: Allusion and Interpretation in the Iliad.* Berkeley.
Smith, P. M. 1981. "Aineadai as Patrons of Iliad XX and the Homeric Hymn to Aphrodite." *HSCP* 85: 17–58.
Smith, R. A. 1997. *Poetic Allusion and Poetic Embrace in Ovid and Virgil.* Ann Arbor.
Smith, R. A. 2005. *The Primacy of Vision in Virgil's Aeneid.* Austin, TX.
Smith, S. C. 1999. "Remembering the Enemy: Narrative, Focalization, and Vergil's Portrait of Achilles." *TAPA* 129: 225–62.
Snodgrass, A. M. 1974. "An Historical Homeric Society?" *JHS* 94: 114–25.
Solmsen, F. 1986. "Aeneas Founded Rome with Odysseus." *HSCP* 90: 93–110.
Sordi, M., ed. 1976. *I canali della propaganda nel mondo antico.* Milan.
Stadler, T. W. 1942. *Vergils Aeneis, Eine poetische Betrachtung.* Einsiedeln.
Stanford, W. B. 1937. "ΤΗΛΥΓΗΤΟΣ." *CR* 51: 168.
Stanford, W. B. 1952. "The Homeric Etymology of the Name Odysseus." *CPh* 47: 209–13.
Stanford, W. B. 1954. *The Ulysses Theme.* Oxford.
Stanford, W. B. 1965. *The Odyssey of Homer.* 2nd ed. 2 vols. New York.
Stanley, K. 1965. "Irony and Foreshadowing in *Aeneid* I, 462." *AJPh* 86: 267–77.
Starry West, G. 1983. "Andromache and Dido." *AJPh* 104: 257–67.
Steinmetz, E. 1894. *Ethnologische Studien zur ersten Entwicklung der Strafe.* Leiden.
Strunk, K. 1958. "ἀπηύρα." *Glotta* 37: 118–27.
Svenbro, J. 1976. *La Parole et le marbre. Aux origines de la poétique Grecque.* Lund.
Taplin, O. 1990. "The Earliest Quotation of the *Iliad*?" In Craik 1990, 111–12.
Thalmann, W. G. 1984. *Conventions of Form and Thought in Early Greek Poetry.* Baltimore.
Thomas, R. F. 1983. "Virgil's Ecphrastic Centerpieces." *HSCP* 87: 175–84.
Thomas, R. F. 1985. "From *Recusatio* to Commitment: The Evolution of the Virgilian Program." *PLLS* 5: 61–73.
Thomas, R. F. 1986. "Virgil's *Georgics* and the Art of Reference." *HSCP* 90: 171–98.
Thomas, R. F. 1991. "Furor and Furiae in Virgil." *AJPh* 112: 261.
Thomas, R. F. 2001. *Virgil and the Augustan Reception.* Cambridge.
Thomas, R. F. 2004. "'Stuck in the Middle with You': Virgilian Middles." In Kyriakidis 2004, 123–50.
Thornton, M. K. 1985. "The Adaptation of Homer's Artemis-Nausicaa Simile in the *Aeneid*." *Latomus* 44: 615–22.
Timpanaro, S. 1986. *Per la storia della filologia virgiliana antica.* Quaderni di 'filologia e critica' 6. Rome.
Trahman, C. R. 1952. "Odysseus' Lies (*Odyssey*, Books 13–19)." *Phoenix* 6: 31–43.
Traiana, A. 1984–91. "Superbia." In Della Corte 1984–91, 4: 1072–76.
Tylor, E. B. 1889. "On a Method of Investigating the Development of Institutions; Applied to Laws of Marriage and Descent." *Journal of the Anthropological Institute of Great Britain and Ireland* 18: 245–72.
Ussani, V. 1947. "Enea traditore." *SIFC* 22: 108–23.
Van Nortwick, T. 1980. "Aeneas, Turnus, and Achilles." *TAPA* 110: 303–14.
Van Ooteghem, I. 1937. "Énée à Buthrotum." *EtCl* 5: 8–13.
Verdenius, W. J. 1985. *A Commentary on Hesiod's Works and Days vv. 1–382.* Leiden.

Vinchesi, M. A. 1984–91. "Patronimici." In Della Corte 1984–91, 2: 1029–32.
Walcot, P. 1977. "Odysseus and the Art of Lying." *Ancient Society* 8: 1–19.
Warde-Fowler, W. 1917. "Duplicated Altars and Offerings in Virgil, *Ecl.* V.65; *Aen.* III.305; and *Aen.* V.77ff." *CR* 31: 163–67.
Weinberg, B. 1961. *A History of Literary Criticism in the Italian Renaissance.* Chicago.
Weiss, M. 1998. "Erotica: On the Prehistory of Greek Desire." *HSCP* 98: 31–61.
West, D. 1969. "Multiple-Correspondence Similes in the Aeneid." *JRS* 59: 40–49.
West, D. 1974. "The Deaths of Hector and Turnus." *G&R* 21: 21–31.
West, D., and T. Woodman, eds. 1979. *Creative Imitation and Latin Literature.* Cambridge.
West, M. L. 2001. *Studies in the Text and Transmission of the Iliad.* Munich and Leipzig.
West, S. 1967. *The Ptolemaic Papyri of Homer.* Cologne.
West, S. 1989. "Laertes Revisited." *PCPhS* 215: 113–43.
West, S. 2003. "Crete in the 'Aeneid': Two Intertextual Footnotes." *CQ* 53: 302–8.
Wheeler, E. L. 1988. *Stratagem and the Vocabulary of Military Trickery.* Leiden.
Whitehead, O. 1984. "The Funeral of Achilles; An Epilogue to the 'Iliad' in Book 24 of the 'Odyssey.'" *G&R* 31: 119–25.
Whitman, C. H. 1958. *Homer and the Heroic Tradition.* Cambridge, MA.
Wickert, L. 1930. "Homerisches und Römisches im Kriegswesen der Aeneis." *Philologus* 85: 285–302, 437–62.
Wigodsky, M. 1972. *Virgil and Early Latin Poetry.* Wiesbaden.
Wijdeveld, G. 1942. "De Vergilii *Aen.* II, 469 sqq." *Mnem.* 10: 238–40.
Wilamowitz-Moellendorff, U. von. 1884. *Homerische Untersuchungen.* Berlin.
Wilamowitz-Moellendorff, U. von. 1927. *Die Heimkehr des Odysseus.* Berlin.
Wilamowitz-Moellendorff, U. von. 1982. *History of Classical Scholarship.* Trans. A. Harris, ed. H. Lloyd-Jones. London.
Willcock, M. M. 1973. "The Funeral Games of Patroclus." *BICS* 20: 1–11.
Willcock, M. M. 1976. *A Companion to the Iliad.* London.
Willcock, M. M. 1983. "Antilochos in the Iliad." In Laffitte 1983, 477–85.
Willcock, M. M. 1987. "The Final Scenes of *Iliad* XVII." In Bremer, de Jong, and Kalff 1987, 185–94.
Williams, G. 1968. *Tradition and Originality in Roman Poetry.* Oxford.
Williams, G. 1983. *Technique and Ideas in the* Aeneid. New Haven.
Williams, R. D. 1960. "The Pictures on Dido's Temple (*Aeneid* 1.453–93)." *CQ* 10: 145–51.
Williams, R. D. 1962. *P. Vergili Maronis Aeneidos Liber Tertius.* Oxford.
Williams, R. D. 1963. "Virgil and the Odyssey." *Phoenix* 17: 266–74.
Williams, R. D. 1972. *The Aeneid of Virgil: Edited with Introduction and Notes.* New York.
Wills, J. 1997. *Repetition in Latin Poetry: Figures of Allusion.* Oxford.
Wiltshire, S. 1989. *Public and Private in Vergil's Aeneid.* Amherst, MA.
Wistrand, E. 1960. "Virgil's Palaces in the Aeneid." *Klio* 38: 146–54.
Wlosok, A. 1986. "*Gemina Doctrina:* On Allegorical Interpretation." *PLLS* 5: 75–84.
Wooding, C. 1990. *Table Talk: Collected Works of Samuel Taylor Coleridge, Volume 14.* Princeton.
Woolsey, R. B. 1941. "Repeated Narratives in the *Odyssey.*" *CPh* 36: 167–81.
Yamagata, N. 1994. *Homeric Morality.* Leiden.

Index of Passages

Homer, *Iliad*
1.2: 55
1.5: 46, 78
1.6: 109
1.8–120: 33
1.189: 111
1.225: 53
1.240–42: 44–45
1.308: 95
1.360–61: 44
1.380–82: 34
1.415–18: 35
1.416–17: 47
1.430: 95
1.505: 47
2.180: 43
2.189: 43
2.260: 36
2.594–600: 78
2.645: 101
2.768–69: 48, 52
2.791–94: 128n25
2.844–45: 99
3.76: 124n73
3.175: 36
3.202: 43, 125n92
3.208: 43
3.212: 43
3.236–42: 36
3.278: 126n102
4.339: 125n92
4.354: 36, 84
5.343–45 34
5.436–37: 43
5.565: 36
6.37–65: 137n102
6.145–49: 33
6.212–36: 34
6.328–29: 99

6.342: 55
6.399–484: 36
6.402: 106
7.54: 124n73
8.135: 46
9.81: 36
9.142: 36
9.145: 36
9.164: 95
9.222–24: 52
9.249–50: 45
9.284: 36
9.287: 36
9.308: 56
9.312–13: 52, 95–96
9.410–16: 59, 95,121n21
9.412–13: 47
9.497: 59
9.624–42: 52
9.632: 59
9.644–45: 52
10.376–457: 137n102
11.430: 54
11.473–86: 53
11.765–69: 41
13.5: 122n34
13.210–515: 101
13.341: 67
13.355: 58
13.392: 50
13.533–35: 128n25
13.621: 98
13.625: 98
14.415: 46
14.489–505: 132n99
14.490–91: 132n99
15.68–71: 127n15
15.339: 128n25
15.570: 48

15.618–21: 27
16.15: 128n17
16.21: 126n106
16.33: 59
16.205–14: 57
16.228: 46
16.248: 122n34
16.272: 122n34
16.431–61: 34
16.485: 50
16.702–3: 43
16.775–76: 124n80
16.784–85: 43
17.17: 43
17.125: 50
17.132: 48
17.165: 122n34
17.274–318: 48
17.279–80: 48, 52
17.642: 48
17.652–53: 48
17.655: 48
17.694–96: 49
17.698–99: 50
17.715–21: 48
18.26–27: 50
18.34: 50–51
18.35–51: 50
18.54–56: 35
18.58–60: 42
18.61–62: 47
18.70–71: 44
18.95: 47
18.98–99: 47
18.104: 126n122
18.120–21: 47
18.155–60: 48
18.330–35: 123n62
18.339–441: 122n47
18.433: 128n17
18.442–43: 47
18.458: 47
18.497–508: 125n95
19.7–8: 44
19.8: 123n61
19.57: 123n61
19.216–19: 57
19.225–29: 58
19.307: 123n61
19.327: 36
19.367: 123n61
19.416–17: 50, 64
20.73: 106
20.74: 106

20.216–18: 101
20.302–8: 63
20.307–8: 4
20.318–29: 110
20.338–39: 84
20.407–23: 100
20.445–46: 43
20.467–68: 43
20.483: 50
21.176–77: 43
21.189: 128n17
21.224: 98
21.414: 98
21.440: 58
21.459: 98
22.31–32: 67
22.93–95: 70, 112
22.115–16: 99
22.134–35: 67
22.250–52: 17
22.317–21: 67
22.358–60: 50, 64
22.365: 72
22.395–405: 16
22.463–65: 16
23.13–14: 119n64
23.46–47: 47
23.51: 126n101
23.65–107: 93
23.72: 57
23.104–4: 57
23.137: 123n61
23.167: 123n61
23.175–77: 69
23.222–23: 124n74
23.276: 58
23.651–99: 10
23.707–39: 54
23.708–9: 54
23.723: 56
23.724–25: 54
23.729–32: 54
23.756: 48
23.80–81: 50, 64, 93
23.97–102: 43
24.14–16: 16
24.127: 44
24.139–40: 46
24.250: 128n25
24.306: 134n17
24.467: 36
24.468–676: 68
24.485–512: 69
24.486: 36

24.487: 74
24.560–70: 68
24.574–75: 124n71
24.772: 123n51

Homer, *Odyssey*
1.2: 91, 98
1.6: 102
1.13–15: 37
1.29–44: 33
1.80–87: 37
1.113–14: 37
1.188–93: 37
1.206–9: 39
1.215–20: 39–40
1.222–23: 40
1.325–27: 78
1.351–52: 78
2.47: 37
2.52–54: 37
2.183–85: 38
2.282: 53
3.36: 41
3.109–12: 48
3.112: 48
3.163: 53
3.191–92: 101
3.230–31: 38
3.401: 41
4.116–19: 131n71
4.155–67: 41
4.187–88: 49
4.202: 48
4.265–89: 93
4.266–89: 65
4.539–40: 125n82
4.555–60: 37
4.658–74: 102
4.704–5: 49
4.790: 99
5.28–115: 81
5.131: 46
5.282–312: 81
5.308–10: 50
6.4–6: 80
6.57: 41
6.102–9: 81
6.119–21: 82
6.175–77: 132n86
6.195: 80
6.204–5: 76
6.243: 76
6.277–79: 130n60
6.280–81: 76

7.18–77: 81
7.61–63: 131n72
7.146: 131n72
7.168: 53
7.186–206: 76
7.199: 77
7.205–6: 131n72
7.237–39: 77
7.238–39: 107
7.240–97: 77
7.244–55: 81
7.248: 108
7.249: 46
7.321–23: 77
7.330–33: 80
8.73–82: 78
8.75: 78
8.77: 78
8.77–82: 84
8.81: 79
8.82: 78
8.83–95: 77
8.97–103: 78
8.100–3: 80
8.132–85: 78
8.215–29: 37
8.219–20: 78
8.241–45: 80
8.250–53: 80
8.431–32: 80
8.493: 86
8.494: 87
8.494–95: 79
8.499–514: 79
8.499–520: 66, 93
8.507: 133n7
8.515: 133n7
8.515–20: 79
8.521–34: 77
8.550: 82
8.550–55: 107
8.550–86: 77
8.555: 82
8.573–75: 82
8.574–77: 107
9.20: 82
9.21: 108
9.33: 55
9.38–39: 134n31
9.116–41: 81
9.173–76: 82
9.252–55: 132n85
10.28–30: 103
10.31–55: 94

Index of Passages

10.50–52: 125n82
10.67: 134n11
10.87–94: 81
10.103–11: 131n80
10.112–13: 124n73
10.493: 126n104
10.526: 126n101
11.34: 126n101
11.84–89: 42
11.87: 44
11.94: 137n85
11.119–37: 64
11.126: 105
11.134: 64
11.164–79: 42
11.195–96: 45
11.200–3: 42
11.202–3: 42, 45
11.206–8: 43
11.210: 44
11.387–89: 48
11.458: 105
11.467–71: 47–48, 51, 125n84
11.467–540: 47
11.472: 57
11.473–76: 56
11.478: 57
11.482–86: 59
11.486: 60
11.488–91: 60
11.492–93: 105
11.492–94: 61
11.508–9: 61
11.511: 71
11.511–12: 133n112
11.512: 61
11.522: 49
11.523–32: 62, 66, 93
11.532–37: 62
11.535: 96
11.538–40: 62
11.539–40: 68
11.541–67: 54
11.543–51: 95
11.545–48: 55
11.548–49: 55
11.548–51: 125n82
11.550–51: 52, 55, 123n67
11.552: 55
11.554–55: 55
11.556–58: 55
11.558–59: 55
11.562: 55
11.565–67: 55

11.601–3: 126n105
11.632:126n101
12.201–59: 106
12.338–73: 94
12.353–88: 103
12.372: 94
12.387: 46
12.415–16: 46
12.417: 46
13.96–104: 81
13.253–86: 80, 135n45
13.259: 101
13.357: 43
13.373: 99
13.403–49: 81
13.415: 40
13.418: 40
13.422–23: 40
14.27: 99
14.192–359: 131n74, 135n45
14.237: 101
14.305–6: 123n60
14.307: 46
14.379–85: 135n45
15.10: 37
15.17: 58
15.53: 60
15.315: 99
15.358: 123n56
16.17–21: 38
16.61–67: 131n74
16.186–219: 39
16.227–31: 80
16.271: 99
16.279: 60
16.420–33: 70
17.251–53: 37–38
17.381: 114
17.454: 114
17.522–27: 131n74
18.32–116: 10
18.167: 99
18.178: 60
18.283: 55
18.379: 84
19.26–28: 38
19.87–88: 38
19.165–202: 135n45
19.181: 101
19.221–48: 135n45
19.268–99: 135n45
19.278–82: 80
19.399–412: 37
19.471–72: 124n75

20.12: 99
20.53: 123n58
20.291: 99
20.338–40: 38
20.379: 127n122
21.393–423: 37
22.1–7: 37
22.35–41: 112
22.115: 53
22.202: 53
22.481–82: 46
22.493: 123n59
23.264–84: 64–65
23.296: 127n4
23.330: 46
23.338–41: 80
23.356: 99
24.14: 57
24.15–18: 48, 125n84
24.17–18: 52
24.18: 123n67
24.36–42: 50
24.47–59: 50
24.78–79: 49, 123n65
24.465–66: 128n30
24.520–25: 70
24.528: 64
24.537–40: 70
24.539: 46

Virgil, *Aeneid*
1.4: 96
1.5: 109
1.6: 103
1.19–31: 96
1.81–123: 81
1.113–19: 83
1.147–48: 69
1.159: 81
1.278: 91
1.302–3: 80
1.308: 82
1.338: 80
1.369–70: 82
1.375–76: 82
1.378–79: 82
1.384–86: 82
1.446–47: 84–85
1.450–52: 83
1.455–56: 84
1.456: 9, 83
1.458: 83
1.463: 83
1.468–78: 83

1.483–84: 16
1.483–87: 83
1.488–93: 84
1.498–505: 81
1.522–60: 85
1.565–78: 85
1.595–96: 85
1.599: 82
1.609–10: 87
1.617: 74, 85
1.623–24: 86
1.625: 85
1.647–56: 83
1.733: 87
1.752: 86
1.753–55: 86–87
1.755: 92, 129n49, 133n8
2.3: 87, 94
2.6–8: 87–88
2.7: 93, 129n44
2.22: 129n36
2.44: 92
2.48: 9, 92
2.54–56: 73
2.56: 129n36
2.90: 129n44
2.164: 129n44
2.191: 129n36
2.228–339: 73
2.244–45: 73
2.260: 93, 133n7
2.261: 93, 129n44
2.263: 67
2.270: 93
2.270–71: 73
2.285–86: 93
2.289: 100
2.290: 93
2.291: 129n36
2.294–95: 93
2.298–308: 130n50
2.299–302: 94
2.300: 74
2.316–17: 74
2.411–12: 92
2.412: 118n34
2.469–558: 66
2.469–70: 67
2.471–75: 67
2.473: 68
2.479: 113
2.489: 92
2.491–92: 95
2.506: 129n45

2.509–11: 69
2.512: 134n17
2.515: 96
2.524–25: 69
2.526–30: 68
2.526–58: 68
2.528: 95, 113
2.530–32: 68
2.532: 69
2.540–43: 68, 112
2.544–46: 69
2.547–50: 71
2.548: 67
2.548–49: 113
2.549: 88
2.550: 96
2.550–53: 68
2.552–53: 113
2.557: 75, 129n42
2.557–58: 72
2.559–60: 73
2.560: 114
2.560–62: 74
2.567–88: 72
2.598–99: 92
2.604–7: 130n50
2.662–63: 75
2.663: 100
2.735: 114
2.735–36: 130n50
2.739: 92
2.750: 94
2.752–53: 94
2.756–57: 94
2.760: 94
2.761: 96
2.761–63: 95
2.762: 129n44
2.766–67: 96
2.774: 74
2.787: 130n53
2.792–94: 119n62
3.1: 129n36
3.1–3: 98
3.3: 99
3.15–18: 99
3.24–25: 99
3.44: 99–100
3.45–46: 135n33
3.48: 74, 135n35
3.55: 100
3.61: 100
3.67–68: 100
3.82–83: 100

3.86–88: 100
3.94: 101, 135n43
3.96–97: 100
3.97–98: 4–5
3.102: 101
3.107: 101
3.109–10: 101
3.121–22: 102
3.123: 102, 104
3.133: 102
3.135–46: 102
3.150–51: 103
3.187: 103
3.209–77: 103
3.272: 135n55
3.272–73: 103
3.273: 129n44
3.291: 104
3.294–505: 104
3.298: 74
3.301: 106
3.302–4: 105
3.305: 105, 136n64
3.310–12: 105
3.331–32: 75
3.339: 105
3.342–43: 105
3.349–50: 105–6
3.374–462: 104
3.388: 105
3.458: 106
3.462: 106
3.469: 112
3.484: 106
3.486: 105
3.488: 106
3.489–90: 105
3.506–47: 106
3.566–67: 119n62
3.569–87: 107
3.582: 107
3.588–691: 107
3.590: 107
3.594: 107
3.613–14: 108
3.690–91: 108
3.707: 108
3.714: 109
3.716: 108
3.717: 88
4.64: 118n35
4.138: 137n89
4.335–36: 87
4.343: 129n36

4.344: 102
4.373–74: 82
4.424: 99
4.537: 118n35
4.538–39: 133n107
4.658: 118n35
4.690–91: 119n62
4.696: 99
5.463: 10
5.607: 118n35
5.756: 102
5.808: 67
5.812: 110
6.89–90: 13
6.89: 109
6.93–94: 109
6.700–1: 119n62
6.776: 129n42
6.865: 118n38
6.875: 118n35
7.1: 6
7.1–5: 13, 111
7.40: 9, 109
7.44: 119n43
7.45: 7
7.246–48: 83
7.321–22: 109–10
7.362: 110
7.473: 138n108
7.54–56: 114
7.586: 26–27
7.649: 138n108

7.783: 138n108
8.9–17: 110
8.564–66: 119n62
9.136–39: 110
9.148: 110, 111
9.343: 129n42
9.600: 110
9.602: 129n44
9.742: 110, 112–13
10.97: 110
10.535–36: 113
10.581: 86
10.635: 118n35
10.662: 118n35
10.685–86: 119n62
10.824: 130n55
10.885–86: 119n62
11.188–90: 17
11.393: 118n35
11.846: 129n42
12.54: 10
12.90–91: 137n93
12.350: 67
12.474: 113
12.476: 113
12.545: 129n36
12.579: 113
12.665–66: 113–14
12.861: 118n35
12.937: 114
12.940: 111
12.946–47: 13, 111

Subject Index

A

Achaeans, 33–34, 44–45, 48, 55, 78–79, 93; best of, 57–59; depicted on temple of Juno, 84–85
Achaemenides, 107–9
Achates, 83
Achilles: abuses Hector's corpse, 16–18, 69, 83–84, 111–12; anger of, 9, 13, 111, 114; best of the Achaeans, 57–59; contest over his arms, 54–55, 95; converses with Odysseus in underworld, 47, 51–52, 56–62, 95–96, 112; death of, 25, 50–51, 63–64; depicted on the temple of Juno, 83; embassy to, 45–46, 52–53, 95; etymological wordplay, 44–45, 60; final duel with Hector, 17, 67–68, 70, 72, 111–12; hears about Neoptolemus from Odysseus, 61–62, 65–66, 72, 76, 96, 105–6; heroic paradigm, 13, 51–58, 63, 66, 68–71, 91, 93–95, 112; interaction with Thetis, 34–36, 42–44, 47; model for Aeneas, 13, 71, 94, 110–13; model for Turnus, 13, 109–13; Odysseus attempts to comfort after Patroclus' death, 57–59; quarrel with Odysseus, 78, 83–84; ransoms Hector's corpse, 13, 16, 33, 36, 44, 46, 68–70, 83–84, 111–12; relationship with Antilochus, 48–51; sorrow of, 44–47, 51, 59–61; subverted model for Neoptolemus, 66–72, 75, 89, 100, 112, 114; visited by Patroclus' ghost, 43, 57, 64, 93
achos, 43–47, 60, 123nn53–54, 56, 61. *See also* sorrow of Achilles
Acroceraunia, 106
Actium, 104
Aeacus, 48, 51–52, 62
Aeneadae, 99
Aeneades, 85
Aeneas: adopts Neoptolemus as model, 71, 110, 112–15; anger of, 15, 111, 114; arrives at Carthage, 80–83; challenges Odysseus' narrative authority, 75–76, 80–81, 85–92, 96–97, 108–9; describes Priam's slaughter by Neoptolemus, 66, 68–74, 100; duel with Turnus, 11, 13, 111–114; encounters Cyclops and Achaemenides, 107–9; encounters Scylla and Charybdis, 97, 106–8; examines temple of Juno, 9, 16, 69, 83–85; failure to defend Troy and Priam, 73–75, 84, 86–87, 92–93, 96; hears Polydorus' ghost, 74, 99–100; in the *Iliad*, 4–5, 34–35, 63, 83–84, 86, 91, 96, 98, 110; meets Helenus and Andromache, 74, 104–6, 109, 112; modeled on Achilles, 13, 71, 94, 110–13; modeled on Hector, 13, 71, 94, 106, 110, 114; modeled on Paris, 13, 109–10; narrates tale to Carthaginians, 27, 85; nearly encounters Phaeacians, 104; *pietas* of, 13, 74–75; reliability as narrator, 73, 97; rescues Anchises, 74–75; sails past Ithaca, 103–4; sees Creusa's ghost, 74; sees Hector's ghost,

162 Subject Index

93–94, 100; sees Odysseus at Troy, 93–96; visits Buthrotum, 104–6, 112; visits Crete, 101–103, 109; visits Delos, 100–101; visits Strophades, 103; visits Thrace, 99–100, 109; visits underworld, 24; wanderings of, 9, 12, 92, 96–97, 109
Aeolus, 73, 94, 103, 107, 125n82, 134n11
Aethiopis, 32, 48–49, 124n70
aftermath: Iliadic, 1, 25, 32–33, 41, 63–66, 88, 91–93, 96, 98–99, 104, 112 ; Odyssean, 64–65. *See also* post-Iliadic
Agamemnon, 33, 84, 100; conflict with Achilles, 15, 34, 44–45, 52–53, 78, 95, 111; daughters of, 36; failed homecoming of, 63, 75, 110, 112; ghost in the *Odyssey*, 25, 48, 50, 105
Ajax (Telamonian), 47–49, 51–56, 59, 62–63, 95–96, 104, 125n82
Alcinous, 41, 76–82, 85, 87, 107–8, 130n51, 131nn71–72, 133n107
allusion: discrete or local, 1, 3, 8–9, 13–15, 27; fragmentary model of Homeric, 13, 15, 22–23, 27; intentional, 2–3, proleptic, 5; two-tier, 20
Amata, 110, 114
Anchises, 24, 74–75, 100–3, 108
Androgeos, 92
Andromache, 104–6, 109–10, 136n64
Anius, 100
Antenor, 86
Anticleia, 41–45, 123n56
Antilochus, 36, 47–51, 123nn64–65, 124n76, 125n82
Antinous, 70, 114
Aphrodite, 34–35, 79, 86. *See also* Venus
Apollo, 4–5, 33–34, 49–50, 58, 78, 100–3
Apollonius of Rhodes, 2, 15, 20, 23
Ares, 79, 86
Arete, 76–77, 79, 107–8
Ariosto, 15
Aristarchus, 5
Aristotle, 29–31, 130n51, 131n71
Arpi, 110
Artemis, 49, 81
Ascanius, 105–6, 136n67
Astyanax, 36, 105–6, 136nn64, 67

Athena, 37, 39–41, 70, 79–81, 101, 112, 123n58
Augustine, 22
Augustus, 2–4, 91
authority of Odysseus' narrative, 75–76, 80–81, 85–92, 96–97, 108–9
Autolycus, 37

B
Barchiesi, Alessandro, 23, 98
belatedness of *Odyssey*, 32, 37, 39, 42, 44, 51, 55, 61–63
bidirectional relationship between Homer and Virgil, 22–23
bipartite model of *Aeneid*, 1, 6–13, 19, 65
book divisions in Homer, 7, 27
borrowing, Homeric, 3–4, 8–10
Briseis, 95, 111
Buthrotum, 104–6, 112
Byron, Lord, 3

C
Caieta, 13, 111, 137n97
Cairns, Francis, 21
Callimachus, 2, 22
Calypso, 37, 77, 81
Carthage, Carthaginians, 73, 81–84, 96–97, 109
Cassandra, 103
Castor and Polydeuces, 36
Castrum Minervae, 106
Catullus, 2
children's perspective in *Odyssey*, 33, 37–38, 41–44, 51, 61–62
Chryses, 15, 33–34
Chryseis, 95
Cicones, 64, 99
Circe, 42, 64, 73
code-model, Homer as, 14–19, 23
Coleridge, Samuel Taylor, 117n6
Conte, Gian Biaggio, 14–15
Coroebus, 92, 133n6
Crete, 101–4, 109, 135n51
Creusa, 74, 92, 94, 96, 114
Cyclic epics, 32, 49, 64–65, 91
cycloidal design: of *Aeneid*, 110; of *Odyssey*, 65–66
Cyclops, 30, 79–82, 97, 107–9

D
Damastes of Sigeum, 90
Dante, 4, 23–24, 120nn88–89, 132n101

Subject Index   163

Dardanus, 101
Delos, 4–5, 100, 102, 104
Demodocus, 11, 66, 73, 77–79, 83–88, 91, 130n65
dialogue, intertextual, 2–6, 8–10, 15–16, 20, 22–27, 63, 115
Diana. *See* Artemis
Dido, 8, 81–88, 92, 94, 96, 99–100, 102, 132n105, 133n107
Diomedes, 4, 33–34, 63, 83–84, 86, 110, 132n105
Dionysius of Halicarnassus, 90–91
Dolopes, 88
Donatus, Aelius, 7, 10, 14, 22
Drepanum, 108

E
Ennius, 2, 15
epic: Homeric mode of, 14–15, 18–19; loser's, 65, 73–74, 85, 88, 101, 110; victor's, 65, 73–74, 80, 97, 101, 110
epilogue, *Odyssey* as, 31–32, 62
epithets, 15, 37, 39, 51, 53–57, 59, 67, 78, 98–99, 108, 125n89, 128n19
Etna, Mount, 107
Eumaeus, 37–38, 40, 101
Eupeithes, 70, 128nn30, 32
Euripides, 100
Eustathius, 29–31
exemplary model, Homer as, 14–19, 22

F
Fowler, Don, 24

G
Glaucus, 33–35

H
Harpies, 103, 107
Hector: absence from the *Odyssey*, 25; corpse abused by Achilles, 16–18, 69, 83–84, 111–12; corpse ransomed to Priam, 13, 16, 33, 36, 44, 46, 68–70, 83–84, 111–12; final duel with Achilles, 17, 67–68, 70, 72, 111–12; model for Aeneas, 13, 71, 94, 106, 110, 114; model for Turnus 13, 111, 114; Neoptolemus as inversion of, 70–72, 112–13; predicts Achilles death, 50, 64; remembered by Andromache, 104–6, 110; visits Aeneas in a dream, 73, 93–94, 100, 103, 106, 110
Helen, 25, 36, 65, 72, 79, 83, 98
Helenus, 74–75, 104–6, 109, 112, 124n73, 136n70
Helios, cattle of, 103, 107
Hellanicus of Lesbos, 90
Hera, 34. *See also* Juno
Hermes, 36. *See also* Mercury
Hinds, Stephen, 23

I
Icarius, 37
Idomeneus, 63, 101–2, 110, 135n51
Ilione, 83
Ilioneus, 85
Ilus, 99
imitation, 2–3, 6, 8, 13–15, 18–21, 26, 28, 90–91
intention, Virgilian, 2–4, 6, 91
intertextuality: active, 14–15, 23; as an aim of *Aeneid*, 2, 14, 18–19, 21, 24–26, 90; in history of Virgilian criticism, 1–4, 6, 8, 13, 20–24; particularized model of, 9, 14; within Homer, 6, 19–21, 23, 26–27, 32, 47, 49, 51, 62, 91
Iopas, 86, 132n104
Italy, 9, 11–12, 68, 81, 90, 97, 101–3, 106, 109–111, 114–15
Ithaca: Aeneas sails past, 103–4; Odysseus' return to, 43, 64, 69–70, 76, 80–81, 88, 91, 97–99, 101–102, 111–12; problem of succession, 36–37
Iulus. *See* Ascanius

J
Juno: hostility toward Aeneas 96, 109–111, 114; sanctuary of, 95–96; temple of, 9, 16, 69, 83–85, 91. *See also* Hera
Jupiter: altar of, 68, 96, 100, 134n13; command to Mercury, 81; prophecy of, 91, 115. *See also* Zeus
Juturna, 113

K
Knauer, Georg, 15

L
Laertes, 37, 41, 45–46, 64, 70, 103–4
Laestrygonians, 81, 124n73, 131n80

164 Subject Index

Laocoon, 9, 92–93
Latinus, 83, 113, 133n4
Lavinia, 109, 111, 114
Liger, 86
Longinus, 30–32
Lycaon, 113

M

Macrobius, 8–15, 21–22, 26–27
Medon, 49–50
Melanthius, 37
Memnon, 49–50
Menelaus: accuses Trojans of defying Zeus, 98–99; model for Odysseus, 111–12; retrieves Helen with Odysseus, 79; carries Patroclus' body, 48–49; reminiscences of, 25, 33, 37, 41, 65; shipwreck of, 63; rescues Odysseus with Ajax, 53; succeeds to Spartan throne, 36
Mentes, 39
Mercury, 80–81. *See also* Hermes
Meriones, 48
Meters of Boethius, 24
modello-codice. *See* code model
modello-esemplare. *See* exemplary model
Myrmidons, 88

N

Naiads, 43
Nausicaa, 41, 76–77, 80–81, 132n86
Neoptolemus: etymology of name, 66–69, 112; mentioned in *Iliad*, 36; Odysseus' report to Achilles, 61–62, 65–66, 72, 76, 96, 105–6; slaughters Priam, 66–76, 88–89, 95, 110, 112–14. *See also* Pyrrhus
Neptune, 110. *See also* Poseidon
Nereids, 50
Nestor, 25, 33, 36–37, 41, 48, 61, 95, 101–2, 104, 126n103
Newton, Isaac, 3
Numanus, 110

O

Odysseus: attempts to comfort Achilles after Patroclus' death, 57–58; contest over Achilles' arms, 54–55, 95; converses with Achilles in underworld, 47, 51–52, 56–62, 95–96, 112; cruelty and deceitfulness in *Aeneid*, 72, 87–88, 96; embassy to Achilles, 45–46, 52–53, 95; encounters Cyclops, 30, 79–82, 97, 107–8; encounters Scylla and Charybdis, 97, 106–8; encounters Cicones, 99; father of Telemachus, 36–37, 39–41; fight with suitors, 10, 46–47, 64, 70, 112, 114–15; founds Rome, 90–93, 115; guards Trojan plunder, 94–96; heroic paradigm, 51, 53–56, 58, 61–63, 66, 68–69, 75, 78–79, 86–87, 91, 93–95, 110, 112, 114; homecoming of, 32, 38, 40, 45–46, 64–65, 75, 80, 98, 103, 111; initial encounter with Phaeacians, 41, 64, 80–82; interaction with Demodocus, 66, 77–79, 85, 87–88; meets Anticleia, 41–45; meets Tiresias, 24, 42, 64–65, 104–5; narrates tale to the Phaeacians, 64, 73, 76–80, 87–89, 101, 104; narrative authority of, 75–76, 80–81, 85–92, 96–97, 108–9; nearly reaches Ithaca, 103–4; quarrel with Achilles, 78, 83–84; reconfigures Iliadic past, 25, 41, 61, 63, 69–70, 110, 112; reports to Achilles about Neoptolemus, 61–62, 65–66, 72, 76, 96, 105–6; rescued by Menelaus and Ajax, 53; reunion with Laertes, 41, 46; reunion with Penelope, 46, 64–65, 80, 101, 112; reunion with Telemachus, 38–41, 80; tells Cretan lying tales, 101–2; transported home by Phaeacians, 7, 80; wanderings of, 9, 12, 37, 76, 91, 97, 103; wrestling match with Ajax, 54
Orestes, 33, 36, 75, 105

P

Pallas, 17–18, 111
Pandarus, 112–13
parental perspective in *Iliad*, 33–37, 41–44, 51–52, 61, 66
Paris, 11, 13, 25, 50, 99, 109–10, 114, 123n74
Patroclus: death of, 35, 42, 44, 46–51, 57–60, 69, 111–12; funeral games of, 11, 54, 86; funeral of, 13, 16–18, 69, 83, 119n64; ghost of, 43, 57, 64, 93; kills Sarpedon, 34

patronymics, 36–37, 39, 41, 51–52, 67, 128n19
Peleus, 41, 52, 61, 67, 69–71
Penates, 103
Penelope: relationship with Telemachus, 40, 49, 70; reunion with Odysseus, 46, 64–65, 80, 101, 112; role in Ithacan succession, 36–37
Penthesilea, 84
Pergama, 100–6, 109–10
Phaeacians: Aeneas' near encounter with, 104; games of, 11; Odysseus' initial encounter with, 41, 64, 80–82; Odysseus' narration to, 64, 73, 76–80, 87–89, 101, 104; transport Odysseus home, 7, 80
Phemius, 78
Phoenicians, 80–81, 85–86, 88–89
Phoenix, 52, 59, 95
Pisistratus, 41
Polydorus, 74, 99–100, 102
Poseidon: Odysseus' sacrifice to, 64; prophecies to Aeneas, 4, 25, 63, 84, 86, 91, 93, 98, 100–1; superiority over Apollo, 58. *See also* Neptune
post-Iliadic: events in the Trojan war, 11, 61, 65–66, 84, 89; experience, 1, 63, 76, 84, 91–92, 96; heritage, 25–26. *See also* aftermath, Iliadic
posteriority of *Odyssey*, 19–20, 31–33, 39
Priam, 4, 83; death of, 66, 68–75, 88–89, 94–96, 100, 110, 112–14; house of, 5, 74, 100; supplicates Achilles, 13, 17, 33–36, 44, 46, 69–70, 72, 111
Propertius, 7
Punic. *See* Carthage, Carthaginians
Pyrrhus, 67–68, 94, 100. *See also* Neoptolemus

Q
Quint, David, 65
Quintilian, 3

R
revision: of Homer in *Aeneid*, 16, 18, 65–66, 68–69, 97, 107, 110, 112; of *Iliad* in *Odyssey*, 20, 51, 56, 62–63, 65–66, 68–69, 97, 110, 112

Rhesus, 83
Rome, foundation of, 90–91, 102, 108–9, 115

S
Sarpedon, 34, 50
Scamander. *See* Astyanax
Scheria, 41, 77, 81–82
scholia, Homeric, 31, 36, 64, 117n15, 124n82, 127n4
Scylla and Charybdis, 97, 106–8
sequel, *Odyssey* as, 20, 25–26, 31–33, 62
Servius, 2–4, 6, 8, 10, 15, 22, 81, 91, 96, 102
Sibyl, 13, 109–10
Sicily, 102, 107–8
Simois, 105
Sinon, 88, 93
Socus, 53–54
sorrow of Achilles, 17, 42, 43–49, 51, 60–62, 66. *See* also *achos*
Sparta, 36, 40–41, 102
Strabo, 5
Strophades, 103
suitors of Penelope, 10–11, 37–38, 46, 64, 66, 70, 78, 81, 99, 102, 112, 114–15
systematic interaction with Homer, 6, 13–15, 18–19, 20–21, 25–27, 90–91

T
Tarentum, 106
Tasso, 15
teknonymic, 36–37, 39, 122n27
Telegony, 64, 91
Telemachus: etymology of name, 37–39, 66; father of, 36–37, 39–41; journey of (*telemachy*), 11, 25, 33, 37–39, 41, 49, 61, 65–66, 78, 101; reunion with Odysseus, 38–41, 80; suitors' plot against, 70, 102, 112
Teucer, 85, 101
Thamyrus, 78
Thersites, 49
Thetis, 34–35, 42–44, 46–47, 49–50, 60
Thrace, 74, 99–104, 109
Thrasymedes, 36
Thrinacia, 73, 94, 103, 107–8
Tiresias, 24, 42, 64–65, 104–5
triplets, Homeric, 13, 17, 44, 49, 52
Troilus, 83

Tros, 99
Troy: destruction of, 9, 11–12, 25, 27, 64–68, 73–75, 84–89, 91–93, 96–100, 108, 112, 114; foundation of new, 75, 97–98, 100, 102, 104–6, 108, 110, 112; walls of, 16–18, 83; war at, 20, 36, 47–49, 52, 56–57, 61, 63, 75–80, 82–83, 101
Turnus, 8, 11, 13, 71, 110–14
Tyndareus, 36

U
Ulixes, Ulysses. *See* Odysseus
unidirectional model of Homeric influence, 1, 3, 8, 10, 13, 25

V
Venulus, 110
Venus, 80–82, 91, 110. *See also* Aphrodite

Vulcan, 111

W
window reference, 20–21, 120n72

X
Xanthus: Achilles' horse, 50, 64; Trojan river, 106

Z
Zeus: Achilles' supplication of, 46–47; allows Sarpedon to die, 34; authority over Poseidon, 58; Odysseus' blame of, 55, 94; prevents Achilles from harming Priam, 68; punishes the Achaeans, 44; relates the story of Orestes, 33; restrains Odysseus, 70, 112; thunderbolt of, 46–47, 64, 123n60; Trojan defiance of, 98; will of, 46–47, 78. *See also* Jupiter